The 'Ars musica' Attributed to Magister Lambertus/Aristoteles

The treatise on *musica plana* and *musica mensurabilis* written by Lambertus/Aristoteles is our main witness to thirteenth-century musical thought in the decades between the treatises of Johannes de Garlandia and Franco of Cologne. Most treatises on music of this century – except for Franco's treatise on musical notation – survive in only a single copy; Lambertus's *Ars musica*, extant in five sources, is thus distinguished by a more substantial and long-lasting manuscript tradition. Unique in its ambitions, this treatise presents both the rudiments of the practice of liturgical chant and the principles of polyphonic notation in a dense and rigorous manner like few music treatises of its time – a conceptual framework characteristic of Parisian university culture in the thirteenth century.

This new edition of Lambertus's treatise is the first since Edmond de Coussemaker's of 1864. Christian Meyer's meticulous edition is displayed on facing pages with Karen Desmond's English translation, and the treatise and translation are prefaced by a substantial introduction to the text and its author by Christian Meyer, translated by Barbara Haggh-Huglo.

ROYAL MUSICAL ASSOCIATION MONOGRAPHS

General Editor: Simon P. Keefe

This series is supported by funds made available to the Royal Musical Association from the estate of Thurston Dart, former King Edward Professor of Music at the University of London. The editorial board is the Publications Committee of the Association.

Recent monographs in the series (for a full list, see the end of this book):

Singing Dante: The Literary Origins of Cinquecento Monody
Elena Abramov-van Rijk

Johann Mattheson's Pièces de clavecin *and* Das neu-eröffnete Orchestre
Margaret Seares

The Politics of Verdi's Cantica
Roberta Montemorra Marvin

Heinrich Schenker and Beethoven's 'Hammerklavier' Sonata
Nicholas Marston

Regina Mingotti: Diva and Impresario at the King's Theatre, London
Michael Burden

ROYAL MUSICAL ASSOCIATION
MONOGRAPHS
27

The 'Ars musica' Attributed to Magister Lambertus/Aristoteles

Christian Meyer, Editor
Karen Desmond, Translator

With an Introduction and Critical Notes by Christian Meyer
translated by Barbara Haggh-Huglo

ASHGATE

© Christian Meyer and Karen Desmond 2015

All rights reserved. No part of this publication may be reproduced, stored in a retrieval system, or transmitted in any form or by any means, electronic, mechanical, photocopying, recording, or otherwise without the prior permission of the publisher.

Christian Meyer and Karen Desmond have asserted their right under the Copyright, Designs and Patents Act, 1988, to be identified as the authors of this work.

Published by
Ashgate Publishing Limited
Wey Court East
Union Road
Farnham
Surrey, GU9 7PT
England

Ashgate Publishing Company
110 Cherry Street
Suite 3-1
Burlington, VT 05401-3818
USA

www.ashgate.com

British Library Cataloguing in Publication Data
A catalogue record for this book is available from the British Library.

Library of Congress Control Number: 2014939820

ISBN 9781472439833 (hbk)

Printed in the United Kingdom by Henry Ling Limited,
at the Dorset Press, Dorchester, DT1 1HD

Contents

Acknowledgements	vii
Introduction *Christian Meyer, translated by Barbara Haggh-Huglo*	ix
Translator's Note *Karen Desmond*	xxxvii
Edition and Translation *Christian Meyer, editor, and Karen Desmond, translator*	1
Tabula abbreviationum	1
Sigla codicum et fontium	5
Explicatio abbreviaturarum	5
Magister Lambertus/Aristoteles, 'Ars musica'	
Musica plana	6
Musica mensurabilis	60
Critical and Explanatory Notes *Christian Meyer, translated by Barbara Haggh-Huglo*	117
Magister Lambertus/Aristoteles, 'Ars musica'	
Musica plana	117
Musica mensurabilis	119
Indexes *Christian Meyer*	123
Liturgical Chants and Polyphonic Compositions	123
Sources and Parallel Readings	124

Acknowledgements

This book would not have seen the light of day had it not been for the assistance and generosity of Prof. Barbara Haggh-Huglo, who initiated the project to publish my edition, translated my French texts, ensured coordination between the collaborators and editors, and took responsibility for the proofreading. I am equally grateful to Dr. Michael Bernhard for his meticulous rereading of my edition and to Dr. Karen Desmond for agreeing to translate the Latin texts, her attentive and critical examination of them, and her fine translation. I also wish to express my thanks to Prof. Mark Everist for his abundant enthusiasm for the project and his advice as we prepared our proposal, and to Mr. Vincent Besson, who engraved the musical examples of the *Musica mensurabilis*, the Centre d'Études Supérieures de la Renaissance (UMR 7323 of the CNRS) at the Université François-Rabelais in Tours, and its director, Dr. Philippe Vendrix. Finally, special thanks go to Kayleigh Huelin of Ashgate Publishing for her patient and vigilant attention during the preparation of this book for publication.

Christian Meyer

I am very grateful to Dr. Leofranc Holford-Strevens who graciously and generously provided assistance and advice regarding the translation of several tricky passages of Lambertus's treatise: in particular, his invaluable interpretation of the passages that open the *Musica plana* and *Musica mensurabilis* and the verses that close each half of the treatise. I would also like to thank Dr. Christian Meyer and Prof. Barbara Haggh-Huglo for their careful reading and rereading of my translation and their prompt and perceptive comments and suggestions at every stage of the project.

Karen Desmond

Introduction

Christian Meyer

The treatise on music presented here in a new edition occupies a unique place in the history of music theory of the last third of the thirteenth century.[1] Whereas most music treatises written at this time survive in only a single copy, with the exception of Franco's work on musical notation written circa 1280, this treatise is distinguished by a relatively substantial and long-lasting manuscript tradition, with two complete copies, one probably accomplished in Paris around 1280 (*P1*) and the other in Italy near the end of the fifteenth century (*Si*), and three incomplete copies, the first a manuscript copied in Germany or in Flanders at the beginning of the fourteenth century (*P2*) that includes only the first part of the treatise, then the copy that Johannes Heerwagen (Johannes Hervagius) reproduced – and possibly reworked – in his monumental edition of the works of Bede published in Basel in 1563 (*Hw*), and finally, an almost complete copy of the *Musica mensurabilis* of the mid-fourteenth century (*Erf*). Above all, this treatise is distinguished by its ambition to set forth a musical *ars* embracing in turn the rudiments of liturgical chants and the principles of polyphonic notation. Furthermore, it maintains, in a dense and consistent manner like few music treatises of its day, a conceptual framework and rigour of expression infused by the university culture of the thirteenth century. Finally, certain aspects of its author's teaching, in particular the theory of the nine rhythmic modes, seem to have enjoyed a certain currency in their time and for a short while thereafter, to judge from the reservations or criticisms that made it their object.

The first complete edition of the treatise was published in 1864 by Charles Edmond de Coussemaker in volume one of his *Scriptores*. He followed the oldest and most complete manuscript (*P1*), filling in *P1*'s lacuna at the beginning of the treatise from Johannes Heerwagen's edition,[2] but he intentionally neglected the readings of *P2*[3] and knew nothing of the existence of the manuscript of Siena (*Si*). Coussemaker

---

[1] A revised edition of the entire treatise was prepared by Gilbert Reaney († 22 March 2008) for the *Corpus scriptorum de musica*, but never published (Mark Everist, 'Music and Theory in Late Thirteenth-Century Paris: The Manuscript Paris, fonds lat. 11266', *Royal Musical Association Research Chronicle* 17 (1981): 42–64, here p. 52, note 1). The treatise was also a planned dissertation topic submitted around 1980 (Murray H. Ralph, 'The *Tractatus de musica* of Lambertus. Edition, Translation, Commentary', Ph.D. diss., New York University), but the dissertation was never completed.

[2] The attribution to Bede was rightly eliminated by Casimir Oudin in his edition of the works of Bede of 1688 (vol. 1, p. 1685, reproduced in *Patrologia latina*, vol. 90 [1850], col. 76c).

[3] Just when the first volume of the *Scriptores* was published, this (no longer extant)

attributed the treatise to a certain Aristoteles, trusting the music theorist Jacobus, who, in his *Speculum musicae* of circa 1330, comments on diverse aspects of *ars mensurabilis* and transmits direct quotations from Lambertus's treatise. This attribution is contradicted by two authors on music, however, the Anonymous of St Emmeram (1279) and Johannes de Grocheio (circa 1300), who each attribute some of these theories, which they cite to support their own, to a Magister Lambertus.

Aristoteles or Lambertus? This question of attribution remains controversial to this day. According to certain historians, Lambertus could be identified as the *Magister* of the same name at the University of Paris, who was also dean of the collegiate church of St Vincent in Soignies (Hainaut), and whom Robert of Sorbon, canon of Notre Dame of Paris and founder of the college of the Sorbonne, had designated as the executor of his testament in 1270.[4] On the other hand, Jacobus's attribution was the subject of various conjectures. According to one, Jacobus would have known the treatise from *P2*, where it appears after the *Secreta secretorum* 'editus ab Aristotele',[5] and deduced the attribution from the proximity of the two texts.[6] According to another, Jacobus's Pseudo-Aristotle was none other than the scribe with the name 'Aristotle' mentioned in a decision of 1282 in the cartulary of the chapter of Notre Dame of Paris.[7]

The problem of the identity of the author is even more difficult to resolve, however, because all past attributions known to this day concern only the section of the treatise on mensural music, and in particular the versified exposition of the author's very singular theory of the nine rhythmic modes, not the *Musica plana*. Yet even if both sections do seem to belong together, Lambertus's contribution to the composition of the first part of the treatise remains an open question. This first part in fact has all of the characteristics of a skilful compilation, juxtaposing its prologue in the form of an *accessus* with an exposition of the fundamentals of music coming from the tradition of teaching of

---

volume disappeared from the manuscript department of the Bibliothèque nationale and then reappeared in the collections of the Count of Ashburnham (see p. xiii further on).

[4] Following Jeremy Yudkin, *'De musica mensurata': The Anonymous of St Emmeram* (Bloomington, 1990), p. 341, Document 1 of 8 April 1270. Also see: Olga Weijers, *Le travail intellectuel à la Faculté des arts de Paris: textes et maîtres (c.1200–1500)*, VI. *Répertoire des noms commençant par L-M-N-O* (Turnhout, 2005; Studia Artistarum, Études sur la Faculté des arts dans les universités médiévales, 13), pp. 47–8.

[5] 'Incipit liber moralium de regimine dominorum qui alio modo dicitur secretum secretorum philosophorum editus ab Aristotele ad honorem Alexandri regis et discipuli sui' (Paris, BnF, latin 6755.1, f. 1r); 'Completus tractatus de signis et moribus naturalibus hominum ad regem magnificum Alexandrum qui dominatus fuit toto orbi monarcha in septentrione. Explicit liber Aristotelis qui intitulatur de secretis secretorum sive de regimine principum vel dominorum' (Paris, BnF, latin 6755.1, f. 34v).

[6] Gordon A. Anderson, 'Magister Lambertus and Nine Rhythmic Modes', *Acta musicologica* 45 (1973): 57–73, here p. 57; Gilbert Reaney, 'The Manuscript Chantilly, Musée Condé 1047', *Musica disciplina* 8 (1954): 73 and note 51.

[7] Jacques Handschin, 'The Summer Canon and its Background (Part 2)', *Musica disciplina* 5 (1951): 83, 107.

Introduction

Johannes de Garlandia, a versified exposition on the modes – which, moreover, seems to have known a rather wide diffusion – and finally, a tonary. For want of other historical indicators, one should no doubt retain for the time being the hypothesis that this treatise took shape in a milieu near the University of Paris and a Magister Lambertus, whose pedagogical core was recorded in the versified treatise on the nine rhythmic modes, and who would then have been the author, all things considered, of the present *Musica mensurabilis*. Then a listener or a pupil of the latter would perhaps have taken the initiative to compose a complete exposition of the *ars musica*, articulating at the centre of the project a *Musica plana* and the *Musica mensurabilis* of Magister Lambertus.[8]

THE MANUSCRIPT AND PRINTED SOURCES OF THE TEXT

1. PARIS, BIBLIOTHÈQUE NATIONALE DE FRANCE, LATIN 11266 (P1)[9]

Parchment volume of 41 folios (149 × 108 mm) of five quaternions with an added folio attached to the last gathering and on a stub. Bound in brown leather of the seventeenth century, restored in 1975. Pastedown and flyleaf of marbled paper. On the verso of the first flyleaf: R. B. n° 4614 / 1848. Second flyleaf: Suppl. Latin 1136. F. 1 Stamp of the Bibliothèque royale. Two back flyleaves, the first blank. On the recto of the second: 'αυΛετησ' three times, then three inscriptions in pencil, in Hebrew, Syriac, and Coptic, respectively; and the name, 'l'abbé de Tersan' (Charles-Philippe Campion de Tersan) in pencil. On the back of the binding: 'Liber de musica et plano cantu' (gold on red background); below: 'Ms. XIVe siècle' (gold on green background). On f. 41r, upper margin, the inscriptions: 'lencoga... (?) nostram [G] et Gobertus de fonte'.

The volume belonged successively to the abbot Charles-Philippe Campion de Tersan (1736–1819),[10] the musician and music historian François-Louis Perne (1772–1821), and finally, to François-Joseph Fétis (1784–1871).[11] It was registered in the national collections on

---

[8] Christian Meyer, 'Quelques remarques à propos du *Tractatus de musica* faussement attribué à Lambert-Aristote', in *Musik des Mittelalters und der Renaissance. Festschrift Klaus-Jürgen Sachs zum 80. Geburtstag*, ed. Rainer Kleinertz, Christoph Flamm, Wolf Frobenius (Hildesheim-Zurich-New York, 2010; Veröffentlichungen des Staatlichen Instituts für Musikforschung, 18 / Studien zur Geschichte der Musiktheorie, 8), pp. 115–27, here p. 123.

[9] Online at http://gallica.bnf.fr

[10] Cf. Jean Chrétien Ferdinand Hoefer, *Nouvelle biographie générale*, vol. 44 (Paris: Didot, 1865), col. 1018. See Lawrence Earp, 'Machaut's Music in the Early Nineteenth Century: The Work of Perne, Bottée de Toulmon, and Fétis', in *Guillaume de Machaut*, ed. Jacqueline Cerquiglini-Toulet and Nigel Wilkins (Paris, 2002), p. 15.

[11] CS 1, p. xvi. The transcriptions of the motets by François-Louis Perne are kept in the Bibliothèque du Conservatoire in Brussels (Ms. 27938). Cf. Lawrence Earp, 'Machaut's Music', p. 15.

The 'Ars musica' Attributed to Magister Lambertus/Aristoteles

26 January 1848 as compensation that Fétis acknowledged he owed to the Bibliothèque nationale de France.[12]

The present copy, in which the treatise (f. 1–35r) is followed by seven three-voice motets (f. 35v–41v), is an example that was relatively rare in the thirteenth century of a book associating theory and musical practice. The text script of the treatise, in two columns, and the more cursive writing of the motet texts permit this small volume to be dated from the years 1275–1290, probably after 1280.[13] According to the analyses of Mark Everist, the two kinds of writing and the style of the manuscript's decoration are similar to those of various manuscripts produced in Parisian workshops,[14] thus suggesting its Parisian origin.

The text of the treatise is incomplete at the beginning as the result of a material lacuna that one can estimate at two folios, a half-quaternion.

Table 1   **Motets in *P1*[15]**

35v–36r	Salve, virgo nobilis Maria / Verbum caro factum est / T. Veritatem [*recte* Verbum]
36r–37r	Quant voi la florete nestre an la prée / Je suis joliete, doucete et plaisant / T. Aptatur.
37r–v	Amor vincens omnia potentia / Marie preconio devotio / T. Aptatur.
38r–39r	L'autrier m'esbatoie et touz seus pensoie / Demenant grant joie, l'autrier m'esbatoie / T. Manere.
39r–v	Se j'ai servi longuement amors / Trop longue<me>nt m'a failli ma dame / T. Pro patribus.
39v–40v	Chorus innocentium sub Herodis / In Bethleem Herodes iratus / T. In Bethleem.
40v–41r	O Maria, mater pia, spes fidelium / Mellis stilla, maris stella, rosa / T. Domino.

[12] Paris, BnF, Département des Manuscrits, registre des acquisitions 1833–1848, n° 4614. This restitution can undoubtedly be situated in the wake of the dispatch, beginning in 1840, of a batch of eighteen works among which figured a 'Traité MS du XIVe siècle'. See François Lesure, 'L'Affaire Fétis', *Revue belge de musicologie* 28–30 (1974–76): 214–21 (in part, p. 220).

[13] Lesure, 'L'Affaire Fétis', p. 55.

[14] Everist, 'Music and Theory in Late Thirteenth-Century Paris: The Manuscript Paris, fonds lat. 11266', *Royal Musical Association Research Chronicle* 17 (1981): 42–64, here pp. 54 and 59: 'The internal evidence of the motet layer of P11266 demonstrates that it was copied under the influence of Franco of Cologne's *Ars cantus mensurabilis*. This fact alone provides a *terminus post quem* of circa 1280 for the second layer of the manuscript. Determining the date of the first layer of the manuscript is more difficult, but it may be placed between circa 1275 and circa ... 1280 ...)'.

[15] Given are the folio numbers that are still legible in italics. Here I wish to thank Marie-Noël Colette, who examined the three volumes and noted where traces of the old foliation occur in the volume.

xii

Introduction

2. Paris, Bibliothèque nationale de France, latin 6755.2 (P2)[16]

The three volumes with the present shelf numbers latin 6755.1, 6755.2
et 6755.3 are all that remains of an otherwise no longer extant volume
of the royal library that had belonged to Cardinal Mazarin and which
the catalogue of Guillaume de Villefroy describes as follows (p. 275, n°
vi M DCCLV):

1. *Aristotelis* liber de secretis secretorum: interprete Philippo, Clerico
   Tripolitano [= latin 6755.1, f. 1 ff.].
2. *Ambrosii Autperti* tractatus de conflictu vitiorum & virtutum
   [= latin 6755.1, f. 37 ff.].
3. Flores è Scriptoribus cum sacris tum profanis collecti.
4. **Anonymi opusculum de musica** [= latin 6755.2, f. 71r–78r] (*olim* f.
   <79> *80 81 82* <83–86>14).
5. Descriptio sanctorum locorum circa Jerusalem [= latin 6755.1,
   f. 61r–v] (*olim* f. <88r–v>).
6. Descriptio urbis Antiochiae [= latin 6755.1, f. 61v–62r] (*olim*
   f. <88v–89r>).
7. Urbium & majorum villarum quas Carolus acquisivit in Hispania
   & Galecia catalogus [= latin 6755.1, f. 62r–v] (*olim* f. <89r>).
8. Sancti *Bernardi* meditationes [= latin 6755.1, f. 63r ff.] (*olim*
   f. <90–97>).
9. Anonymus de constructione & excidio templi Hierosolymitani, &
   de passione Christi [= latin 6755.1, f. 45 ff. + 47 ff.].
10. *Méthodii,* Patarensis Episcopi, oratio de Antichristo & de
    consummatione saeculi [= latin 6755.1, f. 56v ff.].
10. Anonymi dialogus de vitae felicitate [= latin 6755.3].
    Is codex partim decimo tertio, partim decimo quarto saeculo
    videtur exaratus.

That now-missing volume, stolen at an unknown date, had been
acquired by the collector Joseph Barrois (1785–1855) and then
dismembered before he sold it in 1849 to the Count of Ashburnham. In
1888 the Bibliothèque nationale bought it back with other manuscripts
and registered it on 31 January 1889.[17]

From this time on the music treatise appears bound in blue morocco
leather of the nineteenth century and preceded by a flyleaf that has, on
its verso, an illumination representing King David surrounded by four
musicians, and on the recto, an incomplete table of psalms followed
by the beginning of the preface of St Jerome to the Psalter ('Psalterium
Romae dudum positus …'). This folio, which was intended to decorate

[16] Online at http://gallica.bnf.fr
[17] On the fonds Barrois, see Léopold Delisle, *Catalogue des manuscrits des fonds Libri et
Barrois* (Paris, 1888), pp. xxxviii ff., and in the same volume, pp. 216–20, the description of
the manuscript after its return to the national collections.

xiii

The 'Ars musica' Attributed to Magister Lambertus/Aristoteles

the volume, had been cut out of a Bible or a Psalter of the twelfth century. The text presented on f. 71r (col. b) has traces of restoration, no doubt carried out by one or another of the copyists of Joseph Barrois.[18] The text stops near the end of the first part, almost at the beginning of the tonary, and so the verses ('Primum est sexto …') announced on the last line of f. 77v (col. b) were copied on a small additional leaf (f. 78) followed by the incipit of the tonary with space reserved for the music. The verso is covered with fourteenth-century annotations without any relationship to the music. This leaf gives the impression of being an unfinished copy, but it could also be a clever falsification carried out after the dismemberment of the volume. If such were the case, the text may have been followed by these same verses and the tonary. Yet the old pagination, which can be reconstituted from several still readable numbers, seems to exclude the possibility that the present copy was followed by the *Musica mensurabilis*, which was nevertheless announced in the prologue (cf. [mp90]).[19]

The text of the music treatise was copied in a cursive German script[20] at the beginning of the fourteenth century. Given that the volume is a compilation, the hypothesis of a Flemish origin of the music treatise remains fragile, since it rests only on the indications of a colophon appended at a Praemonstratensian abbey of Hainaut in 1267 at the end of the *Meditationes sancti Bernardi*.[21] Michel Huglo advanced the hypothesis of a German origin on the basis of the formula of the tonary summarising the psalmody ('Primi toni melodiam psalles in directo …') whose use was widespread in German-speaking countries.[22]

3. Siena, Biblioteca Comunale degli Intronati, L.V.30 (Si)

The manuscript of Siena is a vast collection (150 folios) of music treatises copied in Italy during the last third or at the end of the fifteenth century.[23] Its origin and provenance are unknown.

It essentially brings together treatises on mensural music, counterpoint, and speculative music theory of the fourteenth and fifteenth centuries, of which most are of French origin, such as the *Musica speculativa* and the *Libellus* of Johannes de Muris, the *Omni desideranti* treatise,[24] or even the short *Musica* of the musician and theorist Bernard

[18] See, for example, f. 71r col. b, where the copyist restored several very effaced lines of text in the document.

[19] See p. xiii above.

[20] According to an evaluation by Gilbert Ouy cited by Michel Huglo in *Les Tonaires* (Paris, 1971), p. 420.

[21] *RISM* B III, 6, p. 183

[22] Huglo, *Les Tonaires*, p. 421. One notes nevertheless that the formula 'Primi toni melodiam …' only figures in *P2*, and in a second hand. The complete tonary (*P1* and *Si*) ignores this formula.

[23] Description in *RISM* B III, 2, pp. 120–23.

[24] This treatise from the Vitrian tradition is edited and discussed in Karen Desmond, 'Texts in Play: The *Ars nova* and its Hypertexts', *Musica disciplina* 57 (2012): 81–153.

xiv

Introduction

de Cligny. The presence of the treatise of Lambertus is anachronistic, to say the least, in this group of texts in which the problems of notation of the *Ars nova* dominate.

4. *JOHANNES HERWAGIUS, OPERA BEDAE VENERABILIS...* (BASEL, 1563), VOL. I, COLS 404–434 (*Hw*)[25]

In many respects, the publication of the treatise of Lambertus within the framework of the *editio princeps* of the works of Bede remains a mystery to this day. The music treatise falsely attributed to Bede consists of a *Musica theorica* (col. 404–414) followed by a *Musica quadrata seu mensurata* (col. 415–435). The first is a cento of glosses on the *De institutione musica* of Boethius,[26] which was rather widely diffused in the tradition of copies of the glosses of the *Musica* of Boethius, but is incomplete except in only one copy of the eleventh century (Paris, BnF, latin 10275) provenant from the abbey of St Willibrord of Echternach.

The editor nowhere explains the reasons that led him to attribute these texts to Bede and says nothing about the sources he used to establish the text. It seems that he only knew the prologue and *Musica mensurabilis* of this treatise, since the *Musica plana* and tonary are absent.

5. *ERFURT, WISSENSCHAFTLICHE ALLGEMEINBIBLIOTHEK, 8° 94 (ERF)*

This last source is an incomplete copy of the *Musica mensurabilis* in what may be an English or Flemish mid-fourteenth-century cursive script of rather mediocre quality. The musical examples, for which space was reserved, were not copied, and the copying was abandoned at the place where the eighth rhythmic mode was to be presented; the study of hocket is missing. This group of pages constitutes the last codicological unit in the center of a composite volume reuniting various treatises of music. This volume is described in the catalogue Amplonius Ratinck made of his collection between 1410 and 1412 as n° 70 among the works on mathematics.[27]

Table 2 gives an overview of the concordances between these five sources.

[25] Online at: https://books.google.fr/books?id=_tBg8_Nxe10C&dq=heruagius+opera+b edae&source=gbs_navlinks_s

[26] Hucbald Pizzani edits and studies these glosses in '[Bedae Presbyteri] Musica theorica sive scholia in Boethii de institutione musica libros quinque', *Romanobarbarica* 5 (1980): 300–61. They were also brought together in *Glossa maior in institutionem musicam Boethii*, ed. Michael Bernhard and Calvin M. Bower (Munich, 1993–96; Bayerische Akademie der Wissenschaften. Veröffentlichungen der Musikhistorischen Kommission, 9–11).

[27] Wilhelm Schum, *Beschreibendes Verzeichniss der Amplonianischen Handschriften-Sammlung zu Erfurt* (Berlin, 1887), p. 808; *RISM* B III, 6, pp. 290–95; *Mittelalterliche Bibliothekskataloge Deutschlands und der Schweiz*, vol. 2: *Bistum Mainz: Erfurt*, ed. Paul Lehmann (Munich, 1928; repr. 1969), p. 31.

xv

Table 2 **Overview of Concordances**

Musica plana	P1	P2	Si	Hw	Erf
[1] Quoniam circa artem musicam	1r–3va (1–38 *om.*)	71r–72v	14r–16r	415–418	–
[92] <I> <De signis et nominibus vocum>	3v	72v–73v	16r–17r	–	–
[108] <II> <De lineis et spatiis>	5r	74r	17r	–	–
[115] <III> <De proprietatibus>	5r–v	74r	17r	–	–
[123] <IV> <De mutationibus>	5v–6v	74r–75r	17r–17v	–	–
[139] Sunt autem species duodecim …	6v–11v	75r–76v	17v–20r	–	–
[215] <De modis>	11v–13v	76v–77v	20r–21r	–	–
[301] Primum querite regnum dei … (tonary)	14r–19v	*om.*	21r–24r	–	–

Musica mensurabilis	P1	P2	Si	Hw	Erf
[1] Cum secundum quod dicit Boetius …	19v	–	24r	418	87r
[7] Discantus vero est … cantus duarum vocum …	20r	–	24r	418	87r
[27] Cum igitur ipsa perfecta figura …	21v	–	25r	420	88r
[85] … de simul ligatis seu coniunctis …	24v	–	26v	423	90v
[193] Modus autem seu maneries …	32r	–	30r	430	96r
[254] … de quadam armonia resecata …	34r	–	31v	*om.*	*om.*

Introduction

The Subject Matter of the Treatise

The *Ars musica* as such – *plana* et *mensurabilis* – is preceded by a vast prologue, which confers authority on the ensemble of the treatise composed with learning and attests to its unity with various remarks.[28] The prologue opens in praise of the wisdom, virtue, and eloquence that divine mercy has accorded to the philosopher to vanquish the evils inherent in human nature. This topos, which spread in the Victorine milieu in the twelfth century and was taken over in the next century by such authors as Raoul de Beauvais, is here surreptitiously turned into a praise of the science of music with a long and hidden but popular citation from Boethius I, 33 ('Quid sit musicus').[29]

It continues with a vast *accessus*, whose structure and principal articulations are borrowed from the chapter on music in the treatise on the division of philosophy by the learned Spaniard, Dominicus Gundissalinus.[30] The adoption of Gundissalinus's structure is noteworthy, since this is the only known attempt in the history of Western music theory to explain the learning and practice of music with the assistance of a grid for reading that was influenced by Arab philosophy. Although several articulations within this classification (*partes* [mp47–50], *species* [mp51–52], *artifex* (composer) [mp85], *officium* (function) [mp86–88]) follow Gundissalinus's text rather faithfully, others were reworked to agree more precisely with the musical material of the time. This is the case, in particular, with the division concerning the '*genus*' [mp44] and the '*materia*' of music [mp45–46], where the question of the manner of organisation and notation of mensural music is especially developed. The same procedure continues in the section concerning the 'utility' of music [mp57–73], where the author defends at length the use of music in the celebration of the divine office, as well as its contribution to the spiritual and physical fulfillment of the individual. Finally, the division of Gundissalinus is augmented by a long section on the invention of music [mp74–84] that invokes the topos that cannot be ignored of Pythagoras's discovery of the harmonic proportions.

---

[28] The '*ars mensurabilis*' is announced at [90], where the question of the function (*officium*) of music comes up for discussion.

[29] On the history of this topos, see Lambert Marie de Rijk, 'Some Notes on the Twelfth-Century Topic of the Three (Four) Human Evils and of Science, Virtue, and Techniques as Their Remedies', *Vivarium* 5 (1967): 8–15.

[30] Dominicus Gundissalinus, *De divisione philosophiae*, ed. Ludwig Baur, *Beiträge zur Geschichte der Philosophie des Mittelalters*, IV/2–3 (Münster, 1903), pp. 96–102 ('*De arte musica*'). On the reception of this text by Lambert, see Gerhard Pietzsch, *Die Klassifikation der Musik von Boetius bis Vgolino von Orvieto* (Halle, 1929), pp. 84–7 and Max Haas, 'Studien zur mittelalterlichen Musiklehre I: Eine Übersicht über die Musiklehre im Kontext der Philosophie des 13. und frühen 14. Jahrhunderts', *Forum musicologicum* 3 (1982): 323–427, here pp. 402–3.

xvii

The 'Ars musica' Attributed to Magister Lambertus/Aristoteles

1. *Musica plana and the Tonary*

The study of the foundations of *musica plana* respects a four-part structure, which successively presents the musical vocabulary ('de signis et nominibus vocum'), the construction of the scale of sounds following the diastematic model of musical notation ('de lineis et spatiis'), the hexachordal structure of the scale ('de proprietate'), and finally the principles of solmisation ('de mutationibus'). These articulations are none other than those of the teaching of Johannes de Garlandia, and the order in which they are presented here is rigorously that of recensions III and IV of Garlandia's teaching, which is transmitted in copies of the second half of the fourteenth and first third of the fifteenth century, respectively (see Table 3).[31] In more than one place, and particularly in the exposition of the principle of hexachordal mutation, the text includes concordances with the redaction of the second of these two *reportationes*.[32]

As in most of the recensions of the teaching of Johannes de Garlandia, the exposition of the four fundamental elements is followed here by a study of the consonances and intervals. Its exposition distinguishes three consonances ('consonanciae'), the fourth, fifth, and octave, and nine intervals as spaces ('spatia'), the unison, semitone, and tone, thirds, sixths, and sevenths. The didactic examples are summarised after the model of the formula 'Ter terni sunt modi ...' attributed to Hermannus Contractus, which was very widely disseminated at the end of the eleventh century and afterwards, particularly in German-speaking regions, but also in northern France, where the incipit was reformulated as 'Ter quaternae sunt species ...'. For the history of the evolution of the theory of intervals, it is interesting to note that this *Musica plana* is one of the rare witnesses – and in every case the oldest – of a list of twelve intervals.[33] A series of ten intervals (without the sevenths) is attested by the compilation manuscript, Thomas 391 of the Universitätsbibliothek in Leipzig,[34] copied in Lotharingia or southern Germany in the fourteenth century, and one knows in addition, but in a relatively late copy, a hybrid series of eleven intervals, including the tritone, an 'exacordum', and an 'eptacordum'.[35] The present series of

---

[31] Trad. Garl. plan. III and IV, ed. Meyer, *Musica plana*, pp. 39–62.

[32] 'Mutatio vero ut hic summitur ... et similiter suo modo descendendo' (p. 256): see Trad. Garl. plan. IV, 76–88 (ed. p. 60).

[33] The nomenclature of the twelve intervals and consonances is still found near the end of the fifteenth century in the *Musica* of Adam de Fulda (cf. GS 3, p. 349); for other sources, see: Basel, Universitätsbibliothek A.IX.2, Nr. 5, ff. 296v–99r (Basel?, *c*.1481–86), but the final formula 'Ter quaterni sunt modi ...' (f. 299r) adds the tritone and consequently realises a series no longer of twelve but of thirteen intervals.

[34] Peter Wagner, 'Aus dem St Thomas-Archiv zu Leipzig', *Zeitschrift für Musikwissenschaft* 12 (1929/30): 130–7, see p. 134.

[35] Vienna, Österreichische Nationabibliothek, Cod. 4774, f. 14v (Bohemia [Prague?], *c*.1450), See Alexander Rausch, *Opusculum de musica ex traditione Iohannis Hollandrini: A Commentary, Critical Edition and Translation* (Ottawa, 1997) (Trad. Holl. VI), section VII (ed.

Table 3   **Comparison of Section Headings**

Trad. Garl. plan. I	Trad. Garl. plan. II	Trad. Garl. plan. III	Trad. Garl. plan. IV	Lambertus
De VII signis Gammatis et VI vocibus	De mutationibus	De signis et nominibus vocum	De signis et nominibus vocum	De significationibus et nominibus vocum
De proprietatibus		De lineis et spaciis	De lineis et spaciis	De lineis et spaciis
De paritate et imparitate		De proprietate	De proprietatibus	De proprietatibus
De mutationibus		De mutationibus	De mutationibus	De mutationibus
De speciebus singulis	De consonantiis			

twelve intervals thus documents a transitional stage in the evolution of the theory of intervals that would stabilise in the fourteenth century, with the incorporation of the tritone, as a series of thirteen intervals.[36] The study of intervals is enriched with explanations that one also finds in the tradition of teaching of Johannes de Garlandia. Of concern is the development following from the study of the semitone, where there is question of *falsa musica* or *falsa mutatio* [mp159–167]. The false mutation that consists of a hexachord built on a degree other than .Γ. .C., .F., .G., .c., .f., or .g., is justified here by the necessity of realising a good consonance. This insistence on 'propter consonantiam bonam inveniendam' should perhaps be situated within the framework of the practice of polyphonic singing, which was concerned with realising fourths and fifths that were correctly tuned.[37]

The study of the twelve intervals is completed by a classification 'secundum auditum' – another Garlandian inheritance – which one finds penned by the (Parisian) author of the treatise said to be from St Emmeram and by Franco of Cologne.[38] According to this classification, the dissonances are ordered as perfect (tone, semitone, and tritone), medial (thirds), and imperfect (sixths), and the consonances in as many categories: perfect (octave and double octave), medial (fifth and twelfth), and imperfect (fourth and eleventh). One should note that although this classification – which is known from other texts[39] – cleverly complements the theory of twelve intervals that has just been presented; it is in any case in disagreement with the customary classifications of the second half of the thirteenth century, those of Johannes de Garlandia, Franco of Cologne, Anonymous IV, and of the Anonymous of St Emmeram.[40]

All things considered, the distinctive feature of the exposition is the author's insistent reference to sensory experience, as in qualifying the dissonance of 'cacophony', for example, as does the commentary of the Anonymous of St Emmeram.[41] Finally, one should note the Aristotelian resonances that enrich this exposition of the classification at the place

pp. 36, 38). Note nevertheless that the author of this compilation presents the 'standard' nomenclature of thirteen intervals a bit further on (cf. p. 44: 'Nota quod tredecim sunt species musice …').

[36] Christian Meyer, 'Le *Tractatus de consonantiis musicalibus* (CS 1 Anonyme I / Jacobus Leodiensis, alias de Montibus): une *reportatio*?', *Revue belge de musicologie / Belgisch Tijdschrift voor Muziekwetenschap* 49 (1995): 5–25.

[37] This practice will be abundantly described in the fourteenth and fifteenth centuries in the short treatises dedicated to *coniunctae* or even more, *coniuncturae*. Cf. Paloma Otaola, 'Les "*coniunctae*" dans la théorie musicale au Moyen Âge et à la Renaissance (1375–1555)', *Musurgia* 5 (1998): 53–69.

[38] See Frank Hentschel, *Sinnlichkeit und Vernunft in der mittelalterlichen Musiktheorie* (Stuttgart, 2000; Beihefte zum Archiv für Musikwissenschaft, 47), pp. 39 and 176–7.

[39] Trad. Holl. VI, chapter 17 (cf. the apparatus of sources of Rausch's edition).

[40] 36 Klaus-Jürgen Sachs, 'Musikalische Elementarlehre im Mittelalter', in *Rezeption des antiken Fachs im Mittelalter* (Darmstadt, 1990; Geschichte der Musiktheorie, 3), p. 140.

[41] See the apparatus of parallel readings. On other uses, see the entries '*cacemphaton*', '*cacephatio*', '*cacophonia*', '*cacophonos*' in LmL, cols 279–80.

Introduction

where the author affirms that all that is composite is grounded in the nature of the extremes [mp213].

The *Musica plana* concludes with an exposition of modal theory that is followed by a brief tonary. A long terminological preamble explains why it is appropriate to speak of mode and not of tones. The recommendation is not new: it circulated in music theory as a consequence of the teachings of Guido of Arezzo and John of Afflighem,[42] but here it assumes a resolutely scholastic emphasis with its emphasised reference to nominalism in the explanation of the term 'modus', which is qualified as 'nomen reale ab antiquis impositum'.

Beyond this preamble, the body of the exposition is presented in the form of a versified summary[43] that outlines fundamental propositions of this theory. At question, first of all, are the eight modes [mp228–235], the regular finals (designated by the syllables *re, mi, fa, sol*, of the hexachord positioned on .C.), and the transposed finals [mp236–245], then the respective ambitus of the authentics and plagals [mp246–261].

Mp262–271 specify the classification of chants of restricted ambitus: the rise to the fifth above the final will be the criterion determining the authentics, and to the second above the final that of the plagals. The general characteristics of the authentics and plagals are described in the eight following verses [mp272–279], that is, the propensity of the authentics to rise above the final, and, inversely, that of the plagals to descend below the final. In mp280–291, the author sets about to examine the cases of chants with an extravagant ambitus, which advance, successively, into the zones proper to the authentic and the plagal modes. According to the author of the summary, two rules can be observed that classify these chants. The first considers the penultimate pitch: when it is above the final, the chant will be called authentic, if it is below, it will be classified as plagal. In other words, a melody that rejoins the final by a descending interval will be called authentic; it will be called plagal in the contrary case. The second rule proposes a decision on the basis of a statistical evaluation: the chants will be classified as authentic or plagal according to the frequency with which they advance into the authentic or plagal zone of the mode. These two rules are unknown elsewhere, but evidently manifest a preoccupation to which Jacobus devotes two chapters of

---

[42] 'Hi sunt quattuor modi vel tropi, quos abusive tonos nominant ...' (GUIDO micr. X, 2 ff.; ed. CSM 4, p. 133), 'X. De modis quos abusive tonos appellamus ... Modi a moderando sive modulando vocati sunt, quia videlicet per eos cantus moderatur id est regitur, vel modulatur id est componitur. Quicumque enim musicae habens notitiam regularem cantum componere curat, prius ad quem tonum eum convenire faciat, secum destinat ...' (Ioн. Cotт. mus. X, 7–8; ed. CSM 1, p. 77).

[43] This structure does not appear in Coussemaker's edition, yet throughout the entire manuscript tradition, the text is copied in the form of verse with capitalised initials. In Paris, BnF, latin 11266, the verses are copied one after another, but each beginning of a verse is signalled by a rubricated initial and sometimes by a sort of 'point of division', which marks the end of the verse. An edition of this abbreviated text is in Meyer, 'Quelques remarques', pp. 124–7).

xxi

The 'Ars musica' Attributed to Magister Lambertus/Aristoteles

the sixth book of his *Speculum musicae*.[44] The summary concludes with the formulas 'Primum cum sexto …' that summarise the rules of psalmody. These formulas were transmitted widely, especially in France and in Italy.

This versified summary, of which this treatise seems to be one of the earliest sources, is also known from three other copies. In the earliest, copied in southern Germany during the first quarter of the fifteenth century (Munich, Bayerische Staatsbibliothek, Clm 24809), all of these verses are found in a compilation of texts concerning the theory of modality. In a manuscript of Italian origin dating from 1463 (Berlin, Deutsche Staatsbibliothek, Mus. ms. theor. 1520) they appear after the rules of solmisation and an exposition on the intervals of chant. A later copy is found in a manuscript of Flemish origin of the second half of the fifteenth century (Venice, Biblioteca Nazionale Marciana, Latin Cl. VIII.24).[45] In this last source, the verses are copied at the beginning of a *Summula musicae* by Henricus Helene, one of the musicians of the 'Collegium musicorum' celebrated in a motet by Bernard of Cluny.[46] This treatise is itself followed by a copy of the *Summa de musica* of Johannes Boen, and finally by the *Musica speculativa* of Johannes de Muris.[47] One can add that the textual environment of this manuscript indisputably situates this summary in a tradition of French or at least Franco-Flemish teaching.

The *Musica plana* is completed with a tonary in which all of the antiphons cited as examples are borrowed from the repertory of sources collated in the *Corpus antiphonalium officii*. These widely diffused pieces hardly permit one to identify or localise the repertory of their origin more precisely.

Although the list of antiphon-types 'Primum quaerite regnum dei …' is equally widely known, the formula '… tonus sic mediatur et sic finitur …' that summarises the rules of psalmody is less common and situates this tonary in an unquestionably French (or at least Romance-language) tradition, of which one of the first sources seems to be the Dominican tonary.[48] The relationship with the tonary of the Dominicans stops there, in any case. The number and usage of the psalm terminations (*seculorum amen*) diverge, and this tonary cites some antiphons that were unknown to the compiler of the Dominican antiphoner.

---

[44] '*De cantuum irregularitate*' and '*De tono cantuum irregularium*' (VI, lxxvii–lxxviii; CSM 3, vi, pp. 221–4).

[45] On these manuscripts, see the notices in *RISM* B III, 2, 3, and 6.

[46] '*Apollinis eclipsatur / In omnem terram / Zodiacum signis lustrantibus*', cf. Frank L. Harrison, *Musicorum collegio. Fourteenth-Century Musicians' Motets* (Monaco, 1986), pp. 7–10 and 37.

[47] Susan Fast classifies this source among the 'Parisian' recensions (A), cf. *Johannis de Muris, Musica 'speculativa'*, ed. Susan Fast (Ottawa, 1994; Wissenschaftliche Abhandlungen / Musicological Studies, 61), p. liv.

[48] Huglo, *Les Tonaires*, pp. 414–19 and Christian Meyer, 'Le Tonaire des Frères prêcheurs', *Archivum Fratrum Praedicatorum* 76 (2006): 117–56, in particular, pp. 138 ff.

Introduction

One should also note that the antiphons of the fifth tone only have a single psalm termination except for the antiphon to the Magnificat, *Alma redemptoris mater*, which is introduced by the psalm termination c c a b a G F.[49] The practice of only admitting a single psalm termination for the fifth mode is proper to the Cistercian and Dominican repertories, in particular, but is even recalled by Jacobus, who also cites the 'special' psalm termination reserved for the intonation of the antiphon, *Alma redemptoris mater*.[50] Later, the German theorist Gobelinus Person (1417) chooses precisely this last psalm termination as an example of those that are appropriate, but not necessary ('competentes et non necessariae').[51]

The antiphons of the sixth tone are likewise sung with a single psalm termination still attested in 1290 in the treatise on the modes by the Amiens theorist, Pierre de la Croix.[52] According to Jacobus, who was writing in the early fourteenth century, the use of this psalm termination, which he attributed to the Ancients, was by his time a thing of the past and must therefore have been abandoned during the course of the last quarter of the thirteenth century.[53] One should observe, finally, that this tonary, curiously, says nothing about the irregular antiphon *Nos qui vivimus* traditionally assigned to the psalm *In exitu Israel* (Ps. 113) sung at Sunday Vespers,[54] and that no commentary is added to the *Gloria patri* of the introits with which the first part of the treatise ends.

This tonary is thus aligned in many respects with a tendency proper to the thirteenth century in France towards the simplification of psalmody, which aimed to reduce the number of psalm terminations in particular.

2. MUSICA MENSURABILIS

The *Musica mensurabilis* of Lambertus occupies a major place in the history of mensural music theory of the last third of the thirteenth century. Situated within the prolongation of the modal theory of the *Ars antiqua* illustrated by Johannes de Garlandia, it introduces innovative elements that would be taken up again and developed by Franco.

The exposition of Lambertus can, in fact, be aligned with writings immediately posterior to the *Ars musice mensurabilis* of Johannes de

[49] See, for example, the antiphoner, Cambrai, Médiathèque Municipale, Ms. 38, f. 156r (at Vespers of the Commemoration of the Virgin; here transposed a fifth higher: g g e fe d c). The same antiphon was copied further on, f. 326 (Vespers of the Nativity of the Virgin), but with the psalm termination g g a f g e.

[50] IAC. LEOD. spec. VI, chap. xcvi, 2 and 7.

[51] Hermann Müller, 'Der *Tractatus musicae scientiae* des Gobelinus Person', *Kirchenmusikalisches Jahrbuch* 20 (1907): 193.

[52] *Petrus de Cruce Ambianensi 'Tractatus de tonis'*, ed. Denis Harbinson (Rome, 1976; Corpus Scriptorum de Musica, 29), p. xxix.

[53] IAC. LEOD. spec. VI, xcvii, 6 (ed. vol. 6, p. 279). According to Jacobus, this psalm termination had been reserved for antiphons beginning with a formula of the type FGa.

[54] On the divergent classifications of this antiphon, see Huglo, *Les Tonaires*, pp. 39, 53, 96, and IAC. LEOD. spec. VI, lxxxvi, 9–14 (ed. vol. 6, pp. 250–51).

The 'Ars musica' Attributed to Magister Lambertus/Aristoteles

Garlandia, even though in many respects it remains separate. Indeed, Johannes de Garlandia in his teaching not only presents the principles of polyphonic notations of the school of Notre Dame, but also treats consonances (chapters IX and X of the Reimer edition), the manners of temporal organisation of the vocal parts of discant, of which the multiple combinations of modes determine just as many elementary polyrhythmic models (chapter XI), and finally, organum. These diverse points of the teaching of Johannes de Garlandia – the theory of consonances, announced in [mm4] but not treated, polyrhythmic models, and organum – are absent from Lambertus's treatise, whose principal and almost exclusive focus is on the notation of durations.

The *Musica mensurabilis* consists of three large parts preceded by a prologue. The first [mm9–160] treats the figures of notes, simple or in ligature, with or without texts. The second [mm161–180] is devoted to time in music, a category that must precede any pronouncement on musical measure. The third [mm181–253] treats the fundamental structures of measured music, that is, the modes or rhythmic schemes. These three parts, which are applied above all to discant, are followed by explanations concerning the procedure and notation of singing called 'cutting up' or 'hocket', which is one of the three genres of mensural music. The study of *organum*, another genre announced in the prologue [mm6], seems to have been abandoned by the author, for the reason perhaps that this genre does not derive from strictly measured music, but from 'partly measured' ('partim mensurabilis') music, according to the classification of Franco.[55]

THE PROLOGUE

The Prologue [mm1–8] opens with a series of philosophical considerations on order, nature, and the principles of knowledge that is founded on the authority of Boethius and situates the present study of mensural music as an extension of the study of the fundamentals of plainchant. The plan sketched out here announces an exposition on the consonances and their mathematical foundation [mm4]. This section is absent in the text that has reached us, but may have resembled the study of consonances as developed by Johannes de Garlandia in chapters IX and X of his treatise,[56] or even the explanations of the fourth chapter of the Anonymous of St Emmeram.[57] Finally, the prologue places the entire exposition within a triple ternary division: that of the genres of mensural music (discant, hocket, and organum), of consonances (fourth, fifth, and octave), and finally of the cognitive categories of mensural music (*figura, tempus,* and *mensura*).

---

[55] 'Dividitur autem mensurabilis musica in mensurabilem simpliciter et partim. Mensurabilis simpliciter est dicantus, eo quod in omni parte sua tempore mensuratur. Partim mensurabilis dicitur organum pro tanto quod non in qualibet parte sua mensuratur'. FRANCO, I, 7–9 (ed. p. 25).

[56] Ioh. Garl. mens., pp. 67–74.

[57] Anon., Emmeram, pp. 258–68 (even-numbered pages).

xxiv

Introduction

I. FIGURA

THE FIGURES OF NOTES (FIGURAE)

This first section aims to establish the repertory of signs used to notate mensural music and their value of duration. The primary definition of the figure and of musical notation with or without text [mm12–15] is borrowed from Johannes de Garlandia and lightly reworked in its formulation.

SIMPLE FIGURES [mm16–85]

Mensural notation relies on three pairs of figures of identical geometrical shape, whose durations are regulated by art [mm16]. The author introduces in this place one of the fundamental and innovative principals of his theory, that is, the primary and triple ternary design of the longest duration in the system, that is, the long (Table 4). According to a simplified passage in the treatise on geometry falsely attributed to Boethius, this figure is to mensural music what the unity is to numbers [mm17–19].

Table 4   The Mathematical Structure of the Durations [mm21–26]

Perfect long	3 *tempora*
Imperfect long	2 *tempora*
'Normal' breve (*recta brevis*)	1 *tempus* (divides itself into two unequal parts)
'Secondary' breve (*altera brevis*)	2 *tempora*
Greater semibreve (*semibrevis maior*)	Greater part of a *tempus* [⅔ of a *tempus*]
Lesser semibreve (*semibrevis minor*)	Smaller part of a *tempus* [⅔ of a *tempus*]

The precedence of number in all things – and in particular of the ternary quality – rests on a series of philosophical and theological considerations [mm27–42] that were widely diffused in medieval commentaries on Aristotelian physics, but also in the commentaries on the *Sentences*: that is, the wisdom, power, and consubstantial grace of the divine nature, but also the immobile principle; God as principle of principles and final cause; the celestial sphere, the mobile principle that governs the movement of all things; and finally, the particular agent that is immediately present when taking effect.

The theory of modal notation distinguishes notations according to whether or not they are accompanied by text (*cum littera*) or not (*sine littera*). In the first case, the notation of durations is interdependent with the syllabification of the text; in the second, it is developed according to a graphic code materialised in the ligatures [mm13–15].

This distinction, which was introduced by Johannes de Garlandia, is echoed for a last time here before it disappears as an operational category with the tradition of teaching recorded by Franco. The rules of

xxv

The 'Ars musica' Attributed to Magister Lambertus/Aristoteles

cum littera notation that were formulated by Lambertus additionally rest on the principle according to which mensural singing proceeds from the unity of the long and is deployed in the framework of this 'perfection'. The idea of the perfection of the long as a single and triune entity imposes itself here as a theoretical tool that breaks with the notion of perfection obtained by amplification, that of the *ultramensurabiles* taught by Johannes de Garlandia and the Parisian author of the Anonymous of St Emmeram, whose principle is here refuted [mm53–55].

The principle of the notation *cum littera* is presented in the form of five rules (*regulae*) organising diverse combinations of figures of longs and breves [mm58–74] (see Table 5).

Table 5   **The Five Rules of Lambertus**

			perfectio	**perfectio**	**perfectio**
1a			L (3)	L	
1b	1B		L B (2+1)	L	
2	2B	L (3)	B B (1+2)	L (3)	
3	3B	L (3)	B B B (1+1+1)	L (3)	
4a	4B	L (3)	B B B (1+1+1)	B L (1+2)	
4b	4B	L B	B B B (1+1+1)	L (3)	
5	5B	L (3)	B B B (1+1+1)	B B (1+2)	

Each example, as is to be expected here, is excerpted from a vocal part of a motet. The example is taken either from the beginning or middle of a piece. The study of the notation *cum littera* is supplemented by two passages, of which the first explains the usage of the duplex longa and the duple subdivision of the breve. For Lambertus, contrarily to Johannes de Garlandia, the duplex longa escapes from the system of mensural notation [mm75–77]. It is reserved for the notation of the sustained notes of chant that support the measured parts. The second passage, on the subdivision of the breve [mm78–84], develops and specifies that which was said just above about this figure [mm26], that is, that every breve divides itself into three semibreves of equal duration or into two semibreves of unequal duration.

COMPOSITE FIGURES (LIGATURES) [mm85–160]
After having studied the forms and function of the simple figures, the author takes on the composite figures corresponding to more than one sound. The minimal form of the ligature is the plica [mm68–97], a simple figure that contains two sounds. Note that the present definition of the plica agrees with the teaching of Johannes de Garlandia, but also refers to the possible intervals between the two sounds constituting this figure. These precise indications can be compared to the explanations given in a brief treatise on the square

xxvi

Introduction

notation of plainchant of the second half of the thirteenth century,[58] in which the author announces four cases [mm90]:

1. The perfect plica, ascending or descending, whose properties are those of the perfect long, subdivided into 1 + 2 tempora [mm91–93].
2. The imperfect plica, ascending or descending, whose properties are those of the imperfect long, subdivided into 1 + 1 tempora [mm94].
3. The plica of the *brevis recta*.
4. The plica of the *brevis altera*.

The explanations concerning the *plica brevis* are nevertheless insufficient: the graphic forms of the descending and ascending plica are given with the title of 'third distinction'. The text omits the presentation of a 'fourth distinction' that is expected here. But it certainly seems that the final presentation ('potestatem autem hec observat regulam et naturam ...') suggests that the two preceding figures [mm95 and 96] must assume, depending on the metrical context, a value either of a *brevis recta* or a *brevis altera*.

Soon afterwards, Franco of Cologne would propose a considerably different system resting on the distinction between the long and the breve, respectively, as realised in the ascending and descending plica, whose graphic shapes would be independent of the values of duration (*longa perfecta/imperfecta, brevis perfecta/imperfecta*) and would indicate only the ascending or descending movement of the sound (see Table 6).[59]

Table 6   Franco's *plicae breves*

longa ascendens (b is the most correct shape)	(a) ♩	(b) ♩
longa descendens	♩	
brevis ascendens	♩	
brevis descendens	♩	

The author next examines (divisions 2 to 5) the ligatures of two, three, four, and five notes respectively. The exposition can be compared, on this point, with the rules of the Anonymous of St Emmeram, who distinguishes the ligatures according to the number of primary signs in subdividing them, as here, into 'distinctions', and uses the same vocabulary (binaria, ternaria, etc.) (Table 7).[60]

---

[58] Christian Meyer, 'La notation carrée du plain-chant. Le témoignage d'un traité inédit, Napoli, Biblioteca Nazionale VIII. D. 12, f. 24r–32r', *Études grégoriennes* 39 (2012): 221–41.

[59] Ch. 6 (pp. 41–3).

[60] The Anonymous of St Emmeram enumerates ligatures of up to ten notes, but examines more precisely only the ligatures consisting of a maximum of seven notes.

xxvii

The 'Ars musica' Attributed to Magister Lambertus/Aristoteles

Table 7   Lambertus' Ligatures

(2) *Ligatures of Two Notes* [mm**98–114**]:
    1.   rB Li (1+2 t.)[61]
    2.   Li rB (2+1 t.)
    3.   rB rB (1+1 t.)
    4.   miS maS or the reverse (1 t.) or B B (1+1 t.)

(3) *Ligatures of Three Notes* [mm**115–131**]:

1. III, II, II	Li rB Li (rB) (2+1+2 t.)
	Li rB Lp (Lp) (2+1+3 t.)
2. II, II, III	rB Li rB
3. I, III, III, III	(Lp) rB aB Lp (1+2 +3 t.)
4. II, III, II, II, III	rB Li + rB aB Lp (1+2 t., 1+2+3 t.)
5.	rB rB rB (*ordo* of the seventh mode)
6.	S S aB (rB)
	S S Lp (Lp)
7.	S S rB (aB)
	S S aB (Lp)
8.	aB S S
9.	S S S

(4) *Ligatures of Four Notes* [mm**132–150**]:

1.	Lp S S aB (3+1+2 t.)
2.	Li S S S (2 + 1 t.)
3.	Li S S aB (B)
	Li S S Lp (L)
4.	rB S S rB
5.	S S S rB (rB)
	S S S aB (L)
6.	rB S S S
7.	B B B Li (B)
	B B B Lp (L)
8.	B B B B
9.	S S Br Br
	S S Ba L

(5) *Ligatures of Five and of Six Notes* [mm**151–155**]:

1.	S S Br Br Li (B)
	S S Br Br Lp (L)
2.	S S S Br Br Li (B)
	S S S Br Br Lp (L)

---

[61] L = *longa*; Lp = *longa perfecta*; Li = *longa imperfecta*; B = *brevis*; rB = *recta brevis*; aB = *altera brevis*; S= *semibrevis*; miS = *minor semibrevis*; ma = *maior semibrevis*.

Introduction

The introduction to the study of the plica in ligatures [mm**156–160**] situates the science of notation as analogous to 'speculative' or theoretical science: the science of notation has no practical finality – it is only the strictly intellectual or theoretical approach of the notator's practice. This last section of the study of ligatures is comparable to the explanations given by the Anonymous of St Emmeram on the same subject.[62] The author only advances a single rule here [mm**160**]: an ascending or descending vertical stroke added to the last note of a ligature of two or more notes, in ascending or descending movement, is a *plica brevis*.

II. Tempus

The examination of the notion of *tempus* [mm**161–180**] begins with the affirmation, in agreement with Johannes de Garlandia, that the *tempus* is consubstantial to the unity of the breve. But, contrarily to Johannes de Garlandia who associates *tempus* with the indivisibility of the breve, Lambertus knows the semibreve but does not give it any value of duration – the idea of *tempus* thus has the basic duration of the smallest divisible unity, the semibreve being indivisible [mm**161**]. Following Johannes de Garlandia, Lambertus also distinguishes three modes of 'performance' of the *tempus*: in full voice, in a child's voice (or perhaps the voice of a falsettist), or by the sound produced artificially on an instrument ('vox cassa'); and finally by the absence of sound ('vox omissa') [mm**163–167**]. The exposition on the notation of silence [mm**168–180**] marks, by comparison with Johannes de Garlandia, the Anonymous of St Emmeram, or even Anonymous IV, significant progress in the rationalisation of their notation. Lambertus establishes, in fact, a strict equivalence between the durations of rests and of notes in developing a scale comprised of five values between 3 *tempora* and ⅓ *tempus* (3, 2, 1, ⅔, ⅓) (Table 8):

Table 8   **Durations of Rests**

four spaces: long	*'perfecta pausa'*
three spaces: altera brevis	*'pausula imperfecta'*
two spaces: recta brevis	*'suspirium breve'*
one space: semibrevis maior	*'semisuspirium maius'*
one half space: semibrevis minor	*'semisuspirium minus'*

This principle of notation would be adopted by the notator of the Bamberg codex and perpetuated by the tradition of Franco with substantial modifications.

---

[62] See the Edition, pp. 158 (l. 1–23) and 180 (l. 25–30) and the Appendix, p. 338.

III. *Mensura*

The study of measure, the third and last point of the exposition on the fundamentals of measurable music [mm181–253], opens with a new philosophical preamble situating measure as the precondition for the existence of all things. In music, measure is of a local order and of a temporal order. The former is that of *Musica plana*: it regulates the distances and relationships of sounds at the heart of the scale; the second is proper to mensural music [mm184–187]. The measure of the temporal order is the correct proportional relationship (*equalitas* [mm188]) between the figures, whatever their number, at the heart of a perfection, that is, the ternary quality of the long. The next part [mm189–190] presents a procedure for ensuring the temporal and harmonic congruence of two or three voices in a given place in polyphony: it suffices to start from a secure place, then to advance, voice by voice, in grouping the notes by ternary unity of perfection.

Measure is thus, in a way, the '*a priori* category' of the rhythmic modes, that is, of those metrical schemes borrowed from the grammarians that guided the composers and notators of *Ars antiqua* polyphony. The theory of the rhythmic modes appears first of all in a short treatise that is known only from the copy that Hieronimus de Moravia gives in his *Tractatus de musica* with the title of a *Discantus positio vulgaris*. This teaching, qualified as 'ordinary' here, states:

these modes number six. The first is composed of a long and a breve, the second of a breve and a long, the third of a long and two breves, the fourth of two breves and a long, the fifth only of longs, and the sixth only of breves and of semibreves.[63]

This teaching was gathered up by Johannes de Garlandia, who introduced a secondary distinction of each mode as perfect or imperfect: the perfect mode begins and ends with the same value of duration (*quantitas*) or the same rhythmic formula (*modus*); it is called imperfect when it finishes with a different value of duration than that by which it began.[64] Lambertus keeps this distinction, but nevertheless modifies its criteria [mm196–197]: the perfect mode observes a regular metrical schema and ends with the same value of duration (*quantitas*), the same rhythm (*numerus*), or the same rhythmic scheme (*maneries*) as this or that by which it begins; the imperfect mode, by contrast, presents rhythmic irregularities. This redefinition of the notion of the perfection and imperfection of the modes gives witness to an original conception of the rhythmic *ordo*, because it abandons the grammatical

---

[63] Christian Meyer and Guy Lobrichon, eds, *Hieronymi de Moravia, 'Tractatus de musica'*, Corpus Christianorum, Continuatio Mediaevalis, 250 (Turnhout, 2012), pp. 179–80 (chapter 26, l. 135–40).

[64] 'Dicitur modus perfectus, ut dicatur prima longa, altera brevis et altera longa, et sic de aliis modis sive maneriebus. Omnis modus dicitur imperfectus, quandocumque ita est, quod aliquis modus desinit per aliam quantitatem quam per illam, qua incipit, ut cum dicatur prima longa, altera brevis, altera longa et altera brevis' (I, 32–34; ed. p. 39).

Introduction

model according to which the rhythmic mode would be a succession of identical feet and introduces the idea of fragmentation or of 'diminution' of the constituent metrical unities of the rhythmic *ordo*.

In addition, Lambertus distances himself from the six modes commonly received, by raising their number to nine (Table 9). This theory of modes would remain singular. It was discussed at length by the Anonymous of St Emmeram[65] and was still recalled around 1300 by the theorist Johannes de Grocheio.[66] The Anonymous of St Emmeram's criticism sought, in particular, to object to the eighth and ninth modes for the reason that they could neither be perfect nor imperfect, given that they were only composed of semibreves, which, minor or major, were imperfect and could not bring forth a perfect *modus*. Curiously, Jacobus – who knew the treatise of Lambertus since he cited it repeatedly and notably on the question of Lambertus's first mode – did not say anything about this important aspect of Lambertus's theory of the rhythmic modes.

In positing as a prior condition that all of the modes derive from the first, which is formed by a continuous succession of perfections, Lambertus distinguishes three principal modes, the first (L L L …), the third (LB, LB …), and the seventh (nine breves), to which the others are subordinate in pairs. Then, in another unique aspect of the exposition, Lambertus gives two examples for each mode (except the first and the last), one with and the other without text (no theorist, in fact, gives examples in ligatures *sine littera*, on this point). The first and last mode nevertheless escape this presentation, however, since the first cannot be written in the form of ligatures as a consequence of the conclusive affirmation according to which 'it [the first mode] can never be reduced' for the reason of its absolute preeminence. As for the last mode, which concerns a combination of semibreves, the notation in ligatures is rather unusual, even though the existence of such ligatures will be explicitly presented further on (cf. [mm**129–131**]).

The system sketched out by Lambertus is remarkable for its mathematical clarity and unfolds within the framework of a large perfection formed of three *longas* (Table 10).

---

[65] ANON. Emmeram. p. 216, l. 25–214, l. 25.

[66] 'Sed Lambertus et alii istos modos ad novem ampliaverunt ex novem instrumentis naturalibus fantasiam adsumentes. Primum enim dixerunt, qui ex perfectionibus continuatur figura simili designatis. Et alios ex tempore et eius partibus composuerunt. Sed forte si aliquis tempus ad perfectionem comparaverit vel e contrario et tempus ad suas partes, inveniet multo plures'. (Ernst Rohloff, *Die Quellenhandschriften zum Musiktraktat des Johannes de Grocheio*, Leipzig, 1967, pp. 164–5.)

xxxi

Table 9   The Nine Modes of Lambertus

Positio vulgaris	5	1	2	3	4	–	6*	–	–
Johannes de Garlandia	5	1	2	3	4	–	6**	–	–
	LLL	LB	BL	LBB	BBL	SSBB	BBB …	SS …	SSS …
Lambertus	**I**	**II**	**III**	**IIII**	**V**	**VI**	**VII**	**VIII**	**IX**
Franco	1a	1b	2	3	4		5***	–	–

* 'ex omnibus brevibus et semibrevibus'.
** 'ex omnibus brevibus'.
*** 'ex omnibus brevibus et semibrevibus'.

Introduction

Table 10   Lambertus' Subdivided Perfection [mm199–253]

Modes	L	L	L
1	3	3	3
2	2, 1	2, 1	2, 1
3	1, 2	1, 2	1, 2
4	3	1, 2	3
5	1, 2	1, 2	3
6	3	½, ½, 1, 1	3
7	1, 1, 1	1, 1, 1	1, 1, 1
8	3 × (⅓, ⅔)	3 × (⅓, ⅔)	3
9	3 × (⅓, ⅓, ⅓)	3 × (⅓, ⅓, ⅓)	3 × (⅓, ⅓, ⅓)

Note: The values of ½, ⅓, and ⅔ are not expressed as such by the author of the treatise.

A few obscure points remain, notably on the question of the number of notes mentioned at almost every mode, beginning with the fourth. Thus, the fourth is said to hold 'a *quaternarius* of figures' that is, four notes (then twice three notes). The fifth would be called thus, because it is formed of five notes. The sixth is composed of six notes, the seventh of seven, and the eighth of eight. The number of notes is given here as a modal characteristic, which is true, in fact, if one considers the examples *sine littera* where the mode is presented in its most rigorous pronouncement. (In the examples *cum littera*, the characteristic rhythm of the mode is sometimes impeded by 'passing notes' that obscure the formulation.) For the seventh mode, nevertheless, the number seven is not found in the *cum littera* example ('O Maria virgo davitica'), nor, moreover, in the example in ligatures. Furthermore, according to the mathematical principal at work here, the number seven is difficult to reconcile with the structure of thrice three breves that characterises this mode. For the eighth mode, the example *cum littera* ('A ma dame …') counts, in fact, eight notes and syllables, but the example *sine littera* has 12 notes (thus, two perfections).

IIII. Armonia resecata
This last point of the exposition [mm254–267] treats the principles of the notation of 'hocket,' which is characterised by use of a single and unique rhythmic mode that produces a strict alternation of sounds and of silences [mm255]. The principle consists of cutting a given note by a fraction of its duration. This cutting up is signalled by a line (rest) placed next to the note whose duration is shortened. According to whether or not this line is placed before or after this note, the silence precedes or follows the note in question. The chosen example is that of the long (*perfectio*) cut by the value of one *tempus*, that is of a *brevis recta* [mm256, mm259 (ex.)]. Finally, one should note that Lambertus only

xxxiii

The 'Ars musica' Attributed to Magister Lambertus/Aristoteles

treats hocket in two voices [mm264], the third voice being present only to ensure harmonic support 'propter consonantiam perficiendam'.

THE EDITION

The text edited here exists in this form only in *P1* (apart from an initial lacuna of one folio) and in the manuscript, *Si*. The other sources transmit only one part of the treatise: the *Musica plana* in *P2*, and the *Musica mensurabilis* in *Erf*. *Hw* only gives some excerpts from the *Musica plana*, but an almost complete text of the *Musica mensurabilis*.

In examining the sources, it appears that the entire tradition derives from a corrupt archetype. A certain number of passages give witness in fact to evident errors, common to the known manuscript tradition, in particular in the *Musica plana* (*P1*, *P2*, *Si*, and *Hw*). Among the most significant indications to be kept in mind are:

1. The lacuna in the exposition of the parts of the theory of music (according to *De ortu scientiarum*): the first part is omitted [mp50].
2. The absence of the verse 'Voce sonat plena ...' in the versified summary on solmisation syllables [mp98–100]; without this verse, attested by the exogenous tradition of this summary, the exposition is evidently incomplete.
3. The absence of explanations concerning the major and minor seventh [mp187], even though this was announced above [mp139].
4. In the description of the octave, the relationship given as an example is that of the double octave [mp190].
5. The end of the explanations dedicated to figures called 'simple' seems irremediably corrupt [mm84].
6. Finally, there are the explanations concerning the notation of the pause of the value of the perfect long [mm175], whose grammar and syntax seem correct, but whose meaning escapes us. Beyond these observations, the examination of the variants – in particular, the errors common to certain manuscripts, authorises several hypotheses of classification.[67]

1. *P1* and *P2*, the two oldest sources:

[mp47] alia practica: alias [sc. partes] practica;
[mp52] similia: similibus (*Si* and in this edition, in agreement with the forms 'psalterio' and 'cythara');
[mp165] de origine al' (sc. de origine alia?, *P1*) de original' (sc. originali?, *P2*): de origine aliarum (*Si* and this edition agree with the exogenous tradition of this passage). The readings of

---

[67] Here, common variants (in orthography, reversed word order ...) that do not change the meaning of the received text or whose meaning (through synonyms, for example) remains admissible are not taken into account.

Introduction

P1 and *P2* seem to translate the hesitation of the scribes at the presence of a written sign or of an altered text.

2. *Si* (end of the fifteenth century)

More than two centuries separate the manuscript from Siena from the presumed date of composition of the treatise, in a time when this treatise and the techniques of notation that it describes already belong to the past. Apart from a large number of correct readings, *Si* agrees with some erroneous readings, sometimes with *P1*, sometimes with *P2*:

a. Errors in common with *P1*:

[mp185] 'intextorum': the right reading is 'intermixtorum';
[mm14] 'his' makes no sense ('huius' is necessary);
[mm100] 'subponitur' is evidently an error, because the note in question is situated well above the preceding note (thus: 'supraponitur').

b. Errors shared with *P2*:

[mp7] omission of 'esse'. 'esse' (to be) is needed here for the meaning and grammatical construction;
[mp31] 'perpensa' evidently results from an erroneous reading of the abbreviation for 'pro' (propensa);
[mp33] 'dicuntur' also results from an erroneous reading of the generally received text 'ducuntur'.

3. *Erf* (mid-fourteenth century)

This source, which only includes the *Musica mensurabilis*, presents unique readings and revisions or omissions of more or less greater amplitude with respect to *P1/Si*. The copy remained unfinished: no musical example – except for the figures of simple notes – was copied in the places set aside for that purpose, and the text is interrupted after the exposition of the nine rhythmic modes. Many variants of *Erf* nevertheless seem to approach the text of *Si*.[68] But one can equally observe that in *Erf* the figures of single note shapes (long, breve, semibreve) copied by the copyist of the text are presented as in *P1*, where each figure is surrounded by a circle.

P1 is the principal source of this edition. It is the oldest witness and one to which the professional calligraphy of the text and music

---

[68] Cf. mm35 et finis] finisque; mm61 appellatur] dicitur; mm74 scire poterit] poterit scire; mm91 ibi] hic; mm96 significans] signantem; mm100 est] etiam; mm107 nisi longa precedat *om.*; mm137 patet *om.*; mm139 patet *om.*; mm144 ascendente] ascendendo; mm165 secundum] per; mm167 vox *om.*

The 'Ars musica' Attributed to Magister Lambertus/Aristoteles

confers great authority. Despite the corrections seemingly contributed by the original copyist, the text presents a certain number of absurd readings, which the manuscript tradition permits one to correct easily. These errors nevertheless betray the work of a copyist little informed in the subject matter of music.[69] One can add that this copyist must have followed a considerably comparable model in two columns.[70]

In this edition, the orthography of Greco-Latin names was normalised (thus, for example: diapente, diatessaron, diapason ..., autentus ... and not: dyapente, dyatessaron, dyapason ... authentus ...). The orthographic variants for these terms were not listed. The musical examples of the *Musica mensurabilis* reproduced in this edition are those of *P1*. It was decided not to edit them here, but a synoptic presentation of these examples in the different sources is online.[71] Last, small black triangles to the right of the text signal associated commentary in the Critical and Explanatory Notes.

Translated by Barbara Haggh-Huglo[72]

---

[69] mp**45** science (*om.*); mp**51** sunt (*om.*); mp**72** quoque (quorum *P1*); mp**74** repertorem (reperatorem *P1*); mp**82** homo (hominum *P1*); mp**85** theorice (theorie *P1*); mp**133** causa descensionis (*om.*); mp**184** tonus (sonus *P1*); mp**190** dupla (duplum *P1*); mp**341** si incipit-ut hic, talis habet (*om.*); mp**342** intonationibus (intonantibus *P1*), officiorum (*om.*); mm**25** maior est (maiore *P1*); mm**26** minor est (minore *P1*); mm**37** trina (trinam *P1*); mm**69** longitudine (longitudinem *P1*); mm que (quod *P1*) non; mm**83** significare (si grate *P1*); mm**89** distantias (*om.*); mm**96** diversos (divisos *P1*); mm**106** quinto (vero *P1*); mm**114** ita (nisi *P1*) quod; mm**160** ultima breviatur (ultima si breviantur *P1*); mm**202** excipitur (exipitur *P1*); mm**283** trina (tertia *P1*); mm**242** subscriptarum (subscripturarum *P1*); mm**251** perficietur (proficietur *P1*); mm**257** principii (percipii *P1*).

[70] Cf., for example, the skip from the same to the same in mp**126/127**.

[71] See Christian Meyer, 'L'"Ars musica" attribuée à maître Lambert / Aristote. I. Introduction et Notes critiques et explicatives, II. Annexe'; in the open-access archive HAL of the French Centre national de la recherche scientifique: http://hal.archives-ouvertes.fr

[72] I wish to thank Dr. Karen Desmond for her helpful comments on my translation.

Translator's Note

Karen Desmond

In translating these two linked treatises, I have followed the Latin word order where possible, especially when the placement of words affects the meaning or emphasis. Terminology that is more easily understood in Latin (due to the history of its use in musicological scholarship) is left in Latin and italicised, for example: *musica mundana, musica humana, musica instrumentalis; durum* and *mollis*; the qualifications of the breve as *recta* or *altera* (understood in the sense that one breve is a proper breve, as opposed to that other sort of breve); *organum*; the rhythmic *ordo* or *ordines*. Similarly, scholastic terms, such as *genus* and *materia*, which are to be understood in their Aristotelian sense, are left untranslated, since the English equivalents, in particular 'matter', would yield an ambiguous translation. The term *proprietas*, again with a scholastic inheritance, is left in the Latin: it is to be understood as an Aristotelian 'property' (which for Lambertus means simply a stroke that is a 'property' or characteristic of a figure). *Proprietas* is left untranslated to avoid any confusion with the current English meaning of 'property' as a possession or good that belongs to someone or something. *Tempus* could have been translated directly as 'time', but *tempus* more accurately conveys the specific mensural meaning that Lambertus employs here. Words that have entered the musicological lexicon but for which there is no direct translation, such as diapente, diapason, or plica, are not italicised.

Sometimes Lambertus will use a single term that has different meanings in different contexts, and in these cases I have guided the reader's interpretation. For example, in certain sections of the *Musica plana*, Lambertus uses 'voces' to refer to solmisation syllables (*ut, re, mi, fa, sol, la*), and so I have used the more specific translation of 'voces' as 'solmisation syllables'; but at mm**163–167** a translation of 'vox' as 'voice' is more appropriate; and elsewhere the more generic translation of 'pitch' suffices. Similarly, 'cantus' is sometimes translated as 'chant' and sometimes as 'song' depending on the particular context. In the *Musica plana*, it was more straightforward to leave *differentia* untranslated, as it is common term used in chant scholarship in discussions of plainchant tonaries; in the *Musica mensurabilis*, however, I translate the term as 'distinction', because here Lambertus uses the term 'differentia' not as a reference to plainchant, but instead to lay out the distinctions between ligatures comprised of two, three, four or more figures.

Lambertus has a tendency, particularly in the *Musica mensurabilis*, to anthropromorphise the elements of musical notation, in particular the figures (*figurae*): they are often described as actually acting themselves, rather than being acted upon (by the notator or singer). For example,

with reference to the perfect long he writes [mm65]: '[the perfect] long does not know how to retain perfection except through some mediating perfection that follows it.' This tendency is evident in the verse passage that concludes the *Musica mensurabilis*. In these cases I have conveyed Lambertus's expression by maintaining the active voice if possible, with the figures themselves as the subjects of the sentences.

For the most part, I have followed the punctuation of the Latin edition, but have split long Latin sentences into separate English sentences if required by sense or readability. I have used square brackets for supplied words that are implicit in the Latin but not stated, or for editorial qualifications of sense or meaning, for example when I have supplied the noun for substantives [*omnia, haec,* etc.] to clarify meaning. Third-person singular verbs have on occasion been translated as plural verbs to allow for gender-inclusive pronouns.

Edition and Translation

Christian Meyer, editor, and Karen Desmond, translator

Tabula abbreviationum

Anderson, Lambertus	Gordon A. Anderson, 'Magister Lambertus and Nine Rhythmic Modes', *Acta musicologica* 45 (1973): 57–73.
Anon. Carthus.	Sergej Lebedev, ed., *Cuiusdam Cartusiensis monachi tractatus de musica plana* (Tutzing, 2000; Musica mediaevalis Europae occidentalis, 3).
Anon. Claudifor.	Karl Rauter, ed., *Der Klagenfurter Musiktraktat von 1430 – Tractatus de musica* (Klagenfurt, 1989).
Anon. Couss.	Charles Edmond Henri de Coussemaker, ed., *Scriptorum de musica medii aevi* (Paris, 1867/repr. Hildesheim, 1988), vol. 4, pp. 434–69.
Anon. Emmeram.	Jeremy Yudkin, ed., *De musica mensurata. The Anonymous of St Emmeram. Complete Critical Edition, Translation, and Commentary* (Bloomington,1990).
August. min.	Michael Bernhard, ed., *Die Thomas von Aquin zugeschriebenen Musiktraktate* (Munich, 2006; Bayerische Akademie der Wissenschaften. Veröffentlichungen der Musikhistorischen Kommission, 18), pp. 90–147.
Bekker	Immanuel Bekker, ed., *Aristoteles, Metaphysica* (Oxford, 1837).
Berno prol.	Alexander Rausch, ed., *Die Musiktraktate des Abtes Bern von Reichenau* (Tutzing, 1999; Musica mediaevalis Europae occidentalis, 5).
Boeth. arithm.	Gottfried Friedlein, ed., *Anicii Manlii Torquati Severini Boetii de institutione arithmetica libri duo. De institutione musica libri quinque* (Leipzig, 1867).
Boeth. Cons.	Ludwig Bieler, ed., *Anicii Manlii Severini Boethii Philosophiae Consolatio* (Turnhout, 1984; CCSL, 94).
Boeth. mus.	Gottfried Friedlein, ed., *Anicii Manlii Torquati Severini Boetii de institutione arithmetica libri duo. De institutione musica libri quinque* (Leipzig, 1867).
CAO	René-Jean Hesbert, ed., *Corpus antiphonalium officii*, 6 vols (Rome, 1963–1979).
Comm. Boeth. II	Matthias Hochadel, ed., *Commentum Oxoniense in musicam Boethii. Eine Quelle zur Musiktheorie an der spätmittelalterlichen Universität* (Munich, 2002; Bayerische Akademie der Wissenschaften. Veröffentlichungen der Musikhistorischen Kommission, 16).

Compil. Ticin.	Michael Bernhard, ed., *Die Thomas von Aquin zugeschriebenen Musiktraktate* (Munich, 2006; Bayerische Akademie der Wissenschaften. Veröffentlichungen der Musikhistorischen Kommission, 18), pp. 17–50.
CS 1	Edmond de Coussemaker, *Scriptorum de musica medii aevi* (repr. Hildesheim, 1963), vol. 1.
CSM	*Corpus scriptorum de musica*
FRANCO	Gilbert Reaney, ed., *Franconis de Colonia: Ars cantus mensurabilis* ([Rome], 1974; CSM 18).
Gennrich, Bibliographie	Friedrich Gennrich, *Bibliographie der ältesten französischen und lateinischen Motetten* (Darmstadt, 1958).
Gloss. Mart. Cap.	Mariken Teeuwen, *Harmony and the Music of the Spheres. The 'Ars Musica' in Ninth-Century Commentaries on Martianus Capella* (Leiden, 2002; Mittellateinische Studien und Texte, 30).
Guido micr.	Joseph Smits van Waesberghe, ed., *Guidonis Aretini Micrologus* ([s·l·], 1955; CSM 4).
Guido prol.	\<Joseph Smits van Waesberghe, ed.\>, *Guidonis Prologus in antiphonarium* (Buren, 1975; DMA A.III).
Guido reg.	\<Joseph Smits van Waesberghe, ed.\>, *Guidonis Aretini Regulae rhythmicae* (Buren, 1985; DMA A.IV).
Gundissalinus	Ludwig Baur, ed., *Dominicus Gundissalinus, De divisione philosophiae* (Münster, 1903). http://hipatia.uab.cat/islamolatina/documents/de_partibus_philosophiae.pdf
Haines, Epyglotus	John Haines, 'Lambertus's Epiglotus', *The Journal of Medieval Latin* 16 (2006): 142–63.
Hugo de Sancto Victore	H. Butimer, ed., *Hugo de Sancto Victore, Didascalicon. De studio legendi* (Washington, 1939; Catholic University of America. Studies in Medieval and Renaissance Latin, 10).
Hugo Spechtsh. comm.	Karl-Werner Gümpel, ed., *Hugo Spechtshart von Reutlingen. Flores musicae (1332/42)* (Wiesbaden, 1958; Abhandlungen der Geistes- und Sozialwissenschaftlichen Klasse/ Akademie der Wissenschaften und der Literatur in Mainz, 1958, 3).
Iac. Leod. spec.	Roger Bragard, ed., *Jacobi Leodiensis Speculum musicae*, 7 vols (Rome, 1955–73; *CSM* 3).
Ioh. Cott. mus.	Joseph Smits van Waesberghe, ed., Iohannes dictus Cotto sive Affligemensis: De musica ([Rome], 1950; CSM 1), pp. 44–162.
Ioh. Garl. mens.	Erich Reimer, *Johannes de Garlandia. De mensurabili musica.* I: *Quellenuntersuchungen und Edition*, II: *Kommentar und Interpretation der Notationslehre* (Wiesbaden, 1972; Beihefte zum Archiv für Musikwissenschaft, 10–11).
Ioh. Mur. comp.	Ulrich Michels, ed., *Joh. de Muris Notitia artis musicae et Compendium musicae practicae. Petrus de S. Dionysio. Tractatus de musica* (Rome, 1972; *CSM* 17), pp. 119–45.
Iohannes Scottus Eriugena	Inglis Patric Sheldon-Williams, L. Bieler, and J.J. O'Meara, eds, *Iohannes Scottus Eriugena, De divisione naturae* (Dublin, 1968–1981).

Isid. etym.	W. M. Lindsay, ed., *Isidori Hispalensis episcopi etymologiarum sive originum libri XX* (Oxford, 1911).
Lad. Zalk.	Michael Bernhard, 'Tractatus ex traditione Hollandrini a Ladislao de Zalka exscriptus', *Traditio Iohannis Hollandrini*, ed. Michael Bernhard and Elżbieta Witkowska-Zaremba (Munich, 2015; Bayerische Akademie der Wissenschaften. Veröffentlichungen der Musikhistorischen Kommission, vol. 24), vol. 6, pp. 301–416.
LmL	*Lexikon musicum Latinum Medii Aevi*, ed. Michael Bernhard (Munich, 1992–).
Ludwig, Quellen	Friedrich Ludwig, 'Die Quellen der Motetten ältesten Stils', *Archiv für Musikwissenschaft*, 5/3 (1923): 185–222 and 5/4 (1924): 273–315 (especially p. 293).
Ludwig, Repertorium	Friedrich Ludwig, *Repertorium organorum recentioris et motetorum vetustissimi stili* (Halle, 1910).
Meyer, Diagramme	Christian Meyer, 'Le diagramme lambdoïde du Ms. Oxford Bodleian Library Auct. F. 3. 15 (3511)', *Scriptorium* 49 (1995): 228–37.
Meyer, Mathématique	Christian Meyer, 'Mathématique et musique au Moyen Age', *Quadrivium. Musiques et sciences* (colloquium: Metz, 8–10 March 1991) ed. Dan Lustgarten, Claude-Henry Joubert, Serge Pahaut, and Marcos Salazar (Paris, 1992), pp. 107–21.
Meyer/Wicker, Leo Hebraeus	Christian Meyer, Jean-François Wicker, 'Musique et mathématique au XIVe siècle. Le *De numeris harmonicis* de Leo Hebraeus', *Archives Internationales d'Histoire des Sciences* 50 (2000) : 30–67.
Nic. Weyts	Charles Edmond Henri de Coussemaker, ed., *Scriptorum de musica medii aevi*, 4 vols (Paris, 1867/repr. Hildesheim, 1988), vol. 3, pp. 262–64.
Nicol. Cap.	Adrien de la Fage, *Essais de diphthérographie musicale* (Paris, 1864), pp. 309–35.
P. Vergilius Maro	Otto Ribbeck, ed., P. Vergilius Maro, *Eclogae sive Bucolica* (Leipzig, 1894).
Petr. Palm.	Johannes Wolf, 'Ein Beitrag zur Diskantlehre des 14. Jahrhunderts', *Sammelbände der Internationalen Musikgesellschaft* 15 (1913–14): 505–34.
Ps.-Boethius. Geometria	Gottfried Friedlein, ed., Anicii Manlii Torquati Severini Boetii, *De institutione arithmetica* (...) (Leipzig, 1867).
Ps.-Phil. lib. mus.	Charles Edmond Henri de Coussemaker, ed., *Scriptorum de musica medii aevi* (Paris, 1867/repr. Hildesheim, 1988), vol. 3, pp. 35–46.
Ps.-Thomas aqu.	Michael Bernhard, 'Die Thomas von Aquin zugeschriebenen Musiktraktate' (Munich, 2006; Bayerische Akademie der Wissenschaften. Veröffentlichungen der Musikhistorischen Kommission), pp. 77–84.

The 'Ars musica' Attributed to Magister Lambertus/Aristoteles

QUAT. PRINC.

Luminita Florea Aluas, 'The *Quatuor principalia musicae*: A Critical Edition and Translation, with Introduction and Commentary' (Ph.d. diss., Indiana University, 1996) (= Charles Edmond Henri de Coussemaker, ed., *Scriptorum de musica medii aevi* (Paris, 1867/ repr. Hildesheim, 1988), vol. 4, pp. 200–98).

RISM

Répertoire International des Sources Musicales

Sachs, Elementarlehre

Klaus-Jürgen Sachs, 'Musikalische Elementarlehre im Mittelalter', *Geschichte der Musiktheorie*, ed. Frieder Zaminer (Darmstadt, 1990), vol. 3, pp. 105–61

TRAD. Garl. plan. I

Christian Meyer, ed., *Musica plana Johannis de Garlandia* (Baden-Baden – Bouxwiller, 1998), pp. 3–21.

TRAD. Garl. plan. III

Ibid., pp. 39–53.

TRAD. Garl. plan. IV

Ibid., pp. 55–62.

TRAD. Holl. V

Christian Meyer, 'Tractatus ex traditione Hollandrini cod. lat. Monacensis 30056 una cum cod. Monacensi 4387, Berolinensi mus. ms. theor. 1590 et Augsburgensi 4° 176', *Traditio Iohannis Hollandrini*, ed. Michael Bernhard and Elżbieta Witkowska-Zaremba (Munich, 2011; Bayerische Akademie der Wissenschaften. Veröffentlichungen der Musikhistorischen Kommission, vol. 21), vol. 3, pp. 7–206.

TRAD. Holl. VI

Konstantin Voigt, 'Tractatus ex traditione Hollandrini (...)', *Traditio Iohannis Hollandrini*, ed. Michael Bernhard and Elżbieta Witkowska-Zaremba (Munich, 2011; Bayerische Akademie der Wissenschaften. Veröffentlichungen der Musikhistorischen Kommission, vol. 21), vol. 3, pp. 207–25.

TRAD. Lamb.

André Gilles, '*De musica plana breve compendium* (Un témoignage de l'enseignement de Lambertus)', *Musica disciplina* 43 (1989): 40–51.

Lambertus, 'Ars musica'

SIGLA CODICUM ET FONTIUM

Erf	Erfurt, Wissenschaftliche Allgemeinbibliothek, CA 8° 94
P1	Paris, Bibliothèque nationale de France, Lat. 11266
P2	Paris, Bibliothèque nationale de France, Lat. 6755.2
Si	Siena, Biblioteca Comunale, L V 30
Be	Berlin, Deutsche Staatsbibliothek, Mus. ms. theor. 1520
Mü	Munich, Bayerische Staatsbibliothek, Clm 24809
Ve	Venice, Biblioteca Nazionale Marciana, Lat. Cl. VIII.24
Hw	Iohannes Herwagius, ed., *Opera Bedae venerabilis* (Basel, 1563), vol. 1, cols 404–34.
Cs	Charles Edmond Henri de Coussemaker, ed., *Scriptorum de musica medii aevi* (Paris, 1867/repr. Hildesheim, 1988), vol. 1, pp. 251–81.

EXPLICATIO ABBREVIATURARUM

add.	addidit
cod.	codex, codice
dub.	lectio dubia
marg.	margine
om.	omisit
ras.	rasura
suprascr.	suprascriptum
Σ consensus	codicum
▶	commentum

Lambertus
(quidam Aristoteles)
<Ars musica>
<Musica plana>

Si 14r/*P2* 71ra/ [1] Quoniam circa artem musicam necessaria quedam ad utilitatem
Cs 251a/*Hw* 415 cantantium tractatim proponimus, necesse est, quod secundum
auctoris intencionem subtilissimas regulas summopere subiectas
intelligere studeamus. [2] Cum humana natura naturaliter omnia scire
desideret, et a primi hominis peccato quatuor sunt mala que
naturam impediunt humanam, scilicet ignorantia, vicium, imperitia
loquendi et indigentia, [3] quibus tamen quatuor bona sunt opposita,
scilicet ignorantie sapientia, vicio virtus, imperitie loquendi
eloquentia, indigentie necessitas, ideoque divina clementia
philosophis peritiam artes inveniendi concessit, [4] ut per earum
notitiam quisque valeat predicta bona comprehendere, et fruendo
hiis lapsam naturam eciam ad meliorem consistentiam sublimare. ▶ *p. 117*
[5] Cumque unum discere valde sit difficile, de multis non est dubium,
quin sit impossibile. [6] In omni tamen arte valde plura sunt que
nostro sensu cognoscimus quam ea que a magistro didicimus. |
Cs 251b [7] Nam sicut in arbore unam natura virtutem multarum regitivam
propaginum complantavit, sic in homine ratio ex unius scientia esse
rerum multarum docuit invenire.

---

1 Compil. Ticin. A 2; Quat. princ. 1, 1 ('necesse est quod quod secundum auctoris
intentionem subtilissimas regulas curiose subiectas intelligere studiam') ‖ **2–4**
Compil. Ticin. A 1; Quat. princ. 1, 1; Trad. Holl. VI 1, 5–7; Nicol. Cap., p. 309 ‖ **2**
(cum natura … desideret) cf. Aristoteles, *Metaphysica* (Iacobus Veneticus transl.),
I, 1 (Bekker 980a) ('Omnes homines scire desiderant natura') ‖ **5** Guido prol. 34
‖ **6** Guido prol. 6; Iac. Leod. spec. 2, 3, 4 *al.* ‖ **7** Quat. princ. 1, 2 ('Nam sicut in
arbore una nulla multarum propaginum virtutem vegitativam complantavit, sic
in homine et racio et exercicium ex unius sciencia docet scienciam multarum
rerum invenire')

1–40 *deest P1* ‖ **1** sancti spiritus adsit nobis gratia *suprascr. Si* | tractatim] tractare
Hw | quod] ut *Hw* ‖ **2** Cum] Quum enim *Hw* | desideret] desiderat *SiHw* |
primi] primis *Hw* | naturam-humanam] naturam humanam impediunt *Si* ‖ **3**
artes] artem *Si* ‖ **4** earum] eorum *Si* eam *CsHw* | notitiam quisque] quisque
notitiam *CsHwP2Si* | fruendo] faciendo *CsHw* | eciam ad] et ad *Hw* ‖ **5** quin]
cum *Hw* | sit] sit quasi *Hw* ‖ **6** in-arte] in omnibus tamen *Hw* | valde *om. Si*
| cognoscimus] agnoscimus *Hw* ‖ **7** unam] una *P2* | natura] naturae *Hw* |
propaginum] propaginem *Hw* | esse *om. P2Si* | rerum *om. Hw*

Lambertus
(A certain Aristotle)
Ars musica
Musica plana

[1] Since we are setting forth, at length, some essential elements of the musical art for the benefit of singers, it is necessary that we strive to understand the most subtle rules laid before us with the utmost diligence, according to the author's purpose. [2] While human nature naturally desires to know all, even from the first sin of humankind on there are four evils which ensnare human nature, that is, ignorance, vice, unskilled speech, and want. [3] To these, however, are opposed four good things, namely: wisdom to ignorance, virtue to vice, eloquence to unskilled speech, necessity to want. And therefore divine mercy has granted to philosophers the skill to discover arts, [4] in order that through knowledge of them anyone may comprehend the aforesaid good things, and by benefiting from them elevate their own lapsed nature to a better state. [5] And since it is difficult to learn one thing well, there is no doubt but that it is impossible to learn many things. [6] Nonetheless, in every art, the things that we recognize from our sense[s] outnumber those we have learnt from a teacher.

[7] For just as in a tree, nature planted one power that governs many shoots, so in a human, reason, from the knowledge of one thing, has taught [us] to find the essence of many things.

The 'Ars musica' Attributed to Magister Lambertus/Aristoteles

[8] Hic etiam illud intuendum est, quod omnis ars omnisque disciplina honorabiliorem naturaliter habeat rationem, quam

P2 71rb artificium quod manu atque | opere exercetur. [9] Multo enim maius atque aptius est scire quod quisque faciat quam ipsum illud efficere quod sciat. [10] Etenim artificium illud corporale quasi serviens famulatur, ratio vero quasi domina imperat, et nisi manus secundum id quod ratio sancit, operetur, frustra fit. [11] In tanto igitur preclarior est scientia musice in cognitione rationis quam in opere efficiendi atque actu, in quanto corpus mente superatur, quod scilicet rationis expers servitio degit. [12] Illa vero imperat atque ad rectum deducit. [13] Quod nisi eius pareatur imperio, expers opus rationis titubabit. [14] Unde fit ut speculatio rationis operandi actu non egeat, manuum vero nulla sint opera nisi ratione ducantur. [15] Iam vero quanta sit gloria meritumque rationis hinc intelligi potest, quod ceteri ut ita dicam corporales artifices non ex disciplina, sed ex ipsis potius instrumentis cepere vocabula. [16] Nam citharedus ex cithara, |

CS 252a tibicen vel auledus ex tibia, ceterique suorum instrumentorum vocabulis nuncupantur. [17] Ratio vero non ab instrumentis sed ad speculatione et scientia denominare voluit musice professores. [18] Si

Si 14v quis ergo | ex improviso discit cantare, qualitates et quantitates,
Hw 416 simi l litudines et dissimilitudines diversorum sonorum, proportiones, tempora et mensuram, necnon et distinctiones longarum breviumque figurarum et semibrevium discernere voluerit, fontem iubilationis huius scientie haureat, et eius suavitatem experietur. [19] Nam qui vineam plantare vult, unam arbusculam inserere, vel unum asinum onerare cognoverit sicut in

P2 71va uno, ita in omnibus | <similiter> facere vel melius non dubitabit.

[20] In principio autem huius scientie scire opinamur quid sit musica, vel quis musicus et unde dicatur, quid genus, que materia, que partes, que species, quod instrumentum, que utilitas, quis artifex, quod officium.

[21] Unde scire debemus quod musica est liberalis scientia perite cantandi copiam subministrans. [22] Sed hec dividitur, quia alia mundana, alia humana, alia instrumentalis. [23] Mundana vero est illa que in complexionali effectu elementorum et temporum atque superiorum corporum iugabilis efficitur. [24] Humana est illa que in

---

8–16 Boeth. mus. I, 34 (p. 223, l. 28–224 , l. 18) ‖ **17** Quat. princ. 1, 3; Anon. Carthus. theor. pr. 5 ‖ **18** cf. Quat. princ. 1, 4; (qualitates quantitates … discernere voluerit) cf. *infra*, mm 4 ‖ **19** Guido prol. 14 ‖ **21** Compil. Ticin. A 15; Trad. Lamb. 1,1,1; Quat. princ. 1, 5, *al.*; Hugo Spechtsh. comm. p. 19 ‖ **23** cf. August. min. BV 13, C 13, D 13 ‖ **24** Quat. princ. 1, 5; Ioh. Mur. comp. 6,4

8 manu atque opere] opere et manu *Si* ‖ **10** quasi[1+2]] quod *Hw* | id quod] quod *Hw* | sancit] canit *HwSi* | operetur] operatur *Hw* ‖ **11** in quanto] quanto *P2* | expers] expres *ante corr.* *P2* | servitio] sine ratione *Hw* ‖ **13** pareatur] perarum *P2* ‖ **14** operandi] aperiendi *P2* | nulla] plura *sub ras.* *Si* ‖ **15** meritumque] multumque *Hw* | quod] qui *Hw* | ipsis] ipsius *P2* ‖ **16** citharedus] citaredus *Si* | ceterique] ceterisque *Hw* ‖ **18** improviso] proviso *Si* | discit] discere *Si* | necnon et] necnon *Si* | distinctiones] distractiones *P2* | discernere] decernere *Si* | haureat] hauriat *HwSi* ‖ **19** vult plantare *Si* | vult] vel *P2* | unam] vel unam *Si* | onerare] hanorare *P2* ornare *Si* | cognoverit] cognovit *Hw* ‖ **20** de multiplicitate nominis musices artis *tit.* *P2* | vel *om.* *Si* | quid genus] quid genus vel quod *Si* quod genus *Hw* | quis artifex *om.* *Hw*

[8] Here too this must be observed, that every art and every discipline naturally possesses a more honorable principle than the craft that is exercised by hand and by work. [9] For it is by far greater and more appropriate to know what someone makes than to know how to produce the actual thing one knows. [10] For this bodily skill does a slave's work like one in service, but reason commands like a mistress. And unless the hand performs that which reason decrees, it is in vain. [11] Therefore, the science of music is as much more illustrious in the knowledge of the principle than in the work of execution and its act, as the body is excelled by the mind, because it is devoid of reason and lives through service, [12] but reason rules and leads back to the right path. [13] For unless her command is obeyed, work devoid of reason will stumble. [14] Whence it comes about that the contemplation of reason does not lack a working act, but that there are no works of the hands unless they are guided by reason. [15] But how great the glory and worth of reason are understood to be even from this, that the other so to speak bodily artisans have taken their names not from an [intellectual] discipline, but rather from the instruments themselves. [16] For *citharedus* from *cithara*, *tibicen* or *auledus* from *tibia*, and the rest are so called from the names of their instruments. [17] But reason chose to call those who professed of music not after instruments but after speculation and science. [18] Therefore, if anyone all of a sudden learns to sing, let them decide to distinguish the qualities and quantities, similitudes and dissimilitudes of various sounds, proportions, times and measures, and also the distinctions of long and short figures and semibreves; let them drink the source of this science's jubilation, and they will experience its sweetness. [19] For let anyone who wishes to plant a vineyard know how to graft one little tree, or to load an ass; as they have done in one [thing], they will not hesitate to do in all things even better.

[20] But to know the beginnings of this science we may ask what music is, or who a musician is, and from there it may be said, what is the *genus*, what is the *materia* [of this science], what are the parts, what are the *species*, what is an instrument, what is [this science's] utility, who is a composer, what is [this science's] function?

[21] From this we ought to know that music is a liberal science furnishing the ability of singing skillfully. [22] But it is divided, for one is *musica mundana*, another is *musica humana*, and another is *musica instrumentalis*. [23] *Musica mundana* is when a union is formed from the combination of the elements and times, and of the heavenly bodies. [24] *Musica humana* is that

The 'Ars musica' Attributed to Magister Lambertus/Aristoteles

coniunctione corporis et anime consistit. [25] Instrumentalis est discernendis et dignoscendis cantibus attributa. [26] Et hec dividitur, quia alia armoniaca, alia ritmica, alia metrica.

[27] Armoniaca vero est illa que discernit inter sonum gravem et acutum, vel armoniaca est illa que consistit in numeris dupliciter et mensuris: una localis secundum proportionem sonorum et vocum, alia temporalis secundum proportionem longarum breviumque figurarum. [28] Et est idem armonia quod discrecio modulacionis et veraciter canendi scientia, et facilis ad perfectionem canendi via, pluriumque vero perdissimilium proportionalis consonantia, et scientia de numero relato ad sonum.

P2 71vb – Cs 252b   [29] Ritmica vero est illa que in scansione verborum requiritur utrum bene vel male cohereant dictiones, | quod cantando | vitandum est tanquam legendo.

[30] Metrica vero est illa que mensuram diversorum metrorum ostendit probabili ratione, ut patet in heroico, iambico et elegiaco metro.

[31] Musicus vero est ille, qui ratione perpensa non solum operis servitio, sed etiam speculationis imperio canendi scientiam manifestat, [32] quod scilicet in edificiorum bellorumque opere videmus, in contraria scilicet nuncupatione vocabuli. [33] Eorum namque nominibus velut edificia inscriberentur vel ducuntur triumphi, quorum imperio hac ratione sunt instituta, non quorum opere servitioque perfecta. [34] Unde philosophus pulchre sic ait:

Si 15r   [35] Musicorum | et cantorum magna est distantia;

[36] Isti discunt, illi sciunt, que componit musica.

[37] Nam qui canit quod non sapit, diffinitur bestia.

[38] Unde versus:

[39] Bestia non cantor, qui non canit arte sed usu;

[40] Non vox cantorem facit artis sed documentum.

P1 1ra   [41] Musica enim dicitur a musis, que secundum fabulam dicuntur filie Iovis, et habet duplicem considerationem, scilicet secundum

---

25 QUAT. PRINC. 1, 6; AUGUST. MIN. BV 8; COMM. Boeth. II, p. 112, 18 et 134, 26; IOH. MUR. comp. 6.4 ‖ **27–30** QUAT. PRINC. 1, 6.- Gundissalinus, p. 99 ‖ **31** (musicus-imperio) BOETH. mus. I, 34 (p. 224, l. 18–20) ‖ **32–33** BOETH. mus. I, 34 (p. 224, l. 20–25) ‖ **35–37** GUIDO reg. 1–3 ‖ **39–40** TRAD. Lamb. 1,2; QUAT. PRINC. 1, 9; Ps.-THOMAS AQU. I 43 *al* ‖ **41** (que secundum … Iovis) TRAD. Lamb. 1,3; COMPIL. Ticin. A 16; (secundum modum et non modum) ANON. Emmeram. VI (p. 282, l. 36)

25 discernendis et dignoscendis] dignoscendis et discernendis *Hw* discernendum et dinoscendis *P2* | dignoscendis] disgnoscendis *Si* ‖ **26** hec] hec etiam *Hw* et etiam *Si* | armoniaca] armonica *Si* | ritmica] rithimica *Si* ‖ **27** sonum] sonos *HwSi* | que consistit *om. Si* | dupliciter] duplex vel dupliciter *Si* | et vocum] vocumque *Hw* ‖ **28** et est idem] et idem *Si* alia, id est *Hw* | veraciter] varietatis *Hw* | facilis) faciliter *P2* | vero *om. Si* | pluriumque] plurimumque *Hw* | perdissimilium] dissimilium *HwSi* | relato] relatu *P2* ‖ **29** scansione] compositione *Si* | requiritur] requirit *HwSi* | quod] quia *Hw* ‖ **30** mensuram] mensura *P2* mensurarum *Si* | heroico] herecco *P2* eroico *Si* | et-metro] et similia *Si* | elegiaco] elore *lect. inc. P2* ‖ **31** Quid sit musicus *tit. P2* | perpensa] propensa *HwP2Si* | manifestat] ministrat *HwP2* ‖ **33** inscriberentur] inscribuntur *Hw* | ducuntur] dicuntur *HwP2Si* | imperio *om. Si* | hac] ac *HwSi* | instituta] infinita *Si* ‖ **34** philosophus-ait] metrice diffinitio sequitur *CsHws* | pulchre *om. Si* ‖ **35** est *om. Si* ‖ **40** vox-artis] verum cantorem facit ars *Hw* verum facit ars cantorem *Cs* | artis *om. Si* ‖ **41** Unde dicatur musica *tit. P2* | enim] igitur *Hw Si om.* | fabulam] fabulas *Si* | Iovis] Iovis et Icos quod est scientia que scientia sumpta de musis *Si*

which results from the joining of body and soul. [25] *Musica instrumentalis* is ascribed to the discernment and discovery of songs. [26] This too is divided, for one is harmonics, another rhythmics, another metrics.

[27] Harmonics is that which discerns between a low and high sound. Or, harmonics is that which consists in numbers and measures in two ways: one is local, according to the proportion of sounds and pitches; another temporal, according to the proportion of long and short figures. [28] And it is the same harmony that is the discernment of modulation and the science of singing correctly, and the easiest path to perfection in singing, and the proportional consonance of the more and the most thoroughly unlike, and the science of number related to sound.

[29] Rhythmics is that which is necessary to the scansion of words, whether the words cohere well or poorly; and what must be avoided in singing just as in reading.

[30] And metrics is that which demonstrates the measure of diverse metres by means of probable reasoning, as is shown in the heroic, iambic, and elegiac metre.

[31] A musician truly is one who makes clear the science of singing through deliberate reasoning, not just through their servitude of work, but also in their command of speculation, [32] since we see, for example, in the work of monuments and of war, a contrast, for example, in the naming of syllables. [33] The inscriptions of these monuments and declarations of triumphs carry the names of those by whose authority and command they were founded, and not of those who completed them with their work and servitude. [34] Whence the philosopher says it beautifully thus:

[35] Between musicians and singers, great is the distance;

[36] The latter teach, the former know, what things music comprises;

[37] For one who sings that which they do not know, is defined as a beast.

[38] Whence the verse:

[39] A beast not a singer, is one who sings not by art but by practice;

[40] It is not the voice that makes the singer, but the lesson of art.

[41] For music is so called from the Muses, who, according to legend, are said to be the daughters of Jupiter, and it is considered in two ways,

The 'Ars musica' Attributed to Magister Lambertus/Aristoteles

Hw 417

modum et secundum non modum. [42] Secundum modum, ut hic sumitur, est longitudo seu brevitas cantus secundum rectam mensuram. [43] Secundum non modum sumi|tur sic respective ut ubi nulla maneriei proprietas est inventa.

P2 72ra

[44] Genus vero huius scientie est peritia modulationis armonice, que ex concordantia plurimorum sonorum vel ex compositione | longarum breviumque figurarum perficitur.

P1 1rb

[45] Materia huius sciencie est sonus ordinatus secundum | modum et secundum non modum. [46] *Sonus* sumitur pro melodie et concordie differentia, *ordinatus* pro numero et mensura locorum et temporum

Cs 253a

in vo|cibus et figuris consistentium, *secundum modum* pro quantitate longarum breviumque figurarum que in vocis accentu et tenore consistit.

[47] Partes autem ipsius alias habet theorica, alias pratica. [48] Partes pratice sunt tres: scientia de gravi sono, et scientia de medio, et scientia de acuto. [49] Et de hiis tractat ostendendo utilitates et comparationes eorum inter se, et quomodo ex hiis componitur omnis melodia. [50] Partes theorice sunt <quinque quarum prima est

P1 1va

sciencia de principiis et primis ... secunda est> de | dispositionibus huius artis inveniendi neumata et cognoscendi numeros eorum, quot sunt, et species eorum, et declarandi proportiones quarundam ad alias <et> demonstrationes de omnibus illis, et docet species ordinum et situum eorum quibus preparantur, ut <unusquisque> accipiat ex eis quod vult et componat ex eis armonias.

[51] Species quoque huius sunt diversitates subiectorum ex quibus fiunt neumata. [52] Nam aliquando voce, aliquando flatu, aliquando tactu exercentur: voce vero ut hominis, flatu ut tibia, tactu ut psalterio vel cythara et similibus.

---

44 Quat. princ. 1, 12; Gundissalinus, p. 96 ('Genus eius est, quod ipsa est sciencia armoniace modulacionis, que ex concordancia plurimorum sonorum vel ex composicione vocum conficitur') ‖ **45** (materia-ordinatus) Quat. princ. 1, 12 ‖ **45–46** (materia huius sciencie est sonus ... que in vocis accentu et tenore consistit) cf. Gundissalinus, p. 96 ('Materia huius artis est tonus. tonus autem est acuta enunciacio uocis. est enim armonia differencia et quantitas, que in uocis accentu et tenore consistit'). ‖ **47–50** Quat. princ. 1, 13 ‖ **48** Gundissalinus, p. 98; cf. *De ortu scientiarum*, ed. Baeumker [1916], p. 19 l. 7 ('sonus qui divisus fuit in tres species, scilicet acutum et gravem et medium inter illos') ‖ **51–52** Quat. princ. 1, 14; Gundissalinus, p. 99

42 secundum rectam mensuram] quae organum (quantum ad nos) generaliter appellatur per certam mensuram de qua nunc supponimus inventionem *Hw* ‖ **43** sic] *Si* sive *CsHwP1P2* | respective] respe⁺ ... ⁺ *P2* | ut *om. Si* | maneriei] materiae *Hw* | inventa] adinventa *P2* ‖ **44** Quid sit genus *tit. P2* ‖ **45** De materia quod sit *tit. P2* | sciencie *om. P1* | et secundum non modum *om. Hw* ‖ **46** ordinatus] ordinatur *HwP2* | pro numero-consistentium] pro numeris temporum in figuris consistentium ante perfectam pausam *Hw* ‖ **47** ipsius] huius *Si* | alias²] habet *add. Si* | que sint partes musice *tit. P2* | autem] vero *Hw* | alias¹] alia *P2* | alias²] alia *P1P2* ‖ **49** componitur omnis melodia] componuntur motelli seu conducti vel organa *Hw* ‖ **50** *om. P2* | theorice sunt] tres scilicet *add. Hw* | de *om. Si* | quot sunt et] et quod sunt *Hw* | demonstrationes (*Hw, lec. inc. P1*)] determinationes *Si* | denumerationes *Cs* | docet] docere *HwP1Si* | situum] scituum *P1* | ut-armonias] ut accipiant ex eis quod volunt et componat ex eis armonias *Si* ‖ **51** Que sint species *tit. P2* | sunt *om. P1* | neumata] scilicet unisonus, tonus, semitonus etc. *add. P2* ‖ **52** vero *om. P2* | ut psalterio] ut in psalterio *Si* | similibus] similia *CsHwP1P2*

Lambertus, 'Ars musica' – 'Musica plana'

namely according to mode and not according to mode. [42] 'According to mode', as it is understood here, is the length or shortness of a song according to a proper measure. [43] With respect to this, 'not according to mode' is thus understood where no *proprietas* of a rhythmic scheme (*maneries*) is found. [44] This science's *genus* is the technique of harmonic modulation, which is perfected from the concord of many sounds or from the composition of long and short figures.

[45] This science's *materia* is ordered sound, according to mode and not according to mode. [46] 'Sound' is understood as the distinction of melody and concord; 'ordered' as the number and measure of locations that exist for pitches and of times that exist within figures; 'according to mode' as the quantity of long and short figures that exists within an accentuated and sustained pitch.

[47] But the theoretical contains some parts of this science, the practical the others. [48] The practical parts are three: the science of low sound, the science of medium sound, and the science of high sound. [49] Science investigates these sounds by showing their uses and comparisons between each other, and how every melody is composed from them. [50] The theoretical parts are five of which the first is the science concerning beginnings and first things ... the second concerns the dispositions of this art through discovering the neumes and knowing the number of them, how many they are, and their *species*, and by revealing the proportions of the neumes to other neumes, and the demonstrations of all those proportions, and it teaches the *species* of *ordines* and the positions by which they are arranged, and let anyone take from these what they want, and let them compose harmonies from them.

[51] Their species too consist in the diversities of acts from which the neumed sounds are made. [52] They are practiced here by voice, now by breath, now by touch: by the voice like a man's, by the breath like a tibia's, by touch like on a psaltery or a *cithara* or similar [instruments].

The 'Ars musica' Attributed to Magister Lambertus/Aristoteles

[53] Instrumentum vero aliud habet pratice, aliud theorice.
P1 1vb [54] Theolrice vero instrumentum est inquisitio et demonstratio ▶ *p. 117*
proportionum sonorum et vocum. Pratice vero aliud naturale, aliud
artificale. [55] Naturale vero est ut pulmo, guttur, lingua, dentes, ▶ *p. 117*
Si 15v palatum et cetera membra spiritualia. | Sed principaliter factor vocis
P2 72rb est epyglotus. [56] Artificiale est ut organa, vielle, | cythara, cytole,
psalterium et similia.

[57] Utilitas autem eius magna est et mirabilis et virtuosa valde, que
fores ecclesie ausa est subintrare. [58] Nulla enim scientia ausa est
subintrare fores ecclesie, nisi ipsa tantummodo musica. [59] Per eam
etenim plasmatorem mundi collaudare debemus et benedicere,
P1 2ra psallendo ei cantilcum novum sicut sancti patres nostri prophete
docuerunt. [60] Nam divina officia per que ad sempiternam
convocamur gloriam, per eam cottidie celebrantur. [61] Etiam testante
Boecio quod inter septem artes liberales musica obtinet principatum,
nichil enim sine illa manet. [62] Etenim ipse mundus quadam armonia
Cs 253b sonorum dicitur esse | constitutus et ipsum celum sub armonie
revolvi modulatione.

[63] Inter omnes enim scientias ipsa liberalior, curialior, iocundior,
letior, amabilior esse probatur. [64] Nam reddit hominem liberalem,
iocundum, curialem, letum, et amabilem. [65] Movet enim affectus
P1 2rb hominum, provocat in dilversum habitum sensus. [66] In preliis

---

53–56 Quat. princ. 1, 15; Gundissalinus, p. 99–100 ('Instrumentum vero aliud
est practice, aliud theorice. -- Instrumentum practice aliud est naturale, aliud
artificiale. naturalis est ut epiglotes, uvula et que sunt in eis et arterie et nasus.
Instrumentum vero artificiale est ut fistule, corde, tuba, timpanum, verba et
similia. Instrumentum theorice est <...>') ‖ **57–58** cf. Quat. princ. 1, 18; Iac.
Leod. spec. 1, 5, 10 ‖ **59–60** Quat. princ. 1, 11 ‖ **61** (Boetio-principatum) Quat.
princ. 1, 19; Trad. Lamb. 1,1 ‖ **61** (nichil ...)-**62** Isid. etym. 3, 17, 1 ‖ **62** Isid. etym.
3, 17, 1; Ps.-Thomas aqu. I 53 ‖ **63–64** Iac. Leod. spec. 1, 5, 13 ‖ **63**, 64–65 Trad.
Lamb. 1,1 ‖ **64–65** Trad. Holl. V pr. 71–72 ‖ **65–73** Quat. princ. 1, 19 (65–67 Isid.
etym. 3, 17, 1–2; **66** cf. Trad. Holl. V pr. 73;

53 Quod sit instrumentum *tit. P2* | vero *om. Si* | pratice *om. P2* | instrumentum]
instrumenta *Hw* | theorice] rhetorice *P2* ‖ **54** demonstratio] demensuratio *Si* ‖
55 vero *om. Si* | ut *om. Hw* | dentes *om. Hw* | spiritualia] alia *Si* | factor] est
factor *Si* | sed-epyglotus] scilicet principaliter sunt vocis et epiglotti *Hw* ‖ **56**
artificiale est] artificiale vero instrumentum est *Hw* | et similia] etc. *P2* | organa]
organum *Hw* | vielle-similia] viola et cythara atola psalterium etc. *Hw* | cytole
om. Si ‖ **57** Que sit utilitas eius *tit. P2* | eius *om. Si* | est et *om. P2* ‖ **58** subintrare]
intrare *Si* | musica] ecclesia musica *ante corr. P2* ‖ **59** eam] ea *Si* | etenim]
rerum *Hw* ‖ **60** per que] quae *Hw* ‖ **61** etiam] et *Hw* | septem] has VII *P2* |
sine] sine sine *P2* ‖ **62** mundus] modus *Si* | et] ut *P2* ‖ **63** omnes enim] enim
omnes *Si* | curialior iocundior] iocundior curalior *Si* | liberalior] laudabilior
Hw | iocundior-amabilior] et iocundior ... et amabilior *P2* | et amabilior *Si* ‖
64 iocundum curialem] curialem iocundum *P2* | et *om. Hw* ‖ **65–66** sensus in
preliis] sicut in preliis *Hw* ‖ **66** etiam] enim *Hw* | concentus] cumcumtus *dub. Si*
| quia] que *P2* | fit *om. Si*

14

[53] Of instruments, one is considered in practice, another in theory. [54] Of instruments 'in theory' is the investigation and demonstration of proportional sounds and pitches. But 'in practice', there is one in nature, another in artifice. [55] 'In nature' is as a lung, throat, tongue, teeth, and other organs of breathing. But principally, the maker of the voice is the epiglottis. [56] 'In artifice' is as an organ, vielle, *cithara*, cytole, psaltery, and similar instruments.

[57] But the utility of music is great and marvelous and strongly virtuous, and that which dared to enter the church doors. [58] There is no science that dared to enter the church doors with the sole exception of music. [59] And through this music, we ought to praise and bless the world's creator, by psalmodizing a new song to Him, just as our Holy Fathers prophetically taught. [60] For the divine offices, through which we sing together glory for all eternity, are celebrated daily through this music. [61] Also, by Boethius's testimony, music maintains first place among the seven liberal arts, for without it nothing remains. [62] For truly this world is said to be established upon a particular harmony of sounds and the heavens themselves to revolve under a harmonic modulation.

[63] Among all the sciences, this music is proven to be more free, more jocular, more joyful, more lovely. [64] For it restores a person as free, jocular, courtly, joyful, and lovely. [65] It stirs people's emotions, it excites the senses into a varying disposition. [66] Now, in wars,

The 'Ars musica' Attributed to Magister Lambertus/Aristoteles

Hw 418 etliam tubarum concentus pugnantes accendit, quia quanto vehementior fuerit clangor, tanto fit animus velocior ad certamen. [67] Quid multa ? Vere musica mortales hortatur ad labores quoslibet tolerandos, et singulorum operum fatigationem vocis modulatio consolatur. [68] Exercitatos quoque animos musica recreat, quoniam dolorem capitis et tristitiam tollit. [69] Immundos spiritus humoresque

P2 72va | pravos et languores depellit. [70] Unde et utilis ad salutem corporis et anime invenitur, eo quod quandoque corpus infirmatur languente

P1 2va anima, et impeditur ipsa existente imlpedita. [71] Unde et curatio corporis sepe fit per curationem anime et per aptationem virium suarum et temperantiam sue substantie <ex> sonis convenientibus <et hoc> agentibus sicut legitur de David, qui regem eripuit Saulem a spiritu maligno arte modulationis. [72] Ipsa quoque reptilia necnon aquatilia verum et volatilia sua dulcedine musica consolantur. [73] Sed et quidquid loquimur et venarum pulsibus commovemur, armonie probatur esse virtutibus sociatum.

[74] Moyses dicit repertorem artis fuisse Tubal qui fuit de stirpe

P1 2vb Cayn ante diluvium. [75] Greci vero Pictagoram dicunt huius arltis primordia invenisse. [76] Nam cum tempore quodam iter ageret, ad quamdam fabricam venit in qua supra unam incudem quinque

Si 16r mallei feriebant, | quorum suavem concordantiam philosophus miratus accepit, primumque in varietate manuum sperans vim soni ac modulationis existere, mutavit malleos. [77] Quo facto suavitas queque secuta est. [78] Subtracto itaque uno qui dissonus erat a ceteris, alios in mirumque modum divino nutu ponderavit, quorum primus

Cs 254a 6 uncias ponderabat, secundus 8, tertius 9, quartus | 12. [79] Cognovit

P2 72vb itaque in numerorum proportione et | collatione musice versari

P1 3r scientiam. [80] Fuit autem | inventa musica, quia tam turpe erat musicam quam litteras ignorare. [81] Nam antiquitus instrumenta erant incerta et canentium multitudo sed ceca. [82] Nullus enim homo vocum differentias ac simphonie discretionem poterat aliqua argumentatione colligere, nec aliquid certum cognoscere, nisi divina

---

68–69 Trad. Holl. V pr. 77; Lad. Zalk. A 14) ‖ **70–73** Gundissalinus, p. 102 ('Unde et utilis est ad salutem corporis, eo quod quandoque corpus infirmatur languente anima et impeditur ipsa existente impedita, unde et curacio corporis fit per curacionem anime et per aptacionem suarum uirium et temperanciam sue substancie et sonis agentibus hoc et convenientibus ad hoc. sic Dauid Saulem a spiritu immundo arte modulacionis eripuit. Ipsas quoque bestias et volucres ad auditum sue modulacionis musica provocat. Set et quicquid loquimur vel intrinsecus venarum pulsibus commovemur per musicos rithmos armonie virtutibus probatur esse sociatum'.) ‖ **71** [sicut legitur ... modulationis] 72–73 Isid. etym. 3, 17, 3; Trad. Holl. V pr. 79) ‖ **74** Isid. etym. 3, 16, 1 ‖ **75** Isid. etym. 3, 16, 1 ‖ **76–79** Guido micr. 20, 4–8 ‖ **80** (turpe erat ...) Isid. etym. 3, 16, 2 ‖ **81** Guido micr. 20, 2 ‖ **82** Guido micr. 20, 2–3

67 vere musica] vere musica vere musica *P2* | vere] verum *Hw* | quoslibet *om. Hw* | quoslibet tolerandos] quosque sustinendos *Si* | modulatio] modulo *Hw* ‖ **68** exercitatos] excitatos *P1P2Si* | excitatos quoque] turbatos *Hw* ‖ **69** languores] pravos *add. Si* ‖ **70** et *om. P2* | corporis et anime] anime et corporis *Si* | ipsa-impedita] ipsa ex consequente impedita *P2* ‖ **71** curatio] causa ratio *Hw* | sepe fit] fit saepe *Hw* | sonis] locis *Hw* | David] Davide *Hw* | eripuit] solavit *Hw* | necnon] ad *add. Hw* ‖ **72** quoque] quorum *P1* | musica *om. Si* | consolantur] consularntur *P2* consolatur *Hw* ‖ **73** armonie] harmonia *Hw* | sociatum] sociatur *P1* ‖ **74–85** *om. Hw* ‖ **74** repertorem] reperatorem *P1* repercionem *P2* | Cayn] de Caym *P2* Caym *Si* ‖ **76** quodam] quoddam *P2* | ad-venit] venit ad quamdam fabricam *P2* | mallei] mallii *P2* ‖ **78** ponderabat] ponderavit *Si* ‖ **79** et] ex *P2* ‖ **82** homo] hominum *P1* | discretionem] indiscretionem *P2* | tandem] quidem *Si*

Lambertus, 'Ars musica' – 'Musica plana'

the noise of trumpets kindles those fighting, since the more furious the clamor, the more swiftly the soul readies for battle. [67] How much more [need I say]? Truly music exhorts mortals to whichever labours must be suffered, and it cheers, by the modulation of pitch, the fatigue of repetitive work. [68] Music also invigorates tormented souls, because it takes away the mind's sorrow and sadness. [69] It dispels foul and petty humours and langours of the spirit. [70] Whence both the usefulness to the health of the body and soul is found, as when the body is made ill by a languid soul, and is shackled by this encumbered existence. [71] Whence both the curing of the body is often made through the curing of the soul and through the adaptation of its energies and the tempering of its nature through the creation of sounds in harmony, just as is written about David, who wrested King Saul from the evil spirit by the art of modulation. [72] Reptiles too, and also aquatic and winged creatures are consoled by music's sweetness. [73] But both that which speaks, and that which is moved by the pulses of veins, are shown to be joined through the powers of harmony.

[74] Moses says the founder of the art [of music] was Tubal who was from the root of Cain before the flood. [75] But the Greeks say Pythagoras discovered the origins of this art. [76] For once upon a time he had gone on a journey and came to a certain workshop above which a forger was making five hammers. The amazed philosopher perceived their agreeable harmony, and at first, believing that the strength of the sound and modulation existed in the variety of hands, he changed the hammers. [77] From this action followed a certain sweetness. [78] And so by removing the one which was dissonant from the rest, he pounded the others in a wonderful way, by a divine intimation; the first which he pounded was 6 *uncias*, the second 8, the third 9, the fourth 12. [79] In this way he knew that the science of music depended on the proportion and collation of numbers. [80] Moreover, music was discovered because so disagreeable was it not to know music than [not to know] letters. [81] For in ancient times, instruments were unreliable and a great number of singers were but blind. [82] For no-one had been able to gather together the distinctions of pitch and the separation of harmony by means of some argument, nor to know it as a certainty, except as a divine goodness,

The 'Ars musica' Attributed to Magister Lambertus/Aristoteles

tandem bonitas suo nutu disponeret. [83] Post quos autem Boecius incipiens, multam miramque difficilem cum numerorum proportione concordiam demonstravit. [84] Et sic usque in hunc diem ars ista paulatim crescendo multis modis est augmentata.

P1 3rb   [85] Artifex autem est ille qui practice for | mat neumata et armonias et eorum accidentia secundum quod sunt, vel qui theorice docet hec omnia fieri secundum artem, que humanos possint movere affectus.

[86] Officium vero aliud practice, aliud theorice. [87] Practice vero est armonias componere secundum artem. [88] Theorice officium est in summa comprehendere cognitionem specierum armoniarum, et id ex quo componuntur, et id ad quod componuntur. [89] Et hoc quantum ad planam musicam. [90] Quid autem sit officium ipsius mensurabilis, in sequentibus cum de ipsa determinabitur, ostendetur.

P1 3va   [91] Cum igitur ista et alia | plura secundum ordinem in hac arte declarantur, primo specialiter videndum est et sciendum quod quatuor sunt partes in musica principales, quarum prima est de signis et nominibus vocum, secunda de lineis et spatiis, tercia de proprietatibus, quarta de mutationibus.

---

83 GUIDO micr. 20, 19 ‖ **84** cf. GUIDO micr. 20, 22 ‖ **85** QUAT. PRINC. 1, 16; Gundissalinus, p. 100 ('Artifex practice est, qui format neumata et armonias et alia accidencia eorum secundum quod sunt in instrumentis, quorum accepcio assueta est in eis. Artifex uero theorice est, qui docet hec omnia secundum artem fieri'.) ‖ **86–90** QUAT. PRINC. 1, 17; Gundissalinus, p. 100 ('Officium autem theorice est in summa comprehendere cognicionem specierum armonicarum et illud a quo componuntur et illud ad quod componuntur et qualiter componuntur, et quibus modis oportet ut sint, quousque faciant operacionem suam penetrabiliorem et magis ultimam. Officium practice est cantilenas secundum artem componere, que humanos effectus possint movere'.)

83 multam *lect. inc. P2* | concordiam] concordantiam (ant *exp.*) *P1* ‖ **85** et[2] *om. P1* | eorum] earum *P2* | theorice] theorie *P1* | possint] nos posuit *P2* | affectus] effectus *P2* ‖ **86** De officio *tit. P2* | officium] officiorum *P2* | practice-theorice] habet practica aliud theorica *Hw* ‖ **87** practice] practica *Hw* | vero *om. Si* | secundum artem] et artem quae humanos possunt movere affectus *Hw* ‖ **88** theorice-est] theorica vero est *Hw* | officium est] est officium *Si* | et id ex] et etiam ex *Si* | id ad] ad id *Hw* | id ad quod] id qualiter *Si* | componuntur[2]] componuntur et qualiter componuntur *Hw* vel est etiam officium figuras longas et breves, necnon corpora et mensuras eorundem qualitates et quantitates ... possit declarare (= mm 4–5) *add. Hw* 89–90 *om. HwP2* ‖ **89** hoc *om. Si* ‖ **90** ipsius *om. Si* ‖ **91** est et sciendum] et sciendum est *Si* | declarantur] declarentur *P2* | est[1] *om. P1* | signis] significationibus *Si* | secunda] est *add. Si* | tercia] est *add. Si* | quarta] est *add. Si* | = Cum igitur illa et alia multa in hac arte secundum ordinem declarantur primo specialiter videndum est et sciendum quod tria tantummodo sunt genera ... *Hw* <*Musica mensurabilis*>, 6 sqq.

Lambertus, 'Ars musica' – 'Musica plana'

by its intimation, were finally to set them in order. [83] But Boethius, beginning after these [individuals], demonstrated great, marvellous, and difficult concord through the proportions of numbers. [84] And thus up to the present day this art, by growing little by little, is augmented in many ways.

[85] But a composer is one who forms – in practice – neumes and harmonies and their attributes according to their definitions, or one who teaches – in theory – how all these things, which can stir human emotions, are to be made according to art.

[86] The function [of this science]: there is one in practice, another in theory. [87] 'In practice' is to compose harmonies according to art. [88] 'In theory' the function is to comprehend, in sum, knowledge of the harmonic species, and from what and for what they are composed. [89] And this insofar as it relates to plainchant. [90] But what function may be as it relates to *musica mensurabilis* will be shown in the following and along with the following it will be determined.

[91] Therefore, since these and many other things in this art are revealed according to order: first, specifically, it should be seen and known that there are four principal parts in music, of which the first concerns the signs and names of the pitches; the second concerns the lines and spaces; the third concerns the *proprietates*, and the fourth concerns the mutations.

<I>

P2 73ra

[92] In prima autem parte sciendum est quod septem sunt littere | latine quibus omnes voces exprimuntur scilicet ·a· ·b· ·c· ·d· ·e· ·f· ·g·. [93] Que etiam claves vocantur, quia sicut per clavem reseratur sera, ita per has litteras reseratur musice melodia. [94] Et sicut clavis in sera revolvitur, ita totus annus et totius anni cantus in istis septem litteris

Cs 254b – P1
3vb

replicatur. | [95] Quibus tamen gamma, id est ·G· | greca littera preponitur, ut ·A·, que est prima littera nostra, altrinsecus tonum habeat, et ·G· grecum ad ·G· latinum diapason introducat.

Si 16v

[96] Preterera quod ·G· greca littera preponitur et latine littere subsequuntur, datur intelligi quod a Grecis | fuit inventa musica, a Latinis consummata. [97] Deinde notandum est quod in istis septem litteris sex voces tantummodo continentur quibus tota musica conformatur, scilicet: *ut, re, mi, fa, sol, la.* Unde versus:

[98] His sex formantur sex motus et variantur:

[99] *Ut* cum *re* plene modulatur, *mi* quoque cum *re*

<Voce sonat plena *fa* cum sol, sol quoque cum *la*>

[100] Dantque semi *mi fa,* nec fit plenus tonus infra.

P1 4ra

[101] Sed queritur | quare plures sint littere quam voces. [102] Cum tamen voces per has litteras exprimantur, videtur enim quod iste due littere, scilicet ·F· et ·G· sint superflue, cum per sex precedentes sex voces lucidissime declarentur. [103] Solutio: sicut tantum sex voces, ita et sex litteras tantum ad exprimendum illas sex voces hoc modo dicimus adinventas, scilicet: Gamma·ut, ·A·re, ·B·mi, ·C·faut, ·D·solre, ·E·lami. [104] Sed quia consideravimus quod tam vocum numerositas quam litterarum paucitas omnium proportiones

P2 73rb

cantuum non sufficeret peragrare, | ·G· latinum in octava clavi locavimus, et eidem tres voces concessimus, scilicet: *sol* et *re* et *ut,*

P1 4rb

quatinus per ipsas | ascensum et descensum competenter ostenderet, et ad ·Γ· grecum ·G· latinum diapason consonaret. [105] Siquidem et ·F· in septima similiter clave locavimus ne non gradatim ad ·G· pareret ascensus ab aliis, et a ·G· quoque descensus ad alias econverso. [106] Cui ·F· duas voces concessimus, scilicet *fa* et *ut,* quatinus cum una possit ad ·G· gradatim ascendere, cum reliqua ad ·E· deinceps descendere competenter.

[107] Et notandum quod iste sex voces septies in palma cursum suum perficiunt, sicut in presenti patet figura:

92–95 Trad. Lamb. 2, 2a; Quat. princ. 3, 1 ‖ **96** Trad. Lamb. 1,3; cf. Quat. princ. 3, 1 ‖ **97** cf. Ps.-Phil. lib. mus. p. 36a ‖ **98** Quat. princ. 3, 2; Trad. Lamb. 2, 2a, 8; Trad. Garl. plan. III 142; Trad. Lamb. 2, 2a ‖ **99** Quat. princ. 3, 2; Trad. Garl. plan. III 142; Trad. Lamb. 2, 2a ‖ **100** Quat. princ. 3, 2; Trad. Lamb. 2, 2a, 8; Trad. Garl. plan. III 142; Trad. Lamb. 2, 2a ‖ **101–106** cf. Iac. Leod. spec. 6, 62, 12–13

92–351 *om. Hw* ‖ **93** clavem] claves *Si* ‖ **94** clavis-revolvitur] in sera revolvitur clavis *Si* | et totius-cantus *om. Si* ‖ **95** ·G·-littera] ·G· que est littera greca *Si* | ·G·²] Γ *P2* | ad] a *P1* ‖ **96** ·G·] Γ *P2* | lictere latine *Si* ‖ **97** VI tantum voces *Si* ‖ **99** plene modulatur] plane modulantur *Si* | Voce-la (cf. Trad. Garl. plan. III 142) *om. Σ* ‖ **100** fit] fa *Si* ‖ **102** exprimantur] exprimuntur *Si* ‖ **103** solutio] sol'o *P1* | ergo *dub. P2* | Gamma ut--E·lami] ·Γ· ·A· ·b· ·C· ·D· ·E· *P2* ‖ **104** consideravimus] consideramus *Si* | numerositas] immobilitas *CsP1P2* mobilitas *Si* | cantuum] cantium *Si* | sufficeret] sufficere *Si* | clavi] clave *Si* | sol-ut] sol re ut *Si* | ipsas] ipsam *Si* | competenter] expetentem *Si* ‖ **105** si quidem] sed quidem *P1P2* | similiter clave] clave similiter *Si* | ne non] necnon (ne cum ?) *P1* | pareret] pateret *P2* ‖ **106** reliqua ad] reliqua nec ad *P1P2Si* | ·E·] ·F· *Si* ‖ **107** sicut-figura] sicut patet in figura sequenti *Si*

<I>

[92] But in the first part, it should be understood that there are seven Latin letters through which all the pitches are expressed, namely, ·a· ·b· ·c· ·d· ·e· ·f· ·g·. [93] They are also called keys, for just as a lock is unlocked with a key, in the same way the melody of music is unlocked with these letters. [94] And just as a key turns in a lock, in the same way the entire year and an entire year's chant is revealed within those seven letters. [95] However, a Greek letter, *gamma*, that is, ·G·, is placed before these, so that ·A·, which is our first letter, can have a tone on each side, and the Greek ·G· to the Latin ·G· makes an octave. [96] In addition, since the Greek letter ·G· is placed before and the Latin letters follow after it, so we are given to understand that music was discovered by the Greeks, and by the Romans perfected. [97] Also, it should be noted that in those seven letters are contained only six solmisation syllables from which all music is fashioned, namely, *ut, re, mi, fa, sol, la*. Whence the verse:

[98] Six motions are formed and varied from these six solmisation syllables:

[99] *Ut* with *re* is fully measured, *mi* also with *re*

With a full pitch *fa* sounds with *sol, sol* also with *la*

[100] And they give the semitone *mi fa*, a full tone is not made between them.

[101] But it is asked why there are more letters than solmisation syllables. [102] For although the solmisation syllables are expressed through these letters, it seems that these two letters, namely ·F· and ·G·, are superfluous, since the six solmisation syllables may be most clearly shown through the six preceding letters. [103] The answer: just as there are six solmisation syllables, so we say six letters were found for expressing those solmisation syllables in this way, namely: *Gamma-ut,* ·A·*re,* ·B·*mi,* ·C·*faut,* ·D·*solre,* ·E·*lami.* [104] But because we deliberated that the numerosity of solmisation syllables compared to the paucity of letters would not have sufficed to traverse the proportions of all songs, we found Latin ·G· in the eighth key, and we yielded three solmisation syllables to the same, namely: *sol* and *re* and *ut*, so through these solmisation syllables it would properly extend through an ascent and descent, and Latin ·G· to Greek ·Γ· would sound an octave. [105] Accordingly we placed an ·F· in a similar fashion on the seventh key so that the ascent from the other pitches to ·G· would not appear out of nowhere, and also the descent from ·G· to the other pitches and *vice versa*. [106] We yielded two solmisation syllables to this ·F·, namely *fa* and *ut*, so that with one solmisation syllable it can ascend to ·G· gradually, with the remaining one it can descend properly to ·E· after the other.

[107] And it should be noted that these six solmisation syllables complete seven times the course on the palm, just as is shown in the present figure:

The 'Ars musica' Attributed to Magister Lambertus/Aristoteles

P1 4v/P2 73v/
Cs 255

e					la	la					e
d				la	sol	sol	la				d
c				sol	fa	fa	sol				c
b♭				fa	mi	mi	fa				b♭
a			la	mi	re	re	mi	la			a
g			sol	re	ut	ut	re	sol			g
f			fa	ut			ut	fa			f
e		la	mi				mi	la			e
d		la	sol	re			re	sol	la		d
c		sol	fa	ut			ut	fa	sol		c
b♭		fa	mi					mi	fa		b♭
a		la	mi	re			re	mi	la		a
g		sol	re	ut			ut	re	sol		g
f		fa	ut				ut	fa			f
e	la	mi					mi	la			e
d	sol	re					re	sol			d
c	fa	ut					ut	fa			c
♭	mi						mi				♭
a	re						re				a
G	ut						ut				G
	♭	n	b	♭	n	b	♭	♭	b	n	♭	b	n	♭

<II>

Cs 255a/P1 5ra/
P2 74ra/Si 17r

[108] Habito de signis et nominibus vocum nunc habendum est de lineis et spatiis. [109] Unde linea et spatium nihil aliud est quam paritas et imparitas. [110] Unde quod dicitur in linea dicitur imparitas, et illud quod dicitur in spatio dicitur paritas. [111] Unde quodlibet signum quod sumitur in loco pari est in spatio. [112] Unde sequitur per numerum naturalem quod si primum sit in linea, semper reliquum erit in spatio, et insuper omne quartum oppositum et omne octavum, sed in illo loco sumitur simile signum. [113] Ergo si primum sit in linea, ▶ *p. 117*

Cs 255b
P1 5rb

semper reliquum erit in spatio, et e | converso. [114] Et hoc secundum qua|dratum vel rectas lineas ipsius manus, secunda regula et prima ▶ *p. 117* tenent, et hoc sufficit.

<III>

---

[115] Ad maiorem autem vocum expressionem perutilis est proprietatum cognitio. [116] Unde proprietas, ut hic sumitur, nihil aliud est quam differentia, et sunt tres species differentiarum, scilicet ·♭· durum, ·b· molle et natura. [117] Unde ·♭· durum dicitur esse tonus ante ·♭· quadratum. ·b· molle dicitur esse semitonium ante ·b· rotundum. [118] Natura dicitur cantus sumptus sine aliquo ·♭·, id est

---

108–114 Trad. Lamb. 2, 2b (**114** 'vel ipsius manus iuncturas rectas quarta regula et prima tenent'.) ‖ **109–113** Trad. Garl. plan. I 145–148; Trad. Garl. plan. III, 129–132; Trad. Garl. plan. IV 61–65; Trad. Lamb. 2, 2b, 2; Quat. princ. 3, 7 ‖ **114** Trad. Garl. plan. I 148; Trad. Garl. plan. III 132; Trad. Garl. plan. IV 65 ‖ **115–119** Trad. Lamb. 2, 3 ‖ **116** Trad. Garl. plan. III 134; Trad. Garl. plan. IV 67–68 ‖ **117** Trad. Garl. plan. III 135; Trad. Garl. plan. IV 69 ‖ **118** Trad. Garl. plan. III 136; Trad. Garl. plan. IV 70; (in eius confinio …) Quat. princ. 3, 8; Trad. Lamb. 2, 3, 3, Iac. Leod. spec. 6, 64, 18

112 erit] sit *Si* | oppositum] opponitur *P1P2* illo] uno *CsP1P2Si* ‖ **114** rectas lineas] lineas rectas *Si* | tenent] teneant *Si* ‖ **116** ·b· molle] et ·b· molle *Si* ‖ **118** id est] et *Si* | eius] eis *P2* | principium habet] habet principium *Si*

22

	C1	C2	C3	C4	C5	C6	C7	C8	C9	C10	C11	C12	
e						la	la						e
d					la	sol	sol	la					d
c					sol	fa	fa	sol					c
b♭					fa	mi	mi	fa					b♭
a				la	mi	re	re	mi	la				a
g				sol	re	ut	ut	re	sol				g
f				fa	ut			ut	fa				f
e			la	mi					mi	la			e
d		la	sol	re					re	sol	la		d
c		sol	fa	ut					ut	fa	sol		c
b♭		fa	mi							mi	fa		b♭
a	la	mi	re							re	mi	la	a
g	sol	re	ut							ut	re	sol	g
f	fa	ut									ut	fa	f
e	la	mi									mi	la	e
d	sol	re									re	sol	d
c	fa	ut									ut	fa	c
♮	mi											mi	♮
a	re											re	a
G	ut											ut	G

♮ n b ♮ n b ♮ ♮ b n ♮ b n ♮

<II>

[108] Having considered the signs and names of the pitches, now the lines and spaces must be considered. [109] Whence a line and a space is nothing other than equality and inequality. [110] Whence that which is said to be on a line is called inequality, and that which is said to be within a space is called equality. [111] Whence whatever sign that is understood to be in an even place is in a space. [112] Whence it follows, according to natural number, that if the first sign is on a line, the following sign will always be in a space, moreover, also each fourth and octave opposite, but in that place a similar sign is used.[113] Therefore, if the first sign is on a line, the remaining sign will always be in a space, and *vice versa*. [114] And this is according to the square or the proper lines of this hand, the second and the first rule holds, and this is enough on this.

<III>

[115] But, for the better delivery of the solmisation syllables, a knowledge of *proprietas* is very useful. [116] Whence *proprietas*, as it is understood here, is nothing other than a distinction, and there are three *species* of distinction, namely ·b· *durum*, ·b· *molle* and natural. [117] Whence ·b· *durum* is said to be a tone before the square ·b·, ·b· *molle* is said to be a semitone before round ·b·. [118] A song is called natural when it is taken without any ·b·, that is,

The 'Ars musica' Attributed to Magister Lambertus/Aristoteles

Cs 256a   sine differentia, et hoc proprie, eo quod omnis cantus | naturalis in eius confinio principium habet et finem. [119] Et notandum quod in quolibet ·C· ·F· ·G· ponitur *ut*, in sequentibus voces sequentes. [120] Unde | regula: omne *ut* incipiens in ·C· cantatur per naturam cum suis sequentibus, in ·F· per b molle, in ·G· per ·♭· durum. Unde versus:

P1 5va

> [121] ·C· naturam dat, ·F· ·♭· molle tibi signat.

P2 74rb

> [122] ·G· quoque ·♭· durum tu | semper habes caniturum.

\<IIII\>

P1 5vb

[123] Mutatio vero, ut hic sumitur, nihil aliud est quam dimissio vocis unius propter aliam sub eodem signo et in eodem sono. [124] Unde sequitur quod ubicumque fit mutatio, oportet quod ibi sint voces due ad minus. [125] Sed in Gamma·ut et in ·A·re et in ·B·mi et in ·e·la, non est mutatio, eo quod istorum quilibet nisi unicam vocem continet, nec similiter in ·b·fa·♭·mi, quoniam ibi | sunt diversa signa et diverse voces. [126] Et quia non ponuntur sub una voce nec se habent sub uno sono, ideo non potuit ibi esse mutatio, quia tunc esset contra diffinicionem. [127] Nam si esset in unisono, tunc deberet dici b.fami ubi nunc dicitur ·b·fa·♭·mi. [128] Et sciendum quod ubicunque sunt due voces, ibi sunt due mutationes, sicut in ·C·faut in quo dicitur *fa ut, ut fa*. [129] Et similiter ubicunque | sunt tres voces, ibi sunt sex mutationes, sicut in ·G·solreut ubi dicitur *sol re, re sol, sol ut, ut sol, re ut, ut re.* [130] Consimili modo fit in omnibus aliis, quoniam ubicunque sunt tres voces, ibi mutatur prima in secundam et econverso, et prima in ultimam et econverso, et secunda in ultimam et econverso. [131] Et hac | ratione due voces non duplicantur per ▸ *p. 117* quatuor sicut tres per sex. [132] Unde regula quod omnis mutatio desinens in *ut, re, mi* dicitur ascendendo | quia plus habet ascendere quam descendere, et omnis mutatio desinens in *fa, sol, la* dicitur descendendo, quia plus habet descendere quam ascendere.

Cs 256b

P1 6ra

Si 17v

---

119 Trad. Garl. plan. I 134; Trad. Garl. plan. IV 57 ‖ 120 Trad. Garl. plan. III 138; Trad. Garl. plan. IV 71; Trad. Lamb. 2, 3, 5; Quat. princ. 3, 8; Trad. Lamb. 2, 3 ‖ 121–122 Trad. Garl. plan. IV 72; Quat. princ. 3, 8; Trad. Lamb. 2, 3 ‖ 123–129, 132, 134–135 cf. Quat. princ. 3, 9 ‖ 123 Trad. Garl. plan. I 151; Trad. Lamb. 2, 4 ‖ 124 Trad. Garl. plan. I 152; cf. Trad. Lamb. 2, 4 ‖ 125 Trad. Garl. plan. I 153–154; Trad. Lamb. 2, 4 ‖ 126 Trad. Garl. plan. I 154 ‖ 127 cf. Trad. Garl. plan. I 155 and Trad. Garl. plan. III 148 ‖ 128–129 Trad. Garl. plan. I 156–157; cf. Trad. Lamb. 2, 4 ‖ 130 cf. Trad. Garl. plan. I 158 ‖ 131 Trad. Garl. plan. I 158, III 151; Trad. Lamb. 2, 4 ‖ 132 Trad. Garl. plan. I 159–160; cf. Trad. Lamb. 2, 4

119 in quolibet-sequentes] ·b· molle non est de origine aliarum clavium *Cs* (cf. ci-dessous 165) | 119 | ponitur *om. Si* | 120 ut *om. Si* | unde[2] *om. P2* ‖ 123 De mutationibus *tit. P2* | propter] prope *P2* ‖ 124 voces due] due voces *P2Si* ‖ 125 Gamma-Ela] ·Γ· ·A· ·♭· (et \<·E·\> *add. marg.) P2* | quilibet] quibus *P1* ‖ 126 non[1]] non non *P2* ‖ 126–127 contra diffinicionem nam si esset in *om. P1* ‖ 127 in unisono] uno sono *Si* | 128 ·C·faut] ·F·faut *P2* ‖ 129 sicut] sic *Si* | ubi] in quo *Si* ‖ 130 omnibus *om. Si* | econverso[1–3]] converso *P2* | et prima] prima *Si* | secuna in ultimam] secuna in primam et ultimam *P1* ‖ 132 regula] regula est *Si* | dicitur ascendendo] ascendendo dicitur *Si*

Lambertus, 'Ars musica' – 'Musica plana'

without a distinction, and by this property, every natural song in its bounds has a beginning and an end. [119] And it should be noted that whether *ut* is placed on ·C· ·F· ·G·, in the following, the solmisation syllables are the following. [120] Whence the rule: let every *ut* beginning on ·C· be sung through the natural [hexachord] with its following solmisation syllables, on ·F· through ·b· *molle*, on ·G· through ·♮· *durum*. Whence the verse:

[121] ·C· gives a natural, ·F· indicates ·b· *molle* to you.

[122] Also, with ·G· you will always have to sing ·♮· *durum*.

<IIII>

[123] And mutation, as it is understood here, is nothing other than the dismissal of one solmisation syllable for another under the same sign and within the same sound. [124] Now it follows that when there is a mutation, there ought to be at least two solmisation syllables there. [125] But there is no mutation on *gamma.ut* and on ·A·*re* and on ·B·*mi* and on ·e·*la*, because each of them contains only one solmisation syllable, unlike ·b·*fa*·♮·*mi*, because in that place there are diverse signs and diverse solmisation syllables. [126] And since they are not placed under one solmisation syllable, nor are they held under one sound, thus there cannot be a mutation there, since that would be against the definition [of mutation]. [127] For if it were on a unison, then it ought to be called ·b·*fami* where it is now called ·b·*fa*·♮·*mi*. [128] And it should be understood that wherever there are two solmisation syllables, in that place there are two mutations, just as on C.*faut* on which is said *fa ut, ut fa*. [129] And likewise, wherever there are three solmisation syllables, in that place there are six mutations, just as on ·G·*solreut* where it is called *sol re, re sol, sol ut, ut sol, re ut, ut re*. [130] Let it be made in a similar fashion in all the others, because wherever there are three solmisation syllables, there the first is changed into the second and *vice versa*, and the first into the last and *vice versa*, and the second into the last, and *vice versa*. [131] And by this reasoning, the two solmisation syllables are not duplicated through four just as three through six. [132] Whence the rule that every mutation ending on *ut, re, mi* is said to be ascending, because it has to ascend more than descend, and every mutation closing on *fa, sol, la* is said to be descending, because it has to descend more than ascend.

The 'Ars musica' Attributed to Magister Lambertus/Aristoteles

P2 74va
P1 6rb

[133] Unde notandum est quod mutatio sumitur dupliciter, aut causa ascensionis aut causa descensionis, ut patet in ·C·faut, quoniam si in illo sumeret aliquis *fa*, scilicet *ut-fa*, posset ascendere ad tertiam vocem, quod si vellet sumere quartam, necesse esset in proprio sumere ·C·faut | *ut*, quod est mutatio de *fa* in *ut*, et similiter suo modo descen|dendo, scilicet *ut fa*. [134] Et in hoc fit compositio gammatis. [135] Unde nihil aliud est gamma quam compositio signorum monocordi cum vocibus, et hoc planius in sequenti figura patebit: ▶ *p. 117–18*

P1 f. 6v
(photo Paris,
BnF),
Cs 256–257

133 Trad. Garl. plan. I 161–162; (unde-in ·C·faut) Compil. Ticin. A 44 ‖ **133–134** Trad. Lamb. 2, 4 ‖ **135** Trad. Garl. plan. I 136
133 causa descensionis *om.* P1 | causa[2] *om.* P2 | sumeret] sumetur *Si* | fa scilicet ut fa] fa P2 | in proprio] inproprie P2 | quod si] quoniam si *Si* ‖ **134** gammatis] canmatis P2 ‖ **135** in-patebit] in sequentibus patet figura P1 *fig. post 135, om. Si*

Lambertus, 'Ars musica' – 'Musica plana'

[133] Whence it should be noted that a mutation is understood in two ways, either on account of an ascent or a descent, as is shown on ·C·*faut*, because if a *fa* were to be understood here, namely, *ut-fa*, it could ascend to a third solmisation syllable, because if it wanted to choose a fourth, it would be necessary, conforming to the *proprietas*, for ·C·*faut* to take *ut*, which is the mutation from *fa* to *ut*, and in a similar way descending, namely *ut fa*. [134] And in this [way] let the composition of the *gamut* be made. [135] Whence the *gamut* is nothing other than a composition of the signs of the monochord with the solmisation syllables and this will be shown more clearly in the following figure:

P1 f. 6v
(photo
Paris,
BnF)

The 'Ars musica' Attributed to Magister Lambertus/Aristoteles

Cs 257a/*P1* 7r [136] In hac igitur figura patet quod viginti claves sive signa sunt in
/ *P2* 75ra numero, quarum octo precedentes graves dicuntur, eo quod omnis
cantus in eisdem gravi sono profertur, [137] septem subsequentes acute
quia omnis cantus in eisdem versatur acuiter, [138] relique vero
superacute quoniam acutiorem sonum reddunt acutius et excellunt
omnia predictis.

*
* *

Si 18r [139] Sunt autem species duodecim quibus omnis cantus contexitur,
scilicet: unisonus, | tonus, semitonium, ditonus, semiditonus,
diatessaron, diapente, tonus cum diapente, semitonium cum
P1 7rb diapente, ditonus cum diapente, semiditonus cum diapente, ulti | ma
diapason.

[140] Unisonus autem dicitur sonus unius vocis a qua non fit
progressio. [141] Si vero progrediatur a quadam voce vocem tangendo
propinquam, tunc aliquando fit tonus, aliquando semitonium. [142] Et
ponitur unisonus in quacumque clave fuerit necessarius.

[143] Tonus autem est perfectum spatium duarum vocum, duo
semitonia continens non equalia. [144] Est enim tonus quedam
percussio aeris indissoluta usque ad auditum, sicut de gravi ad
acutum, videlicet de ·G· ad ·a· et econverso, et fit tali modo, scilicet:
ut re, re ut, re mi, mi re, fa sol, sol fa, sol la, la sol. [145] Et dicitur a *tono,*
P1 7va *tonas,* | eo quod perfecte tonat, id est perfecte ostendit distantiam |
Cs 257b inter duas voces. [146] Ubicumque enim due voces a linea in spatio
continuantur vel econverso ibi est tonus, preterquam in semitonio.
Et habet fieri in sesquioctava proportione. [147] Sicut enim in numeris
P2 75rb vi | demus quod aliquis numerus continet alium numerum et
octavam partem eius, sicut novem continet octo et eius octavam
partem que est unitas, sic quando vox una super aliam in octava
parte elevatur, hic proprie tonus appellatur. [148] Et quod hoc verum
sit, hoc manifeste demonstrat Boetius in monocordo et in aliis
musicis instrumentis secundum mensuram localem ita videlicet, |
P1 7vb [149] quod si accipiatur corda alicuius instrumenti, utpote cythare,
vielle vel cytole, et ·G· grecum in capite ipsius corde ponatur, [150] et
inde in linea que sonanti corde subiacet, novem partes dividantur
equales, et in termino prime partis iuxta gammam ·A· prima littera
nostra ponatur, et erit tibi tonus. [151] Ab ·A· similiter usque ad finem
novem partes divide et in termino prime partis ·B· secundam
litteram pone, et fit tibi tonus secundus.

136–138 (in eisdem-predictis) Trad. Lamb. 2, 2a ‖ **139** Trad. Lamb. 3, 1 ‖ **140**
Trad. Lamb. 3, 2 ‖ **140–142** Compil. Ticin. A 50–53 ‖ **142** Trad. Garl. plan. IV 98 ‖
143 Quat. Princ. 3, 14 ‖ **144–146** Compil. Ticin. A 69–70 (**139** percussio-auditum:
Boeth. mus. I, 3[p. 189, l. 22–23]; Quat. Princ. 3, 14) ‖ **145** Trad. Lamb. 3, 3;
Quat. Princ. 3, 14 ‖ **146–147** (et habet fieri-unitas) Quat. Princ. 3, 14 ‖

136 patet quod … sunt in] quod *?* patet sunt … in *Si* | quarum] quorum *P1*
| octo] si *P2* | precedentes] quatuor (*exp.*) *add. P2* **139** De speciebus *tit. P2* |
ditonus semiditonus] diptonus semidiptonus *Si* | ditonus²] diptonus *Si* ‖ **140**
sonus-vocis] unius vocis sonus *P2* ‖ **144** fit *om. P2* ‖ **145** tonas] as *Si* ‖ **146** voces
om. Si | semitonio] semitonis *Si* | et] sicut *Si* | sesquioctava] sesquitertia *P1* ‖
147 et eius octavam partem] et octavam partem eius *P2Si* | que est unitas *om. Si*
| hic] hoc *Si* ‖ **148** hoc¹⁺² *om. Si* | Boetius] Betius *P1* | monocordo] monacordo
P1 monochordo *P2* ‖ **149** quod *om. P2* | corda *om. Si* | cythare-vielle] vielle
cythare *Si* ‖ **150** inde in linea] inde linea *Si* ‖ **151** ·B·] ♮ *Si* | et-secundus] et ibi
tonus est secundus *Si* ‖

Lambertus, 'Ars musica' – 'Musica plana'

[136] This figure shows that there are twenty keys or signs in number, of which the eight preceding are called low, because every song is delivered on these same keys by a low sound, [137] the seven subsequent ones are called high because on these same keys every song is transformed into a high range, and the remaining [keys] are superacute, [138] because they render an even higher sound in a higher range and they surpass all the preceding keys.

*

* *

[139] There are twelve species [of intervals] from which every song is woven, namely: unison, tone, semitone, ditone, semiditone, diatessaron, diapente, tone with a diapente, semitone with a diapente, ditone with a diapente, semiditone with a diapente, the last is a diapason.

[140] But a unison is said to be a sound of one pitch from which no motion is made. [141] And if there is motion from a particular pitch by approaching the pitch next to it, then it is sometimes a tone, sometimes a semitone. [142] And a unison is placed on whatever key necessary.

[143] But a tone of two spaces of pitches is perfect, containing two unequal semitones. [144] And a tone is a certain percussion of air, that is undissolved all the way up to the hearer, just as from a low sound towards a high, for example from ·G· towards ·a· and *vice versa*, and let it be made in the following way, namely: *ut re, re ut, re mi, mi re, fa sol, sol fa, sol la, la sol*. [145] And it is named from *tono, tonas*, because it 'tones' perfectly, that is, it extends perfectly [through] the distance between two pitches. [146] And when two pitches are continued from a line into a space or *vice versa* there is a tone, beyond that a semitone. And it has to be made in the sesquioctave proportion. [147] For just as we see in numbers that some number contains another number and an eighth part of it, so nine contains eight and the eighth part of it, which is the unity, thus when one pitch is raised above another pitch in an eighth part, this is rightly called a tone. [148] And that this is true is clearly shown by Boethius in the monochord and on other musical instruments according to local measure. So, for example, [149] if you take a string of some instrument, for example, the cithara, vielle, or cytole, and place Greek ·G· at the top of the string, [150] and from there on a line, which is placed under the sounding string, let nine equal parts be divided, and in the terminus of the first part, next to the gamma, let ·A·, the first of our letters, be placed, and this will give you a tone. [151] From ·A· likewise divide nine parts from the end and in the terminus of the first part place ·B·, the second letter, and this will give you a second tone.

The 'Ars musica' Attributed to Magister Lambertus/Aristoteles

P1 8ra
Cs 258a

[152] Semitonium est imperfectum spatium duarum vocum quod secundum vocem hominis non licet dividi vel ponere medium. [153] Unde sciendum est quod nunquam fit semitonium, nisi de *mi* in *fa* vel econverso. [154] Et dicitur semito|nium a *semus, sema, semum*, quod est *imperfectum*, et *tonus*, | quasi imperfectus tonus. [155] Boetius autem determinavit semitonium esse in <sesqui>XVII^a proportione, quam divisit in duas partes, unam minorem et alteram maiorem. [156] Minorem appellavit dyesim, id est minus semitonium, maiorem apothome vocavit, id est semitonium maius. [157] Differentia autem inter minorem et maiorem comma nuncupatur, id est differentia.

Si 18v
P2 75va

[158] Post hoc autem ad gamma<m> recurrens et ab ipsa | usque ad finem quatuor partes | equales divide, et in termino prime partis tertiam ·C· litteram pone, et habebis semitonium.

P1 8rb

[159] Nunc autem oritur questio quid vel que sit necessitas in mu|sica regulari de falsa musica, seu de falsa mutatione, cum enim nullum regulare debeat accipere falsum, sed pocius verum. [160] Ad hoc dicendum est quod mutatio <falsa> sive falsa musica non est inutilis, immo necessaria propter consonantiam bonam inveniendam, malam autem econverso vitandam. [161] Nam si velimus habere diapente de necessitate, oportet quod habeamus tres tonos cum semitonio, ita quod si aliqua figura sit in ·b·fa·b·mi sub ·b· quadrato, et alia sit in ·f·faut acuto per naturam, [162] tunc non est ibi consonantia sed dissonantia cum semitonio pessima, quia non sunt ibi tres toni cum semitonio, sed duo tantummodo cum duplici semitonio. [163] Verum tamen | fieri potest ibidem, sed hoc per falsam musicam. <'Per falsam musicam'> fieri appellamus scilicet quando facimus de semitonio tonum, vel econverso. [164] Non tamen est falsa, sed inusitata. [165] Unde notandum quod b mollis non est de origine aliarum clavium. [166] Hoc autem cognoscitur per signum ♮ quadrati vel ·b· rotundi in loco inusitato locatum, ita quod dicamus *mi* durum in ·f· acutam cum signo ♮ quadrati, vel <*fa*> si ·b· rotundum ponamus in ·b·fa·b·mi vel in consimilibus ita quod sit in toni proportione, et tunc erit diapente consonantia. [167] Et ideo falsa musica quandoque necessaria est, etiam et ut omnis consonantia seu melodia | in quolibet signo perficiatur.

P1 8va

P1 8vb

▸ *p. 118*

---

152 Quat. Princ. 3, 13 ‖ **153** Compil. Ticin. A 54 ‖ **154** Compil. Ticin. A 55; cf. Trad. Lamb. 3, 4a ‖ **155** (Boetius autem determinavit) Compil. Ticin. A 56 ‖ **159–167** Compil. Ticin. A 60–68, Trad. Garl. plan. IV 111–17 (159–64 Trad. Lamb. 3, 4b, ‖ **165** Trad. Lamb. 2, 3; 166–67 Trad. Lamb. 3, 4b)

152 De semitonio *tit.* P2 | imperfectum spacium] spacium imperfectum *Si* ‖ **154** semus-semum] semus ma mum *Si* | quasi] quod *Si* ‖ **156** vocavit *om. Si* ‖ **157** minorem et maiorem] maiorem et minorem *P2* | nuncupatur] nuncupabatur *P2* ‖ **158** post hoc] postea *Si* | autem *om. P2* | tertiam ·C·--pone] tertiam pone litteram *Si* ‖ **159** seu] vel *Si* ‖ **160** hoc] quod *Si* | est *om. Si* | malam-vitandam *om. CsP2* ‖ **161** sit² *om. Si* | ·f·faut] Effaut *P1* ·F· *P2* ‖ **162** cum semitonio] est semitonio *P2* | non sunt ibi] ibi non sunt *P2* | tantummodo] tantum *Si* ‖ **163** ibidem *om. P2* | scilicet] sed *P2* ‖ **164** inusitata] mutata *Cs* ‖ **165** *om. Cs* | notandum] notandum est *Si* | mollis] molle *P2* | de origine aliarum] de origine al' *P1* de original' *P2* ‖ **166** inusitato] mutato *Cs* | in f] in fa *ante corr. P1* | acutam] acutum *P2* | et tunc] tunc *P1P2* ‖ **167** necessaria est] est necessaria *P2* | etiam *om. P2* | et *om. Si* | omnis consonantia] omnis cantus consonantia *Si*

Lambertus, 'Ars musica' – 'Musica plana'

[152] The semitone is the imperfect space between two pitches, which, according to the human voice, cannot be divided or a midpoint placed [in it]. [153] Whence it should be understood that a semitone ought never be made, except from *mi* to *fa* or *vice versa*. [154] And it is called a semitone from *semus, sema, semum*, that is, 'imperfect', and *tonus*, as if an 'imperfect tone'. [155] But Boethius determined that a semitone was in a *sesquiXVII*[a] proportion, which he divided into two parts, one minor and another major. [156] The minor he called *dyesim*, that is, a minor semitone; the major he called an *apothome*, that is, a major semitone. [157] But the distinction between a minor and a major semitone is called a *comma*, that is, a 'distinction'. [158] But after this, returning to the *gamma*, divide from here to the end into four equal parts, and place the third letter ·C· on the terminus of the first part, and you will have a semitone.

[159] But now the question arises as to how or what need there is in music to regulate false music, or false mutation, since nothing ought to be regulated to be taken as 'false', but rather as 'true'. [160] To this it must be said that false mutation or false music is not of no use, nay indeed it is necessary for finding good consonance, but also the converse, for avoiding bad [consonance]. [161] For if (of necessity) we should want a fifth, we ought to have three tones with a semitone, so that if some figure is on ·b·*fa*·b·*mi* under square ·b·, and another on high f.*faut* through the natural, [162] then there is not a consonance found there but the worst dissonance with a semitone, because there are not three tones there with a semitone, but only two with a doubled semitone. [163] It is true, however, that it can be made here, but this is through false music. We say it is made 'through false music' namely when we make a tone from a semitone, or *vice versa*. [164] It is not false, however, but unusual. [165] Whence it should be understood that ·b· *mollis* is not from the origin of the other keys. [166] But this is known through the square ♮ sign or a round ·b· found in an unusual place, so that we may say *mi durum* on high ·f· with a square ♮ sign, or *fa* if we should place round ·b· on ·b·*fa*·b·*mi* or similarly so that it would be in the proportion of a tone, and then there will be a consonance of a fifth. [167] And so there is false music when there is a need for it, and so every consonance or melody may be perfected in whatever sign.

The 'Ars musica' Attributed to Magister Lambertus/Aristoteles

P2 75vb
Cs 258b

[168] Ditonus est spatium inter duas voces continens duos tonos, videlicet ascendendo | *ut mi, fa la,* econverso descendendo. [169] Et dicitur ditonus a *dia* | quod est *duo,* et tonus, eo quod in se continet duos tonos.

[170] Semiditonus est spatium inter duas voces continens semitonium et tonum, vel econverso, et fit duobus modis, scilicet *re fa,* vel *mi sol,* et econverso.

P1 9ra

[171] Diatessaron est quedam consonantia, que inter duas voces continet tantumdem sicut ditonus et semitonium. [172] Et dicitur diatessaron a *dia* quod est *de,* et *tetra* quod est *quatuor,* et *saron* | quod est *vox,* quasi de quatuor vocibus constituta. [173] Et fit tribus modis, ascendendo scilicet, *ut fa, re sol, mi la* et totidem descendendo. [174] A qualibet enim voce quarta fit diatessaron preter ab ·F· grave in ·♮· acuta quadrata, vel ab eadem ·♭· rotunda in ·e· acuta. [175] Fieri

P2 76ra

Si 19r

tamen potest | ibidem et in consimilibus, si necesse fuerit, per falsam musicam supradictam. [176] Est autem diatessaron in sesquitertia proportione quemadmodum quaternarius numerus ad ternarium, | qui continet tria et terciam partem trium, ut ecce si digitum supra quartam partem corde posueris, reddetur tibi consonantia diatessaron.

P1 9rb

[177] Diapente est quedam con|sonantia que inter duas voces tres tonos continet et semitonium intermixtum, ascendendo videlicet *ut sol, re la,* et totidem descendendo. [178] Et dicitur diapente a *dia* quod est *de* et *penta* quod est *quinque,* quasi de quinque vocibus constituta.

[179] A qualibet enim voce quinta fit diapente, nisi a ·♭· gravi ad ·F· gravem, vel a ·♮· acuto ad ·f· acutum. [180] Fieri tamen potest ibidem et in consimilibus per falsam musicam supradictam. [181] Fit autem diapente in sesquialtera proportione quemadmodum se habet unus numerus ad alium, ut senarius ad quaternarium et novenarius ad senarium. [182] Et vocatur numerus sesquialter quasi continens illum

P1 9va

numerum | et eius medietatem. [183] Sic etiam quando vox super aliam in medietate acuitur, dicitur esse diapente, nam si supra tertiam partem corde digitum posueris, reddetur tibi consonantia diapente.

Cs 259a

[184] Tonus autem cum diapente inter duas voces transcendit per spatium quatuor tonorum cum semitonio intermixto, scilicet *ut la,* etc.

168–169 Compil. Ticin. A 72 (**168** cf. Trad. Lamb. 3, 5) ‖ **170** Compil. Ticin. A 71 ‖ **171–172** cf. Trad. Lamb. 3, 8 ‖ **172–175** Compil. Ticin. A 74–78 (**172, 174–175** Trad. Lamb. 3, 8) ‖ **177–180** Compil. Ticin. A 80–83; Trad. Lamb. 3, 9 ‖ **184** cf. Trad. Lamb. 3, 10

168 De ditono *tit.* P2 |ditonus] diptonus *Si* ‖ **169** ditonus *om.* P2 | diptonus *Si* ‖ **170** De semiditono *tit.* P2 | semiditonus] semidiptonus *Si* | vel mi] et mi *Si* ‖ **171** De dyatesseron *tit.* P2 ‖ **172** diatessaron *om.* P2 | de] duo P2 | saron] seron P2 ‖ **173** quadrata] quadrato *Si* | vel *om.* P2 ‖ **174** quadrata] quadrato *Si* | acuta] accuta P2 | eadem … rotunda] eodem rotundo *P1P2Si* ‖ **175** in *om. Si* ‖ **176** videlicet] scilicet *Si* ‖ **178** quod est *om. Si* ‖ **179** acutum] acutam *Si* ‖ **180** potest] posset P2 | in *om. Si* ‖ **181** sesquialtera] sexquialtera *Si* ‖ **182** et vocatursesquialter] et sextum P2 | sesquialter] sexqualiter P1 sexqualter *Si* | quasi] quod ? *Si* ‖ **183** sic] sicut *Si* | in medietate *om. Si* ‖ **184** De tono cum dyapente *tit.* P2 | tonus] sonus P1 | intermixto] intermixti *Si*

[168] A ditone is the space between two pitches containing two tones, namely, ascending *ut mi, fa la,* and *vice versa,* descending. [169] And it is called a ditone from *dia,* that is 'two', and 'tone', because it contains within it two tones.

[170] A semiditone is the space between two pitches containing a semitone and a tone, or *vice versa,* and it may be made in two ways, namely, *re fa,* or *mi sol,* and *vice versa.*

[171] A diatessaron is that consonance, which contains the equivalent of a ditone and a semitone between its two pitches. [172] And it is called a diatessaron from *dia,* which is 'from', and *tetra,* which is 'four', and *saron,* which is 'pitch', as if it was created from four pitches. [173] And it can be made in three ways: ascending, namely *ut fa, re sol, mi la* and descending just as many. [174] Beyond these, a particular diatessaron can be also made from a fourth pitch from low ·F· to high square ·♮·, or from the same round ·♭· to high ·e· [175] It can be made there, however, and similarly, if there is a need, through the aforementioned false music. [176] And the diatessaron is in a sesquitertia proportion as the number four to three – the three contains the third part of three – so that if you place a finger there above the fourth part of the string, it will return to you the consonance of the diatessaron.

[177] The diapente is that consonance which contains between its two pitches three tones intermixed with a semitone, ascending, namely *ut, sol, re, la,* and descending, just as many. [178] And it is called a diapente from *dia,* that is 'from', and *penta,* that is 'five', as if created from five pitches.

[179] For a fifth from any pitch makes a diapente, except from low ·♮· to low ·F·, or from high ·♮· to high ·f· [180] However, it can be made here, and in similar places, through the aforesaid false music. [181] But the diapente is made in the sesquialteral proportion that one number has to another, as six is to four and nine is to six. [182] And it is called a sesquialteral number as if it contains this number and its half. [183] And so whenever a pitch is raised above another by a half, it is called a diapente, for if you will have placed a finger above the third part of the string, it will give you a consonance of a diapente.

[184] But a tone with a diapente between two pitches traverses through the space of four tones intermixed with a semitone, namely *ut la,* etc.

[185] Semitonium cum diapente transcendit per spatium trium tonorum et duorum semitoniorum per medium intextorum, sicut ab ·E· gravi ad ·c· acutam. [186] Ubi enim talis modus evenerit, ibi est semitonium cum diapente. [187] Et notandum quod tonus cum diapente et semitonium cum diapente rarissimi sunt in cantu | propter gravem accentum.

P1 9vb

<Ditonus cum diapente ...>

<Semiditonus cum diapente ...>

[188] Diapason autem est quedam consonantia que inter duos unisonos a qualibet littera ad consimilem elevatur et deponitur econverso. [189] Et dicitur diapason a *dia* quod est *de*, et *pan* quod est *totum* vel *omnis*, et *son* quod est *vox*, eo quod in se continet omnes voces et consonantias, seipsam videlicet et diatessaron et diapente.

[190] Fit autem diapason in proportione dupla ad sonos quemadmodum se habent numeri quidam ad aliquos, sicut <...>

P2 76rb aliquis numerus se habet | ad alterum in quadrupla proportione, ▶ *p. 118* sicut XVI ad IV. [191] Et hoc patere potest per instrumenta musicalia, si

P1 10ra quis inspexerit diligenter. [192] Nam si quis | digitum in medio corde alicuius instrumenti posuerit, duobus passibus equaliter partitis, fiet diapason consonantia.

[193] Preterea sunt nonnulli qui tritonum inter predictas species enumerant. [194] Ad quarum cognitionem discernendum et multorum etiam errorem destruendum, eas iterum cum probatione et opere ▶ *p. 118* reformamus.

Si 19v/Cs [195] Ter qua-ter-ne sunt spe-ci-es qui-bus o-mnis can-ti-le-na
259–260

P1 10rb con-te-xi-tur, | sci-li- cet u-ni-so-nus, to-nus, se-mi-to-ni-um,

Cs 259b | di-to-nus, se-mi-di-to-nus, di-a-tes-sa-ron, di-a-pen-te,

P2 76va to-nus cum di-a-pen-te, se-mi-[di]-to-nus | cum di-a-pen-te,

P1 10va di-|to-nus cum di-a-pen-te, se-mi-di-to-nus cum

di-a-pen-te ad hec so-nus di-a-   pa-son.

185–186 Q∪ᴀᴛ. Pʀɪɴᴄ. 3, 16 ‖ **187** Tʀᴀᴅ. Lamb. 3, 11; (propter gravem accentum) cf. Q∪ᴀᴛ. ᴘʀɪɴᴄ. 3, 17 ‖ **188–189** Tʀᴀᴅ. Lamb. 3, 14; Q∪ᴀᴛ. Pʀɪɴᴄ. 3, 18 ‖ **190** (fit-dupla) Tʀᴀᴅ. Lamb. 3, 14 ‖ **193–194** Tʀᴀᴅ. Lamb. 3, 1 ‖ **195** Aɴᴏɴ. Claudifor. 3, 2, 6

185 De semitonio cum dyapente *tit. P2* | interxtorum] intermixtorum *P2* ‖ **187** Et notandum-diapente *om. Si* | rarissimi] rarissime *P2* ‖ **188** De dyapason *tit. P2* | autem est] est autem *P2* ‖ **189** et pan] et spa *Si* ‖ **190** dupla] duplum *P1* | potest] posset *P2* ‖ **191** medio] media *P2* ‖ **193** enumerant] enuntiant *P1Si* ‖ **194** etiam *om. P2* | cum probatione] in probatione *P2* | improbatione *Si* ‖ **195** ter quaterne] sex quaterni *P1* ter quaterni *P2*

Lambertus, 'Ars musica' – 'Musica plana'

[185] A semitone with a diapente traverses through the space of three tones and two semitones inserted in the middle, just as from low ·E· to high ·c· [186] Where [an interval of] such a kind should occur, there is a semitone with a diapente there. [187] And it should be noted that a tone with a diapente and a semitone with a diapente are the most rare in chant on account of the heavy sound.

Ditone with a diapente …

Semiditone with a diapente …

[188] But a diapason is a particular consonance, which is elevated and laid down between two unison pitches from any letter to a similar one, and *vice versa*. [189] And it is called diapason from *dia* that is 'from', and *pan*, that is 'whole' or 'every', and *son*, that is 'pitch', because it contains in itself all the pitches and consonances, namely itself, and the diatessaron and diapente.

[190] But a diapason is made in a duple proportion to the sounds in the same way that certain numbers relate to others, just as some number relates to another in a quadruple proportion, just as 16 is to 4. [191] And this can be shown through musical instruments, if anyone were to examine this with care. [192] For if someone were to place a finger in the middle of a string of some instrument, by two steps parted equally, it will make the consonance of a diapason.

[193] Beyond this there are several who enumerate the tritone among the aforementioned *species*. [194] In order to separate the knowledge of these *species*, and to destroy the error of many, we amend these again with our proof and work.

[195] Three (by) four are the *species* by which every song

is woven, namely, unison, tone, semitone,

ditone, semiditone, diatessaron, diapente,

tone with a diapente, semiditone with a diapente,

ditone with a diapente, semiditone with

a diapente, to these the sound of the diapason.

The 'Ars musica' Attributed to Magister Lambertus/Aristoteles

P1 10vb

Cs 260a

P2 76vb
P1 11ra

[196] Istarum autem specierum quedam sunt concordantes, quedam discordantes, quedam magis, quedam mi|nus. [197] Concordantia vero dicitur esse, quando due voces in eodem tempore compatiuntur ita quod una cum alia secundum auditum suavem reddat melodiam, tunc est consonantia. [198] Discordantia vero per oppositum dicitur, [unde] cum discordantia concordantie opponatur, et unum oppositum preter alterum complete sciri non possit. [199] Unde discordantia est duorum sonorum sibimet permixtorum ad aures pervenientium dura collisio, scilicet quando due voces in eodem iunguntur, ita quod secundum auditum una cum alia non compatitur, tunc est dissonantia. [200] Nam quidam sonus gravis cum

P1 11rb acuto | commixtus propter aliquam specialem concordantiam, ▶ *p. 118* statim offenditur anima et generatur in sensu particulari utpote in aure dissonantia, quae cacophonos appellatur a *cacos*, quod est *malum*, et *phonos* quod est *sonus*, quasi malus sonus.

[201] Quarum autem quedam dicuntur imperfecte, quedam medie, et quedam perfecte. [202] Imperfecte vero sunt tonus, semitonium et tritonus, quia quanto propinquiores inveniuntur eo tanto peiores, et ▶ *p. 118* quanto remotiores tanto meliores. [203] Medie vero sunt ditonus et ▶ *p. 118* semiditonus. [204] Perfecte sunt tonus cum diapente et semitonium cum diapente.

196–214 Trad. Holl. VI 17, p. 46 ‖ **196–198** cf. Anon. Emmeram. IV (p. 258, l. 15–20) ‖ **199** (discordantia-collisio) Petr. Palm. p. 518 ‖ **200** (offenditur-cacophonos) Anon. Emmeram. IV (p. 268, l. 1–3 'Nam voces ab invicem discordantes offendunt animam, in sensu particulari, utputa in aure, chacephaton generantes, et sic auditum impediunt et perturbant'.) ‖ **201** (quedam … perfecte) Ioh. Garl. mens. 9, 26

197 vero *om. Si* | tempore *om.* P2 ‖ **198** per oppositum dicitur] dicitur per oppositum *Si* | sciri] scire P1 ‖ **199** quando due] quandocumque P1 ‖ **200** specialem concordantiam] concordantiam specialem *Si* | cacophonos] cassenphaton P1 cacophaton P2 cachenphaton *Si* | cacos] cachos *Si* | quod est² *om.* P2*Si* | quasi] quod *Si* ‖ **202** sunt] dicuntur *dub. Si* | eo *om. Si* ‖ **203** semiditonus] semitonium P1 semiditonium P2 semiditonum *Si* ‖ **204** et semitonium cum diapente *om.* P2 | cum diapente] et dyapente *Si* | et semitonium cum diapente *om. Si*

Lambertus, 'Ars musica' – 'Musica plana'

[196] But of these species some are concordant, some discordant, some more, some less. [197] A concord is said to be when two pitches are held together at the same time so that one with another returns a sweet melody, according to the sense of hearing, then it is a consonance. [198] A discord is said to be its opposite, [whence] a discord is placed against a concord, and the one opposite cannot be fully known beyond its alternate. [199] Whence a discord is a harsh collision of two sounds mixed together striking the ears, namely when two pitches are joined in the same [sound], so that according to the sense of hearing one is not compatible with the other, then it is a dissonance. [200] For any low sound mixed together with a high sound according to any special concord is immediately offensive to the soul, and a dissonance is generated within the particular sense, being hearing, and which is called cacophony from *cacos*, which is 'bad', and *phonos*, which is 'sound', as if a 'bad sound'.

[201] But certain of these dissonances are called imperfect, certain medium, and certain perfect. [202] The tone, semitone, and tritone are imperfect, because the closer they are found together, the worse they are, and the further apart they are, the better they are. [203] The ditone and the semiditone are the medium dissonances. [204] The tone with a diapente and the semitone with a diapente are the perfect dissonances.

The 'Ars musica' Attributed to Magister Lambertus/Aristoteles

P2 77ra – P1
11va Cs 260b
Si 20r

[205] Sciendum est autem | quod sicut sex sunt | voces quibus tota musica conformatur, ita et sex tantummodo sunt concor|dantie quarum tres prime genera sunt generalissima | omnium ▸ *p. 118* concordantiarum. Alie vero sunt aliene. [206] Prima scilicet est ▸ *p. 118* diatessaron, secunda diapente, tertia diapason, quarta diatessaron cum diapason, quinta diapente cum diapason, sexta bisdiapason. [207] Harum autem prima et quarta secundum quod in se sunt, imperfecte dicuntur. Secunda et quinta sunt medie. Tertia et sexta perfecte sunt consonantie. [208] Secundum Boetium diatessaron cum ▸ *p. 118* diapason se habet in proportione dupla superbipartiente tertias, sicut 8 ad 3. [209] Nam si tollatur medietas corde alicuius instrumenti et quarta pars residui, erit diatessaron cum diapason. [210] Diapente cum

P1 11vb diapason se habet in | tripla proportione ad sonos sicut inter tres et unum. [211] Nam si dividatur corda in duas partes equales, in tertia parte residui erit diapente cum diapason. [212] Bis diapason habetur in quadrupla proportione ad sonos, sicut est inter quatuor et unum. [213] Et hoc manifeste patet in simplicibus, nam omne compositum debet sapere naturam suorum extremorum et hoc probatur. [214] Nam si dividatur corda in duas partes equales et altera pars similiter in duas et super ultimam digito tangatur, erit bis diapason. Et hoc sufficit ad presens.

<De modis>

[215] Sequitur videre de modis, qualiter omnis cantus ecclesiasticus se
P1 12ra – P2 habeat et in quo differat. | [216] Quos quidam minus periti | musici
77rb secundum usum modernum tonos asserunt appellandos, quos contradicimus autenti ratione, quod non debent vocari toni, immo potius modi, videlicet [217] propter nomen reale ab antiquis impositum, quoniam modus dicitur discretio modulationis a moderando, eo quod omnis cantus regularis ecclesiasticus et quelibet res naturalis per modum seu per modos regulariter discernitur ac moderatur, [218] et propter etiam secunde speciei differentiam, que tonus ▸ *p. 119* appellatur, eo quod perfecte tonat, id est perfecte ostendit distantiam tantummodo inter illas duas voces de quibus dictum est superius.

---

205 (generalissima omnium concordantium) Ioh. Garl. mens. 9, 13 ‖ **213** (nam omne compositum … extremorum): cf. Raimundus Lullus, *Liber de venatione substantiae, accidentis et compositi (op. 130)*, dist. 7, pars 4, l. 227 (ed. A. Madre, Turnhout, 1998; CCCM, 114): 'Et respondendum est, quos sunt de suis specificis praemissis; quoniam omne medium oportet sapere naturam suorum extremorum'.

205 tota *om. Si* | conformatur] formatur *P2* | tantummodo sunt] sunt tantummodo *P2* | sunt *om. Si* ‖ **208** dupla *om. Si* ‖ **209** pars] partem *P1* parte *Si* | erit] erat *dub. Si* ‖ **214** ultimam] alteram *Si* ‖ **215** De modis *tit. P2* ‖ **216** autenti] audenti *P1* evidenti *P2* ‖ **217** regularis ecclesiasticus] ecclesiasticus regularis *Si* | modos] modum *P2* ‖ **218** et etiam propter *Si* | etiam *om. P2* | quod] quot *P2* | illas duas] duas illas *P2*

Lambertus, 'Ars musica' – 'Musica plana'

[205] Now it should be understood that there are six solmisation syllables from which all music is formed, so there are only six concords, of which the first three are the most general types of all the concords. The others belong with another. [206] Namely: the first is the diatessaron, the second the diapente, the third the diapason, the fourth the diatessaron with diapason, the fifth the diapente with the diapason, the sixth the bisdiapason. [207] But of these, the first and the fourth, according to how they are in themselves, are called imperfect. [208] According to Boethius, the diatessaron with a diapason has within itself a duple proportion superbipartiens to three, just as 8 to 3. [209] For if the midpoint of some instrument's string is taken, and there is a fourth part remaining, it will be a diatessaron with a diapason. [210] The diapente with a diapason has within itself a triple proportion to its sounds just as between three and one. [211] For if a string is divided into two equal parts, in the remaining third part will be a diapente with a diapason. [212] A bisdiapason will be contained in a quadruple proportion to the sounds, just as there is between four and one. [213] And this is clearly shown in single things, for every composite ought to know the nature of its extremes and this is proven. [214] For if a string is divided into two equal parts and the other part likewise into two and it is touched by a finger above the last part [of the string], this will be a bisdiapason. And this suffices for now.

<On the Modes>

[215] It follows to look into the modes, how each ecclesiastical chant possesses them, and into which modes the chant is separated. [216] Certain less skilled musicians claim that these modes should be called tones, according to modern practice. [217] We contradict this with a valid reason: they ought not to be called tones, nay rather modes, that is, according to the imposition of its proper name by the ancients, because the discernment of modulation by *mode*rating [governing] is called 'mode'; because every regular ecclesiastical chant and any natural thing is discerned and governed through a mode or modes by rule, [218] and now according to the distinction of the second species, which is called 'tone', by which is meant that it 'tones' perfectly, that is, it extends precisely the distance between two pitches, about which was spoken of above.

The 'Ars musica' Attributed to Magister Lambertus/Aristoteles

Cs 261a *P1* 12rb

[219] Unde sciendum est quod quatuor tantummodo modi principaliter a Grecis erant | adinventi, videlicet prothus, deuterus, tritus atque tetrardus, quos Greci authentos appellabant. [220] Videntes autem Latini quatuor minus sufficere ad omnium cantuum genera discernendum, alios quatuor eisdem addiderunt et eosdem plagales sive subiugales vocaverunt. [221] Unde notandum quod omnes modi tam autenti quam plagales quatuor finales habent, scilicet ·D·, ·E·, ·F·, ·G· graves. [222] Prothus autentus et primus plagalis finiunt in ·D· gravi. [223] Deuterus autentus et secundus plagalis finiunt in ·E· gravi. [224] Tritus autentus et tertius plagalis finiunt in ·F· gravi. [225] Tetrardus

P1 12va

autentus et quartus plagalis | finiunt in ·G· gravi. Unde versus:

P1 P2 Si, Be Mü Ve

[226] Dicitur esse modus in cantu regula quedam

[227] qua cantus regitur, discernitur ac moderatur.

[228] Octo vero modi sunt quorum quilibet impar

P2 77va – *Si* 20v

[229] dicitur autentus | a Grecis nam adinventus.

[230] Primus tertius indeque quintus, septimus hii sunt.

[231] Postea tunc sequitur quod par vero quilibet horum

[232] collateralis erit qui dicitur esse secundus,

[233] quartus cum sexto, quibus octavus sociatur.

[234] Impar quisque parem sibi postulat associari,

[235] qui secum possit in eodem fine morari.

[236] Voces finales illorum sunt *re mi fa sol*.

[237] Sedes finales horum ·D· vel ·E· simul ·F· ·G·.

P1 12vb

[238] Primus finitur in ·D· pariterque secundus.

[239] Tertius et quartus ·E· sumpserunt sibi finem.

[240] Quintus in ·F· finit sextusque sibi sociatur.

[241] Septimus in ·G· cadit, octavus iungitur illi.

[242] Quarti vero modi finis quandoque repertus

[243] est in a.lamire cui donat regula nomen

[244] quod per ·b· mollem finire videtur ibidem.

[245] Sic sexti finis cesolfaut est aliquando

[246] Nature talis autentus esse probatur

[247] ut queat ad finem protendi vocibus octo,

[248] Huicque licentia dat vocem contingere nonam,

[249] undecimamque licet sibi quandoque tangere vocem.

[250] Voceque sub fine tantum deponitur una.

[251] Est quoque natura data collateralibus hec ut

---

219 authentos] autentos *Si* ‖ **220–221** sive subiugales-quam plagales] appellaverunt qui *Si* ‖ **221** habent *om. Si* ‖ **227** discernitur] decernitur *Ve* ‖ **229** nam adinventus] nam et inventus *Be* namque repertus *Mü* sunt que reperti *Ve* ‖ **230** primus-quintus] tertius et primus hiis quintus *Be* ‖ **231** quod par vero] quod parvus *Be* quoque par quod *Mü* ‖ **232** erit *om. Be* | qui dicitur esse] sicut finit ipse *Ve* ‖ **234** associari] sociari *Be* ‖ **235** eodem] eadem *P2* ‖ **237** vel *om. Be* | simul *om. Mü* | ·G·] ac alamire per re licet hiis dare finem *add. Mü* ‖ **239** ·E·] in ·E· *Be* ‖ **240** sextusque] et sextus *Be* | sociatur] sociabit *Ve* ‖ **242–245** *om. Be* ‖ **242–243** repertus-est in] reperta est in *MüP1* ‖ **244** per ·b· mollem] ·b· molle *S* ‖ **245** cesolfaut] csolfaut *VeP2* ‖ **246** autentus] autenticus *P2* ‖ **248** Huicque licentia dat] Hiisque licenciam datur *Be* ‖ **249** *om. Be* | undecimam quandoque licet contingere vocem *Mü* | sibi quandoque] aliquando *Ve* ‖ **250** voceque] vocemque *Be* deponitur] supponitur *Ve* ‖ **251** Est] E *Be*

Lambertus, 'Ars musica' – 'Musica plana'

[219] Whence it should be understood that there were only four modes first found by the Greeks, namely *prothus, deuterus, tritus,* and *tetrardus,* which the Greeks called 'authentic'. [220] But the Latins, seeing that four would not suffice for discerning the classes of all chants, added others to these four and they called them plagal or subjugated [modes]. [221] Whence it should be noted that all the modes, authentic and plagal, have four finals, namely low ·D·, ·E·, ·F·, ·G·. [222] Authentic *protus* and the first plagal finish on low ·D·. [223] Authentic *deuterus* and the second plagal finish on low ·E·. [224] Authentic *tritus* and the third plagal finish on low ·F·. [225] Authentic *tetrardus* and the fourth plagal finish on low ·G·. Whence the verse:

[226] A mode is said to be a certain rule in a chant

[227] by which the chant is ruled, known, and governed.

[228] There are eight modes, of which each odd-numbered one

[229] is called 'authentic', for it was discovered by the Greeks.

[230] These are the first, the third and also the fifth and seventh.

[231] Then afterwards it follows that any even-numbered one

[232] will be 'collateral', the one that is called the second,

[233] the fourth, with the sixth are called, to which the eighth is joined.

[234] The uneven demands that the even be coupled with it,

[235] so that it may dwell with it on the same final.

[236] Their final pitches are *re mi fa sol.*

[237] Their final seats are ·D· or ·E· likewise ·F· ·G·.

[238] The first is finished on ·D· and equally the second.

[239] The third and fourth have taken ·E· as a final for themselves.

[240] The fifth finishes on ·F· and the sixth is coupled with it.

[241] The seventh falls on ·G·, the eighth is joined with it.

[242] The final of the fourth mode is sometimes found,

[243] on ·a· *lamire* to which the name gives by rule

[244] because it is seen to end there by way of ·b· *molle.*

[245] In the same way the end of the sixth is sometimes ·c· *solfaut.*

[246] The authentic is shown to be of such a nature

[247] that it seeks the final by stretching over eight pitches,

[248] and it is given licence to extend to a ninth pitch,

[249] and now and then allows itself to reach an eleventh pitch.

[250] And [the authentic] is lowered by one pitch beneath the final.

[251] This nature is also given to the collateral modes so that

The 'Ars musica' Attributed to Magister Lambertus/Aristoteles

P1 13ra

[252] ad quintam vocem possint a fine levari.

[253] Hiisque licentia dat vocem contingere sextam,

[254] octavamque licet hiis quandoque tangere vocem,

Cs 261b

[255] cum sub fine queant vocem contingere quintam.

[256] Sic bis sex voces retinet, nam sepe videmus

[257] offertoria cum gradualibus officiisque,

[258] alleluiaque vel antiphonas responsaque quedam,

[259] et tractus voces cantari per duodenas.

[260] Et sic quemque licet duodenis vocibus uti,

[261] tot vero voces cantus non postulat omnis.

[262] Multotiens et enim cantus quidam reperitur,

[263] qui nondum per tot voces protenditur,

P2 77vb

[264] ut per ascensum possit autenticus esse,

P1 13rb

[265] nec descendit idem quod sit iam collateralis

[266] propter descensum. De quo fit questio cuius

[267] debeat esse modi, que soluitur hac ratione:

[268] sicut transire metas aliquas prohibetur,

[269] cantus quilibet et aliquas sic adire iubetur.

[270] Quilibet autentus ascendere namque tenetur

[271] trans finem quintam, plagalis vero secundam.

[272] Protendi semper autenticus optat in altum,

[273] raroque descendit. E contra collateralis

[274] sepius ima tenens, raro se tollit in altum.

[275] Hinc quoque de facili sciri poterit cito cuius

[276] debeat esse modi si caute respiciatur

[277] an magis alta petat cantus quam tendat ad ima.

P1 13va

[278] Nam magis alta tenens | autenticus esse probatur,

[279] sepius ima tenens est collateralis habendus.

[280] Rursus multotiens alium cantum reperimus,

[281] qui primo sicut autenticus obtinet alta,

[282] postea descendit ut collateralis ad ima,

[283] vel vice conversa prius ima, de hinc petit alta.

[284] De quo si querit quis cuius iure modi sit,

[285] sic respondetur, quod cantus quilibet eius

[286] esse modi possit in quo finire videtur:

[287] nam punctus preiens extremum, si situetur

---

252 possint a fine] possunt a suo fine *Be* ‖ **254** octavamque licet] octavam quoque *S* | licet hiis quandoque] licet quandoque *Be* licet hiis interdum *Mü* licet aliquando *Ve* ‖ **255** vocem-quintam] quintam contingere vocem *Mü* | contingere] deponere *Be* ‖ **256–269** *om. Be* ‖ **256** retinet] retinent *Ve* ‖ **257** cum] tum *P2* ‖ **263** qui] quod *P1 Ve* ‖ **263–265** esse-idem] esse nec idem tantum descendit *Ve* ‖ **265** nec-sit] nec idem tantum descendit ut sit *P1* ‖ **266** cuius] talis *P1* | **267** hac] ac *P2* ‖ **269** cantus-adire] omnis cantus sic aliquas et *Mü* ‖ **271** trans finem] transire *Be* ‖ **272** optat] tensat *? ante corr. P1* ‖ **274** ima] imo *P1* | se tollit] tendit *Be* ‖ **275–276** *om. Be* ‖ **275** Hic docet iudicare an sit autenti vel plagalis. Hinc … *Ve* | sciri poterit] poterit scire *P1P2* ‖ **279** an] cum *Be* | petat] petit *Be* | quam tendat] quem *? tendit BeVe* | Auctentus talis econtra collecteralis *add. Be* ‖ **278–286** *om. Be* ‖ **280** Proprietates diversorum cantuum. Rursus … *Ve* ‖ **281** obtinet] optinet *VeP1* ‖ **282** ad ima] in yma *P1* ‖ **284** sit] sunt *P2* ‖ **285** quod] quia *P1P2Si* ‖ **287** punctus] punctum *BeMü* | si situetur] sic acuetur *Be*

42

Lambertus, 'Ars musica' – 'Musica plana'

[252] they can be raised to a fifth pitch from the final.
[253] And to these licence is given to extend to a sixth pitch
[254] and now and then allows these to reach an eighth pitch
[255] since they can reach a fifth pitch beneath the final.
[256] Thus it retains twice six pitches, for often we see
[257] offertories with graduals and introits,
[258] and alleluias or antiphons and certain responses,
[259] and tracts to be sung over twelve pitches.
[260] And so it is allowed for each chant to use twelve pitches,
[261] but not every chant requires so many pitches.
[262] And often a certain chant is found,
[263] which is not yet stretched over so many pitches,
[264] so that through its ascent it is able to be authentic,
[265] and it does not descend in the same way for it to be a collateral
[266] because of its descent. From which we may ask the question – which
[267] mode ought it to be, which is answered by this reasoning:
[268] just as it is prevented from crossing some boundaries,
[269] so any chant is ordered to approach some other boundaries.
[270] For every authentic is required to ascend
[271] beyond the final fifth, but the plagal to the second.
[272] The authentic always desires to be extended upwards,
[273] and rarely it descends. And against this, the collateral
[274] more often holding the depths, rarely raises itself aloft.
[275] From this too it will be easy to know quickly of which
[276] mode it ought to be, if one carefully examines
[277] whether a chant seeks heights more than it strains towards the depths.
[278] Since the one that holds the heights more is proved to be authentic,
[279] that which holds the depths more must be accounted collateral.
[280] Again many times we find another chant,
[281] which first, like an authentic chant, obtains the heights,
[282] afterwards it descends as a collateral to the depths,
[283] or *vice versa*: first it seeks the depths, then the heights.
[284] From this, if anyone asks of which mode a chant rightly is,
[285] thus the answer will be that each chant
[286] can be of the mode in which it seems to end:
[287] for the note going before the last, if it is located

The 'Ars musica' Attributed to Magister Lambertus/Aristoteles

Si 21r   [288] altior extremo, merito tunc esse meretur

[289] autentus talis, e contra collateralis,

[290] aut eius de quo plus accipit, esse probatur.

[291] Precipue cantus hiis versibus examinetur.

P1 13vb   [292] Nunc autem videre sequitur ǀ in quibus clavibus modi incipiant et in quo differant et quot differentias habeant et quomodo psalmi cuiuslibet modi incipiant vel moderantur et ubi distinguantur vel mediantur. [293] Primo igitur quisque scire poterit de intonationibus per hos versus:

Cs 262a   [294] Primum cum sexto *fa sol la* semper habeto

[295] Tertius octavus capit *ut re fa* sicque secundus

[296] *la sol la* quartus, *ut mi sol* tibi quintus

[297] Septimus *fa mi fa sol* sic omnes esse recordor

[298] Septimus et sextus dant *fa mi re mi* quoque primus

[299] Quintus et octavus *fa sol fa* sicque secundus

[300] *Sol fa mi fa* ternus *re ut mi re*que quaternus.

<I>

P1 14ra   [301] Pri-mum que-ri-te re-gnum de-i.

[302] Pri-mus to-nus sic me-di-a-tur et sic fi-ni-tur.   Si-cut e-rat in prin-

P1 14rb   ci-pi-o et nunc et sem-per et in se-cu-la ǀ se-cu-lo-rum. A-men.

[303] e u o u a e.   e u o u a e. e u o u a e.   e u o u a e.   ▶ *p. 119*

Cs 262b   e u o u a e.   e u o u a e.

---

289 collateralis] collecteralis *Be* ‖ **290** probatur] meretur *Be* probetur *P1* ‖ **292–293** *des. BeMüVe* ‖ **292** clavibus] cantibus *Si* ‖ **293** quisque scire] scire quisque *Si* ǀ intonationibus] intonantibus *P1* ‖ **294–300** *des. Be ab alia manu P2* ‖ **295** capit *om. Ve* ‖ **296** tibi] dat tibi *Ve* ‖ **297** fa] est *MüP2* ‖ **300** reque] re sicque *P2* ‖ **301** *sine notis P2* ǀ ⸙] ⸙ *Si* ‖ **302–344** *des. P2*

[288] higher than the last, deservedly then such a chant deserves to be
[289] authentic, and from its contrary, the collateral,
[290] or it is proved to be the one from which it takes more.
[291] Above all let the chant be tested by these verses.

[292] But now it follows to see in which keys the modes may begin; in which they may be separated; how many *differentiae* they may have; how the psalms, in any mode, may begin or are governed; and where they may be distinguished or sung at their midpoints. [293] So, first, everyone will be able to know the intonations through these lines of verse:

[294] The first, with the sixth, which always has *fa sol la*;
[295] The third, the eighth takes *ut re fa* and so the second,
[296] The fourth, *la sol la*; the fifth is to you *ut mi sol*;
[297] The seventh, *fa mi fa sol* thus is all I remember it to be;
[298] Seventh and sixth give *fa mi re mi*, also the first;
[299] The fifth and the eighth, *fa sol fa* and so the second;
[300] *Sol fa mi fa* the third; and *re ut mi re* the fourth.

<I>

[301] *Pri-mum que-ri-te re-gnum de-i.*

[302] And so the first tone is sung at its midpoint and so it is finished.

Si-cut e-rat in prin-ci-pi-o et nunc et sem-per et in se-cu-la \ se-cu-lo-rum. A-men.

[303] *e u o u a e.   e u o u a e.   e u o u a e.   e u o u a e.*

e u o u a e.   e u o u a e.

[304] Prima differentia primi modi talis est, quod quandocumque antiphona incipit in ·C·, ut hic:

A-ma-vit. Ec-ce ve-ni-et. O be-a- ta tale habet e u o u a e.

P1 14va [305] Secunda sequitur differentia primi modi, videlicet quando antiphona incipit in ·D·, ut hic:

Si 21v   Ec-ce no-men do-mi-ni. Se-de a dex-tris me-is. | O pa-stor

tunc habet tale e u o u a e.

[306] Tertia differentia primi modi talis est quando antiphona incipit in ·D· et statim gradatim ascendit in *sol*, verbi gratia ut hic:

Co-gno-ve-runt o-mnes. Eu- ge. E u o u a e

[307] Talis est differentia quarta primi modi quod quandocunque antiphona incipit in ·F· et a *fa* descendat in *ut* vel in *re*, verbi gratia:

Cs 263a   A-ve Ma-ri- a. Pa-ter. Chri-sti vir<go>

P1 14vb tunc habet tale | e u o u a e.

[308] Quinta differentia primi modi talis est, quod quando antiphona incipit in ·F· et statim *mi re* sequatur post *fa*, vel de *fa* saliat in *la*, vel de *fa* per *sol* ascendat in *la*, ut hic:

Vo-lo pa-ter. E-sto-te. Do-mi-nus.   E u o u a e.

[309] Sexta differentia primi modi talis est, quod quando antiphona incipit in ·a· acuto et statim de *la* descendet in *sol*, ut patet hic:

P1 15ra   Vi-di do-mi-num.| Sci-o cu-i cre-di-di. Ut non de-lin-quam

<tale habet> e u o u a e

304 Amavit eum dominus … (CAO 1360); Ecce veniet propheta magnus … (2552); O beata et benedicta et gloriosa … (3992) ‖ **305** Ecce nomen domini … (2527); Sede a dextris meis … (4853); O pastor eterne o clemens … (4051) ‖ **306** Cognoverunt omnes … (1849); Euge serve bone … (2732) ‖ **307** Ave Maria gratia plena … tu in mulieribus (1539); Pater manifestavi … (4237); Christi virgo nec terrore … (1787) ‖ **308** Volo pater … (5491); Estote fortes … (2684); Dominus defensor vite mee (2404) ‖ **309** Vidi dominum … (5404); Scio cui credidi … (4831); Ut non delinquam in lingua … (5294)

304 Ecce veniet] ⸺ (Similabo) ⸺ (s·l·) *add. Si* ‖ **305** Sequitur secunda *Si* | ut hic] verbi gratia ut hic *Si* | Sede a dextris] ⸺ (Beatus) ⸺ (Gloria) *add. Si* | O pastor] ⸺ | tunc habet *om. Si* ‖ **306–307** quando antiphona-primi modi *om.* P1 ‖ **306** ⸺] ⸺ *Si* ‖ **307** quandocunque] quando *Si* | vel in re *om. Si* | gratia] ut hic *add. Si* | tunc habet *om. Si* ‖ **309** quod *om. Si* | Scio-delinquam] Ut non delinquam Scio cui credidi *Si* | ⸺ (Aiutorium) ⸺ (Domine hodie Christe) *add. Si*

[304] The first *differentia* of the first mode is as follows: where an antiphon begins on ·C·, as here:

A-ma-vit. Ec-ce ve-ni-et. O be-a- ta has the following *e u o u a e*.

[305] The second *differentia* of the first mode follows, namely, when an antiphon begins on ·D·, as here:

Ec-ce no-men do-mi-ni. Se-de a dex-tris me-is. O pa-stor

then it has the following *e u o u a e*.

[306] The third *differentia* of the first mode is as follows: when an antiphon begins on ·D· and immediately ascends stepwise to *sol*, for example, as here:

Co-gno-ve-runt o-mnes. Eu- ge. *E u o u a e*

[307] So follows the fourth *differentia* of the first mode: whenever an antiphon begins on ·F· and descends from *fa* to *ut* or to *re*, for example:

A-ve Ma-ri-a. Pa-ter. Chri-sti virgo

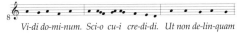
then it has the following *e u o u a e*.

[308] The fifth *differentia* of the first mode is as follows: when an antiphon begins on ·F· and immediately *mi re* follows after *fa*, or from *fa* it may leap to *la*, or it may ascend from *fa* through *sol* to *la*, as here.

Vo-lo pa-ter. E-sto-te. Do-mi-nus then it has the following *e u o u a e*

[309] The sixth *differentia* of the first mode is as follows: when an antiphon begins on the high ·a· and immediately descends from *la* to *sol*, as is shown here.

Vi-di do-mi-num. Sci-o cu-i cre-di-di. Ut non de-lin-quam

it has the following *e u o u a e*

\<II\>

Cs 263b

³¹⁰ Se-cun-dum au-tem si-mi-le est hu-ic.

P1 15rb

³¹¹ Se-cun-dus mo-dus sic me-di-a-tur et sic fi-ni-tur. Si-cut e- rat

in prin-ci-pi-o et nunc et sem-per et in se-cu-la se-cu-lo-rum.

A- men.

³¹² Antiphone vero secundi modi ubicumque incipiantur, tantummodo unicum habent *seculorum amen*, preter ad Magnificat et ad Benedictus.

\<III\>

Si 22r

³¹³ Ter-ti-a di-es est quod hec fa-cta sunt.

P1 15va/Cs 264a

³¹⁴ Ter-ti-us mo-dus sic me-di-a-tur et sic fi-ni-tur. | Si-cut e-rat

in prin-ci-pi-o et nunc et sem-per et in se-cu-la se-cu-lo-rum. A-men.

³¹⁵ Prima differentia tertii modi est quando antiphona incipit in ·E· et de *mi* per *re* ascendit in | *sol* et ultra in ·c·, ut hic:

P1 15vb

Quan-do na-tus es. E u o u a e

³¹⁶ Item, quando antiphona incipit in ·c· acuto, ut hic:

U-num o-pus fe-ci, Do-mi-ne mi rex tale habet e u o u a e.

³¹⁷ Quando antiphona incipit in ·G· et inde ascendit per *re* in *fa*, vel de *sol* saliat in *fa*, ut patet hic:

▶ *p. 119*

P1 16ra

Sur-ge. Vi-vo e- go. | Qui se-qui-tur me tunc tale habet e u o u a e.

---

316 Unum opus feci ... (5275); Domine mi rex ... (2358) ‖ **317** Surge et in eternum serva ... (5072); Vivo ego dicit dominus ... (5481); Qui sequitur me ... (4496)

312 ubicumque] utcumque *Si* | unicum habent] habent unicum *Si* ‖ **313** (facta sunt) ⸫] ⸫ *Si* ‖ **315** est] talis est *Si* | in ·c·] in ·G· *Si* ‖ **316** unum opus feci *om. Si* | tale habet *om.* P1 ‖ **317** fa] verbi gratia *add. Si* | patet *om. Si* | Surge] ⸫ (fidelis servus) *add. Si* | vivo ego] ⸫ (quoniam) *add. Si* | qui sequitur me] ⸫ (Si quis diligit me) ⸫ (Orietur) *add. Si*

\<II\>

[music notation]
310 Se-cun- dum au-tem si-mi-le est hu- ic.

[music notation]
311 So the second mode is sung at its midpoint and so it is finished.

[music notation]
Si-cut e-rat in prin-ci-pi-o et nunc et sem-per et in se-cu-la se-cu-lo-rum.

[music notation]
A- men.

312 No matter where antiphons of the second mode may begin, they have only one *seculorum amen*, except for the *Magnificat* and *Benedictus*.

\<III\>

[music notation]
313 Ter-ti-a di-es est quod hec fa-cta sunt.

[music notation]
314 So the third mode is sung at its midpoint and so it is finished.

[music notation]
Si-cut e-rat in prin-ci-pi-o et nunc et sem-per et in se-cu-la se-cu-lo-rum. A-men.

315 The first *differentia* of the third mode is when an antiphon begins on ·E· and ascends from *mi* through *re* to sol and beyond this to ·c·, as here:

[music notation]
Quan-do na-tus es. e u o u a e

316 Likewise, when an antiphon begins on high ·c·, as here:

[music notation]
Unum opus feci.   Domine mi rex has the following *e u o u a e*.

317 When an antiphon begins on ·G· and ascends from there through *re* to *fa*, or leaps from *sol* to *fa*, as shown here:

[music notation]
Sur-ge. Vi-vo e-go.   Qui se-qui-tur me then it has the following *e u o u a e*.

The 'Ars musica' Attributed to Magister Lambertus/Aristoteles

Cs 264b ³¹⁸Quando antiphona incipit in ·E· et statim de *mi* in *fa* vel in *sol* ascendit, ut hic:

▶ *p. 119*

Fe- lix nam-que. Len-tis qui-dem <tunc tale habet> e u o u a e.

<IIII>

³¹⁹Quar-ta vi-gi-li-a ve-nit ad e-os.

P1 16rb – *Si*
22v

³²⁰Quar-tus mo-dus sic me-di-a-tur et sic fi- ni-tur. I Si-cut

e-rat in prin-ci-pi-o et nunc et sem-per et in se-cu-la se-cu-lo-rum.

A-men.

³²¹ Prima differentia quarti modi est quando antiphona incipit in ·F· descendendo in *re*, I vel in *mi* vel in *re* ascendendo, verbi gratia:

P1 16va

Cs 265a   Au-ro vir-gi-num. Na-tu-re. O ve-ra. I Vi-gi-la-te.

Ru-bum quem vi-de-rat. Tri-du-a-num. E u o u a e.

³²² Quando vero antiphona incipit in ·C· gravi ascendendo, ut hic:

P1 16vb   Beth-le-em. I Ho-di-er-na. <tale habet> e u o u a e.

³²³ Quando antiphona incipit in ·E· vel in ·G· gravibus, ut hic:

Fi-de-li-a. Cru-cem tu-am. In man-da-tis. <tale habet> e u o u a e.

---

318 Felix namque es beata virgo … (2860); Lentis quidem sed iugibus … (3605) ‖ **321–325** cf. Iac. Leod. spec. 6, 94, 8–11 ‖ **321** Auro virginum … (1534); Nature genitor conserva … (3855); O vera summa sempiterna trinitas … (4086); Vigilate animo in proximo … (5418); Rubum quem viderat … (4669); (Triduanum) Triduanas a domino … (5185) ‖ **322** Bethleem non es minima (1737); Hodierna (not identified) ‖ **323** Fidelia omnia mandata … (2865); Crucem tuam adoramus … (1953); In mandatis eius volet nimis (3251)

318 sol-ut hic] ascendit in sol verbi gratia ut hic *Si* I quidem] quidam *P1* ‖ **319** ad eos] neuma *add. Si* ‖ **321** prima *om. Si* I est] talis est *Si* I gratia] ut hic *add. Si* I Auro-Triduanum] ‖ 8♭⸱ Virgo virginum. Nature genitor. Laudabo*. O vera*. Vigilate* Inventus Ihesus ‖ 8♭ Rubum quem viderat Innuebant Triduanum *Si* *Laudabo, O vera, Vigilate notés par erreur à la tierce supérieure (G GF E … etc.) ‖ **322** 81 8♭ (Tulit ergo) (Bethleem Hodierna) Ne reminiscaris E u o u a e *Si* ‖ **323** Fidelia] (In domum. A viro) *add. Si* I Crucem] Vocem *Si* I In mandatis] (Impleatur) *add. Si*

Lambertus, 'Ars musica' – 'Musica plana'

[318] When an antiphon begins on ·E· and immediately ascends from *mi* to *fa* or to *sol*, as here:

Fe- lix nam-que. Len-tis qui-dem then it has the following *e u o u a e*

<IIII>

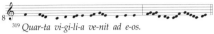

[319] Quar-ta vi-gi-li-a ve-nit ad e-os.

[320] So the fourth mode is sung at its midpoint, and so it is finished.

Si-cut e-rat in prin-cipi-o et nunc et sem-per et in se-cu-la se-cu-lo-rum.

A-men.

[321] The first *differentia* of the fourth mode is when an antiphon begins on ·F· by descending to *re*, or to *mi*, or by ascending to *re*, for example:

Au-ro vir-gi-num. Na-tu-re. O ve-ra. Vi-gi-la-te.

Ru-bum quem vi-de-rat. Tri-du-a-num. *e u o u a e.*

[322] And when an antiphon begins on low ·C· by ascending, as here:

Beth- le-em. | Ho- di-er-na. <tale habet> *e u o u a e.*

[323] When an antiphon begins on either low ·E· or ·G·, as here:

Fi-de-li-a. Cru-cem tu-am. In man-da-tis. has the following *e u o u a e.*

51

[324] Quando vero antiphona incipit in ·a· et in ·c· acutis que semper habent finire per b molle in ·a· acuta, verbi gratia:

Cs 265b

Be-ne-di-cta tu <tale habet> e u o u a e.

P1 17ra [325] Quando vero antiphona incipit | in ·F· et de *fa* descendat in *ut*, verbi gratia ut hic:

Que-ri-te do-mi-num. <tale habet> e u o u a e.

<V>

Si 23r

[326] Quin-que pru-den-tes in-tra-ve-runt ad nu-pti-as.

[327] Quin-tus mo-dus sic me-di-a-tur, et sic fi-ni-tur.

P1 17rb

Glo-ri-a pa-tri et fi-li-o et spi-ri-tu san-cto. Et hoc est e u o u a e.

Cs 266a [328] Omnes autem antiphone quinti modi, ubicunque incipiant, unicum tantummodo habent *seculorum* | *amen*, preter hanc antiphonam *Alma redemptoris mater*, que cantatur ad Magnificat, cuius differentia patet:

Se-cu-lo-rum a-men.

<VI>

[329] Sex-ta ho- ra se-dit su-per pu-te-um.

P1 17va

[330] Sex-tus mo-dus sic me-di-a-tur, et sic fi-ni-tur. Si-cut e-rat in prin-

ci-pi-o et nunc et sem-per et in se-cu-la se-cu-lo-rum. A-men.

[331] Omnes autem antiphone sexti modi tam autenticales quam collaterales unicum habent tantummodo *euouae*, ut hic:

Se-cu-lo-rum a-men.

324 Benedicta tu in mulieribus … (1709)

324 antiphona incipit *Si* | verbi gratia] verbi gratia in ·a· acuta ut hic ‖

Dignare me. Post partum. Rorate celi. Benedicta tu. E u o u a e tale habet ‖ **325** antiphona--F·] in ·C·. incipit *Si* | Querite. Dominum. Simon. E u o u a e tale est *Si* ‖ **326** nuptias] neuma *add. Si* ‖ **327** Gloria-euouae] ‖ Sicut erat in principio et nunc et semper et in secula seculorum amen. *Si* ‖ **328** autem *om. Si* | ubicunque incipiant *om. Si* | tantummodo habent] habent tantummodo *Si* | amen *om. Si* | redemptoris mater] red. *P1* ‖ **331** autem *om. Si* | unicum] unice *P1* unum *Si* unicam *Cs* | Seculorum amen *om. Si*

[324] And when an antiphon begins on either high ·a· or ·c·, which always has to end through ·b· *molle* on high ·a·, for example:

Be-ne-dic-ta tu has the following e u o u a e.

[325] And when an antiphon begins on ·F· and and descends from *fa* to *ut*, as here, for example:

Que-ri-te do-mi-num has the following e u o u a e.

<V>

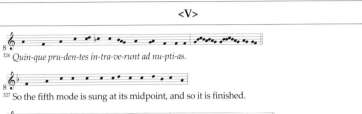
[326] *Quin-que pru-den-tes in-tra-ve-runt ad nu-pti-as.*

[327] So the fifth mode is sung at its midpoint, and so it is finished.

Glo-ri-a pa-tri et fi-li-o et spi-ri-tu san-cto. And this is the e u o u a e.

[328] But all antiphons of the fifth mode, wherever they may begin, have only one *seculorum amen*, except this antiphon, *Alma redemptoris mater*, which is sung to the Magnificat, whose *differentia* is shown:

Se-cu-lo-rum a-men.

<VI>

[329] *Sex-ta ho- ra se-dit su-per pu-te-um.*

[330] So the sixth mode is sung at its midpoint and so it is finished.

Si-cut e-rat in prin-ci-pi-o et nunc et sem-per et in se-cu-la se-cu-lo-rum. A-men.

[331] But all antiphons of the sixth mode, both authentic and collateral, have only one *e u o u a e*, as here:

Se-cu-lo-rum amen.

The 'Ars musica' Attributed to Magister Lambertus/Aristoteles

\<VII\>

Cs 266b/P1 17vb

[332] Se-ptem sunt spi-ri-tus an-te tro-num de-i.

[333] Se-pti-mus mo-dus sic me-di-a-tur et sic fi-ni-tur. Si-cut e-rat in prin-

ci-pi-o et nunc et sem-per et in se-cu-la se-cu-lo-rum. A-men.

P1 18ra [334] Quando antiphona septimi modi incipit in ·G·, non statim saliendo in diapente, sed melodiam ascendendo perficiente, verbi gratia:

De-scen-di in or-tum. Pon-ti- fi-ces. Sa-pi-en-ti-a.

\<habet tale\> e u o u a e.

Si 23v [335] Sed si statim salit in diapente ut hic:

Cs 267a Ba-pti-sta tunc habet tale I e u o u a e.

P1 18rb [336] Et quando incipit in ·d· acuta descendendo in *fa*, vel I in *mi*, vel in ·♭· quadrato:

An-ge-li ar-chan-ge-li. Ar-gen-tum. Re-dem-pti-o-nem.

\<habet tale\> e u o u a e.

---

334 Descendi in ortum ... (2155); Pontifices almi divina revelatione ... (4310); Sapientia edificavit sibi domum ... (4810) ‖ **335** Baptista contremuit et non audet ... (1552) ‖ **336** Angeli archangeli throni ... (1398); Argentum et aurum ... (1480); Redemptionem misit dominus populo ... (4587)

333 8 (...) secu- lorum amen *Si* ‖ **334** gratia] ut hic *add.* *Si* I 8 ‖ **335** salit] saliat *Si* I tunc habet tale *om.* *Si* ‖ **336** vel in mi ... Redemptionem] 8 vel *mi* verbi gratia ut hic *Angeli archangeli* vel in ♮ quadrato verbi gratia ut hic *Argentum.* *Redemptionem Si*

54

\<VII\>

[332] Se-ptem sunt spi-ri-tus an-te tro-num de-i.

[333] So the seventh mode is sung at its midpoint and so it is finished.

Si-cut e-rat in prin-ci-pi-o et nunc et sem-per et in se-cu-la se-cu-lo-rum.   A-men.

[334] When an antiphon of the seventh mode begins on ·G·, not by leaping up immediately to a fifth, but perfecting the melody by ascending, for example:

De-scen-di in or-tum.   Pon-ti-fi-ces.   Sa-pi-en-ti-a.

it has the following *e u o u a e.*

[335] But if it immediately leaps to the fifth, as here:

Ba-ptis-ta then has the following *e u o u a e.*

[336] And when it begins on high ·d·, descending to *fa*, or to *mi*, or to square ·♮·:

An-ge- li ar-chan- ge-li.   Ar- gen- tum.   Re-dem-pti- o-nem.

it has the following *e u o u a e.*

339 Ego plantavi Apollo … (2580); Dominus ab utero vocavit me … (2400) ‖
340 Hodie celesti sponso … (3095) ‖ **341** Deo nostro iocunda sit laudatio …
(2148); Dominus dixit ad me filius … (2406) ‖ **339** Ego plantavi Apollo … (2580); ‖
Dominus ab utero vocavit me … (2400) ‖ **340** Hodie celesti sponso … (3095) ‖ **341**
Deo nostro iocunda sit laudatio … (2148); Dominus dixit ad me filius … (2406)

\<VIII\>

[337] *O-cto sunt be-a- ti- tu-di-nes. Neuma.*

[338] So the eighth mode is sung at its midpoint and so it is finished.

Si-cut e-rat in prin-ci-pi-o et nunc et sem-per et in se-cu-la se-cu-lo-rum.

A-men.

[339] Every antiphon beginning on low ·G· by leaping to high ·c· or by descending to low ·D·, as here:

E-go plan-ta-vi. Do-mi-nus ab u-te-ro. has the following *e u o a e.*

[340] If it begins on low ·F·, as here:

Ho-di-e has the following *e u o u a e.*

[341] If it begins on low ·c·, for example as here:

De-o no-stro has the following *se-cu-lo-rum a-men.*

[342] And if it begins on high ·c· by descending as here:

Do-mi-nus di-xit has the following *e u o u a e.*

[343] It follows to look at the intonations of the offices.

[344] *Glo-ri- a pa-tri et fi-li-o et spi-ri-tu-i san-cto | si-cut e-rat in prin-ci-pi-o*

et nunc et sem-per, et in se-cu-la se-cu- lo-rum. A-men.

[345] *Glo- ri-a pa-tri et fi-li-o et spi-ri-tu-i san-cto*

and this is the *e u o u a e*

The 'Ars musica' Attributed to Magister Lambertus/Aristoteles

Lambertus, 'Ars musica' – 'Musica plana'

<Musica mensurabilis>

Cs 269a/*Erf* 87r/ *P1* 19va/*Si* 24r

[1] Cum, secundum quod dicit Boetius, nichil *est quod* non *retinet ordinem servatque naturam,* summopere in cunctis actibus humanis ordo considerari debet, ne quod actum est nihil esset. Per dictum Boetii 'profectu ordinis' arguatur: [2] sicut enim in effectibus nature cause sunt priores, sic in actibus rationis illa priora sunt et prius sciri

P1 19vb desiderant, que posterio|ribus et ipsa consequentibus cognitionis principium amministrant. [3] Cum igitur in cognoscendo musicam

Si 24v mensurabilem sit ipsa plana musica fundamentum, | et de ipsa in precedentibus convenienter existimamus esse tractatum, consequenter causa salvandi ordinis artem mensurabilis musice postponamus, [4] in qua tam theorice quam practice quis possit in summa comprehendere cognitionem specierum armoniarum, qualitates et quantitates, similitudines et dissimilitudines proportionum, sonorum et vocum, necnon figuras longas et breves, tempora et mensuram, ac etiam orthographiam cognoscere et

P1 20ra conservare, et regulariter eam discri|bere, [5] ita quod omnis cantus, qualitercunque fuerit diversificatus, usque ad extremitatem, etiam in modum vielle, congrue per illam possit declarari.

Hw 418, l. 40 [6] Primo igitur sciendum est | quod tria tantummodo sunt genera per que tota mensurabilis musica discurrit, scilicet discantus, ▸ *p. 119* hokettus et organum.

---

1 (nihil... actibus humanis) Boeth. Cons. lib. 4, prosa 2, l. 96 ('est enim quod ordinem retinet servatque naturam; quod vero ab hac deficit esse etiam, quod in sua natura situm est, derelinquit'.) ‖ **4** (qualitates et quantitates... tempora et mensuram) cf. supra mp 18

1–3 *om. Hw* ‖ **1** esset] esse *CsErfP1Si* | profectu] perfectum *Cs Erf* per defectum *ErfS* ‖ **2** sunt priores] priores sunt *Erf* | prius] prima *Erf* | sciri desiderant] desiderantur sciri *Si* | que] quam *Si* | consequentibus] q⁺ ... ⁺tibus *Erf* ‖ **4** in qua-orthographiam] Theorica vero est in summa comprehendere cognitionem specierum harmoniarum et id ex quo componuntur et ad id quod componuntur et qualiter componantur vel est etiam officium figuras longas et breves necnon corpora et mensuras eorundem, qualitates et quantitates, similitudines et dissimilitudines proportionum, sonorum et vocum, et orthographiam *Hw* | ac] et *Si* | discribere] describere *Erf* ‖ **5** ita *om. Hw* | qualitercunque] qualiscunque *Hw* | usque-vielle *om. Hw* | possit per illam *Si* ‖ **6** primo igitur sciendum est] Cum igitur illa et alia multa in hac arte secundum ordinem declarantur primo specialiter videndum est et sciendum *Hw* | tantummodo sunt] sunt tantummodo *Erf* | discurrit] transcurrit *Hw* | hokettus] hocetus *Hw* hocketus *Si*

Musica mensurabilis

[1] Since, according to Boethius, 'that which does not retain its order and maintain its nature' is nothing, so order ought to be thoroughly examined in all human acts, lest that which has been completed be nothing. By Boethius's phrase 'by the advance of order' let it be argued: [2] for just as in effects of nature, there are prior causes, so in acts of reason those things are prior and wish to be known first that themselves supply the beginning of knowledge to the later things that follow from them. [3] Therefore, since *musica plana* is the basis for knowing measurable music, and we reckon that we have suitably covered this in the preceding, for the sake of preserving order let us place the art of measurable music afterwards, [4] so that in both theoretical and practical terms, anyone may in sum grasp knowledge of the harmonic species, grasp the qualities and quantities, similarities and dissimilarities of proportions, sounds, and pitches, as well as longs and breves, *tempora* and measure, and also know and preserve and write down according to rule music's orthography, [5] so that every piece of vocal music, however varied it may be, may be known right to the end, even in the instrumental style, and may be revealed through it.

[6] First then, it should be understood that there are only three classes through which all measurable music traverses, namely, discant, hocket, and *organum*.

The 'Ars musica' Attributed to Magister Lambertus/Aristoteles

[7] Discantus vero est aliquorum diversorum generum cantus duarum vocum sive trium in quo trina tantummodo consonantia, scilicet diatessaron, diapente et diapason, per compositionem longarum breviumque figurarum secundum dualem mensuram naturaliter proportionata manet. [8] Unde notandum est, quod tres genera I lissime sunt species per quas omnes modi, id est omnis can I tus, in quo consistit maneries, dignoscuntur et discernuntur ac etiam moderantur, scilicet figura, tempus et mensura.

P1 20rb
Erf 87v

[9] Et quoniam huiusmodi discantus per dictam compositionem, sub certa dimensione temporis seu temporum, per diversa capitula declaratur, [10] ideo primo de representa I tione formaque figurarum tam de simplicibus quam de compositis, quot tempora quelibet figura pro sua parte continet in se, [11] ac etiam de plicis et de proprietatibus et distinctionibus earumdem videamus, I et quomodo per huius<modi> figuras denotetur longitudo seu brevitas cantus.

Cs 269b

Hw 419

[12] Unde figura I est representatio soni secundum suum modum et secundum equipollentiam sui equipollentis. [13] Sed huiusmodi figure aliquando ponuntur cum littera, aliquando sine: cum littera vero ut in motellis et similibus, sine littera ut in neumatibus conductorum et ▸ *p. 119* similibus. [14] Inter enim figuras que sunt cum littera vel sine, talis datur differentia: quoniam ille que sunt sine littera, debent prout possunt amplius ad invicem ligari, sed huiusmodi proprietas aliquando omittitur propter litteram his figuris associatam. [15] Et huiusmodi figurarum proprietas tam littere sociatarum quam non, dantur divisiones ac I etiam regule sequentes.

P1 20va

P1 20vb

---

7 IAC. LEOD. spec. 7, 5, 8: 'Quod autem tres tactae consonantiae principaliter in discantibus observari debeant, approbat Aristoteles qui discantum describens dicit sic: Discantus est aliquorum diversorum generum cantus duarum vocum sive trium in quo terna tantummodo consonantia, idest diatessaron, diapente et diapason, per compositionem longarum breviumque figurarum, secundum debitam mensuram, naturaliter proportionata manet'. ‖ **8** ANON. Emmeram. I (p. 86, l. 5–7 '... quoniam sunt tres generalissimae species e quibus omne genus cantuum efficitur et habetur, scilicet figura, tempus et mensura') ‖ **10–11** (ideo primo... brevitas cantus) ANON. Emmeram. I (p. 86, l. 11–16); (de representatione... et quomodo...) IOH. GARL. mens. 2, 1 ‖ **12–15** IOH. GARL. mens. 2, 2–6 ‖ **12** cf. IOH. GARL. mens. 1, 4 ('Discantus est aliquorum diversorum cantuum sonantia secundum modum et secundum aequipollentis suis aequipollentiam'); (figura-modum) IAC. LEOD. spec. 7, 20, 5 ‖ **13–15** ANON. Emmeram. I (p. 88, l. 1–9)

7 est *om. Erf* I duarum] due scilicet *Erf* I sive] seu *Hw* I trina tantummodo] termino *Hw* I consonantia] concurrit *add. Si* I et *om. Hw* I scilicet-diapason] scilicet diapente diapason et diatessaron *Si* I et diapason per compositionem] et dyapason etiam aliquando ditonus semiditonus qui perfecte consonancie non sunt ⁺se con sui quid⁺ per compositionem *Erf* I dualem] dulcem *Hw* ‖ **8** id est] et *Si* I omnis] omnes *Hw* I consistit] consistet *Si* I dignoscuntur] dinoscuntur *Si* I et discernuntur *om. Si* I ac etiam] ac ter *Erf* I scilicet figura] per figuram *Hw* ‖ **9** quoniam] prout *dub. Erf* I huiusmodi] huius *ErfHwfP1* ‖ **10** ideo] quadeo (?) *ante corr. Erf* I formaque] et forma *Hw* I de compositis] compositis *Si* I figurarum-compositis] figurarum simplicium secundo de figuris similiter pariterque ligatis seu iunctis *Hw* I quot] quae *Hw* I et de] et *Erf, om. Hw* ‖ **12** figura est] figuras *Hw* ‖ **13** huiusmodi figure] huius *Si* I cum littera vero *om. Erf* I ut in] in *Si* I motellis] modulis vel motellis *Si* I neumatibus] neumis *Hw* I conductorum] conductuum *Si* I similibus] similia *HwP1* ‖ **14** huiusmodi] huius *ErfP1Si* I que-sine] cum litteris et sine litteris *Erf* I amplius *om. Si* I propter] super *Hw* I his] huius *P1Si* huius⁺ ... ⁺ *Erf* ‖ **15** huiusmodi] huius *HwP1*

Lambertus, 'Ars musica' – 'Musica mensurabilis'

[7] Now discant is a song [comprised] of some various vocal lines (of two or three voices), in which such a threefold of consonance (namely, the diatessaron, diapente, and diapason) remains proportional by nature according to a twofold measurement in the arrangement of long and short figures. [8] Whence it should be noted that there are three most general *species* through which all the modes (that is, all song in which a rhythmic scheme [*maneries*] occurs) are recognized, discerned, and governed: namely the figure, *tempus*, and measure.

[9] And since this kind of discant, by the said arrangement under a particular measurement of *tempus* or *tempora*, is explained in a variety of chapters, [10] for that reason let us look first at the representation and form of the figures, both simple and composite, at how many *tempora* any figure contains in itself for its part, [11] and also at the plicas and their *proprietates* and distinctions, and at how the length and brevity of a song may be denoted through these figures.

[12] Whence a figure is a representation of a sound, according to its mode, and according to the equipollence of its equipollents. [13] But figures of this type are sometimes placed with text, sometimes without: with text, as in motets and the like; without text, as in the *neumae* of conductus and the like. [14] The distinction between figures with text or those without is given as follows: because these figures are without text, accordingly they can be joined together more often, one after another, but *proprietas* of this sort is sometimes omitted when text is associated with these figures. [15] And there is a sort of *proprietas* of figures as joined to text as [those which are] not, and so the following divisions are given and also the rules.

The 'Ars musica' Attributed to Magister Lambertus/Aristoteles

[16] Quapropter ad omnia discernenda prolata scire debemus quod sex tantummodo figure sunt adinvente, quarum bine et bine semper sunt affines etiam in forma et quantitate consimiles, sed in potestate, ▶ *p. 119* arte, regula differunt et natura.

[17] Quarum igitur prima super omnes fons est et origo ipsius scientie atque finis, que perfecta longa merito vocatur. [18] Nam a *Si* 25r perfectione trine equalitatis nomen habere sumpsit, eo quod sub *P1* 21ra certa dimentione longitudinis unius per vocis accentum, [19] in mora *Erf* 88r trium temporum equaliter proportionata manet, seipsamque ǀ in IX ▶ *p. 119* partes diminuendo dupliciter parǀtiens. [20] Cuius forma quadrangularis ǀ efficitur, comam <habens> semper in eius latere ▶ *p. 119* dextro fixam, per quam naturam etiam longitudinis habere meretur. [21] Que patet in presenti: ¶

[22] Secunda vero imperfecta longa ab *in* quod est non, et *perfecta*, quasi non perfecta dicitur, eo quod nisi duo tempora continet in se, affinitatem in forma et proprietate perfecte figure tenens, ut hic: ¶

Cs 270a [23] Tertia recta brevis dicitur ab eo quod unum rectum et integrum continet in se tempus, seipsamque in duas diminuens partes non equales vel in tres tantummodo equales et indivisibiles, cuius forma quadrangularis omni carens proprietate patet: ▪

P1 21rb [24] Quarta altera brevis appellatur, eo quod duas rectas breves tenet et quod semper alterum occupat locum, affinitatem recte brevis tam in forma quam in proprietate verum et societate tenens, ut hic: ▪

[25] Quinta semibrevis maior dicitur, et hoc a *semus, sema, semum*, quod est imperfectum, et brevis quasi imperfecta semibrevis, et maior est quoniam maiorem partem retinet recte brevis, ut *Hw* 420 predictum est, cuius forma ǀ talis est: ◆

---

16 Anon. Emmeram. I (p. 98, l. 38–42) ‖ **17** (fons est et origo) cf. Ps-Boethius, Geometria (ed. Friedlein, p. 397 l. 19–398 l. 1 'Primum autem numerum id est binarium, unitas enim, ut in arithmeticis est dictum, numerus non est, sed fons et origo numerorum...') ‖ **18–19** Anon. Emmeram. I (p. 102, l. 46 + p. 104, l. 1–5 'quoniam quidam in suis artibus maiorem longam perfectam solummmodo vocaverunt, eo quod a perfectione trinae aequalitatis nomen habere sumpsit, eo quo sub certa diminutione longitudinis unius per vocis accentum in mora trium temporum aequaliter proportionata manet, se ipsamque in novem partes diminuendo dupliciter partiens'.)

16 sunt adinvente] adsunt invente *Si* ǀ etiam] et *Erf om. Hw* ǀ quantitate] in quantitate *Erf* ǀ sed] scilicet *Hw* ǀ et natura] ac natura *Erf* ‖ **17** Quarum] harum *Erf* ǀ igitur] autem *Erf* et *Hw* ǀ super omnes *om. Si* ǀ merito] minuta *Hw* ǀ vocatur] appellatur *Erf* ‖ **18** trine] trines *ante corr. P1* ǀ trine-nomen] circa equalitatem aliquid *Hw* ǀ habere *om. Erf* ǀ dimentione] dimensione *Erf Si* diminutione Anon. Emmeram. ǀ vocis] voces *ante corr. Si* ǀ accentum] accidentiam *Hw* ‖ **19** trium temporum] circa ipsum *Hw* ǀ partes *om. Erf* ǀ dupliciter] duplicatur *Si* ‖ **20** naturam] natura *P1* ǀ naturam etiam] etiam nomine *Erf* etiam naturam *Si* etiam nomen *Hw* ǀ habere meretur] meretur habere *Erf* ‖ **21** que] ut *ErfHw* ǀ in presenti] hic *Erf* ‖ **22** longa *om. Si* ǀ ab-quasi] aliquando etiam non est perfecta quod *Hw* ǀ quasi] quod *Si* ǀ in forma] forma *P1* ǀ ut hic] ut patet *Hw* ‖ **23** integrum-tempus] integrum tempus continet in se *Si* ǀ vel in] vel *Si* ǀ tantummodo equales] equales tantummodo *Erf* ǀ indivisibiles] divisibiles *Si* ǀ patet] ut hic *Hw* ǀ quadrangularis] quadrangularis est *Hw* ǀ omni ... proprietate] omnis ... proprietas *Erf* ‖ **24** et quod] atque *Hw* ǀ in proprietate] proprietate *P1* ǀ verum *om. Hw* ‖ **25** quinta] quinta vero *Hw* ǀ et-semum] et habet a se minus magnum *Hw* ǀ semus-semum] semus ma mum *Si* ǀ semum *om. Erf* ǀ quod est] quod etiam *Hw* ǀ imperfectum] imperfectum ta tum *Si* ǀ quasi] quia *Hw* quod *Si* ǀ imperfecta semibrevis] imperfecta scientia brevis *Hw* ǀ semibrevis] brevis *Erf* ǀ et maior-recte brevis *om. Si* ǀ maior est] maiore *P1* ǀ talis est] patet hic *Erf*

Lambertus, 'Ars musica' – 'Musica mensurabilis'

[16] For the purpose of discerning all durations we ought to know that only six figures are found, of which two and two are always affinities and very similar both in form and quantity, but they differ in power, art, rule, and nature.

[17] Therefore, the first above all of these, the source and origin of this very science, and its end, is appropriately called a perfect long. [18] The name was taken from the perfection of threefold equality, by this [we mean] that it is under a particular measurement of length through the accent of one pitch, [19] it lasts for a delay equally proportionate to three *tempora*, and parting itself two times, divides into nine parts. [20] Its form is made from a quadrangle, always having a stem fixed on its right side, through which it too deserves to have the nature of length. [21] This is shown in the following: ◗

[22] And the second is the imperfect long, from *in*, that is 'not', and 'perfect' as if it is said to be 'not perfect', because it contains within itself but two *tempora*, holding an affinity with the form and *proprietas* of a perfect figure, as here: ◗

[23] The third is said to be a *recta* breve because it contains within itself one proper and integral *tempus*, dividing itself into two unequal parts or into no more than three equal and indivisible parts; its form, quadrangular and lacking all *proprietas*, is shown: ▪

[24] The fourth is called an *altera* breve, because it holds two *recta* breves and it always occupies an 'alternate' place; it bears an affinity to the *recta* breve both in form and *proprietas* truly through a relationship [with it], as here: ▪

[25] The fifth is said to be a major semibreve: this is from *semus, sema, semum*, that is, imperfect, as if the semibreve is an 'imperfect breve', and 'major' because it fills the major part of a *recta* breve, as was said before; its form is as follows: ◆

The 'Ars musica' Attributed to Magister Lambertus/Aristoteles

[26] Sexta semibrevis minor consimili modo dicitur, et minor est eo quod minorem in se continet partem recte brevis, tenens affinitatem in forma et quantitate precedentis, ut hic: ◆

P1 21va   [27] Cum igitur ipsa perfecta figura manens in unitate sit fons et origo ipsius scientie et finis propterea quod omnis cantus ab eadem procedit et in eadem replicatur, [28] et ipsa in numeris consistit, temporibus et mensuris, et trinam in se continet equalitatem, [29] videre sequitur quod ipsa ceteris prior esse videtur, eo quod mundi conditor deus omnia in numero, pondere et mensura constituit. [30] Et hoc principale extitit exemplar in animo conditoris.
[31] Nam quecumque a primeva rerum origine formata sunt,

Erf 88v   numerorum ratione videntur | esse constituta. [32] Et ideo numerus
P1 21vb   omnem creaturam natura precedit et in singulis ternarius inve|nitur, quia ab ineffabili trinitate, que cuncta condidit, essentialiter non recedit. [33] Unde illud in auctoribus legitur: numero deus impare gaudet ternario. [34] Itaque hic numerus inest rebus omnibus, cuius principium unitas est, que grece *monas* dicitur. [35] Ipsa vero non numerus, sed fons et origo numerorum, principium et finis omnium.

Cs 270b   [36] Et ideo non | immerito ad summam refertur trinitatem, quia res quelibet naturalis ad similitudinem divine nature ex tribus constare invenitur.

29–30 (mundi conditor... conditoris) cf. Sapientia 11, 20 ('sed omnia mensura et numero et pondere disposuisti') ‖ **30–31** cf. Boeth. arithm. I, 2 ('Omnia quaecunque a primaeva rerum natura constructa sunt, numerorum videntur ratione formata. Hoc enim fuit principale in animo conditoris exemplar', p. 12, l. 14–17) ‖ **32** (numerus-precedit, quia-recedit) 33 (unde illud, numero-gaudet) 34 (numerus-omnibus) Gundissalinus, p. 95 ‖ **33** P. Vergilius Maro, *Eclogae sive Bucolica*, ed. O. Ribbeck (Leipzig, 1894), 8, v. 73 (p. 45) ‖ **34–35** cf. Iohannes Scottus Eriugena, *De divisione naturae*, III (ed. Sheldon-Williams, 1981), p. 104 'Si unitas quae a Grecis dicitur monas omnium numerorum principium est et medium et finis...'

26 consimili] et simili *Si* | consimili-quod] consimile vero et eciam minor quia *Erf* | et minor est] et minore *P1* in minore *Si* | in se *om. Erf* | recte brevis *om. Si* | precedentis] in forma *add. Si* precedens *Hw* | *ex. om. P1* ‖ **27** ipsa *om. ErfHw* | sit] sic *Hw* | procedit] propterea *ante corr. P1* | in eadem] eadem *Erf* ‖ **28** ipsa] ipsa manens *Erf* | consistit] consistat *Si* | in se continet] continet in se *Erf* ‖ **29** ceteris prior] prior ceteris *Hw* ‖ **30** principale] prin^c *Erf* ‖ **31** rerum] orbis *Hw* | videntur] universa *Hw* ‖ **32** ideo] omnis *Si* | singulis] singulis numeris *Erf* | ineffabili] effabili *ante corr. P1* ‖ **33** illud *om. Erf* | numero] summe *Erf* quomodo *Hw* | impare] imperare *Hw* ‖ **34** itaque] ita *Hw* | inest] mensurabilis *Si* | monas] monos *ErfHw* ‖ **35** et finis] finisque *ErfSi* ‖ **36** immerito] merito *P1* | invenitur] annuitur *Hw*

Lambertus, 'Ars musica' – 'Musica mensurabilis'

[26] In a very similar way, the sixth is said to be a minor semibreve, and it is 'minor' because it contains within itself the smaller part of a *recta* breve; holding an affinity with the form and quantity of the preceding semibreve, as here: ♦

[27] Therefore since this perfect figure, remaining within the unity, is the source and origin of this very science, and beyond this its end, as all song arises from, and is revealed by the same [figure],[28] and this [figure] occurs in numbers, *tempora*, and measures, and it contains within itself a threefold equality; [29] it follows that this figure seems to be prior to the others, because God, the world's creator, establishes all things in number, weight, and measure. [30] And this first prototype exists in the soul of the creator. [31] For whatever things were formed from the very beginning of creation seem to have been established through the reasoning of numbers. [32] Thus in nature number is prior to every creature and the ternary is found in each, since number does not in essence withdraw from the ineffable Trinity, which created all things. [33] Whence that is read in the authorities: 'God rejoices in the ternary, an odd number'. [34] And so this number is present in all things, whose beginning is unity (which in Greek is called *monas*). [35] This unity is not a number, but the source and origin of numbers, the beginning and end of all things. [36] Thus it is not without cause that it reverts to the highest Trinity, because everything in nature is found to accord with the likeness of the divine nature in threes.

The 'Ars musica' Attributed to Magister Lambertus/Aristoteles

[37] In vocibus etiam sonis et rebus omnibus trina tantum existit consonantia, scilicet diatessaron, diapente et diapason. [38] Hanc igitur

P1 22ra trinitatem omnia naturaliter formata con|sequntur, [39] quoniam rebus omnibus ab origine prima naturaliter inherentem in summo et primo artifice fuisse imperitos necessario credere oportet, [40] cum nil possit fieri nisi prius sit in artifice faciendi potentia, nichil sapienter sine sapientia, et cum nullo indigeat, nichil ab eo fiat nisi ex gratia. [41] Cum igitur ab eo fiant omnia, manifestum est sapientibus quod

Si 25v hec tria, | scilicet sapientia, potentia et gratia, sunt in divina essentia, quia ad summum perfectumque bonum plura non sunt necessaria. [42] Et rerum omnium prima principia sunt tria: principium immobile, deus principiorum principium, principium mobile, celestis spera

P1 22rb cuius motu moventur omnia, | et agens particulare.

[43] Et ut breviter dicamus: omnis cantus mensurabilis ab ipsa figura procedit et dividitur et in eadem replicatur, et omnes figure subsequentes ad eandem propter equipollentiam retinendam recurrunt. [44] Eius autem regula talis est et natura, quod

Erf 89r quandocunque longa reperta est ante longam | semper tria tempora tenet, verbi gratia ut hic: ♩♩♩ |♩♩♩♩ |♩♩♩♩♩♩|

Hw 421 [45] Affinitas autem eius, que in forma sibi con|similis efficitur, sequitur. Cuius regula talis est et natura, [46] quod semper ante brevem vel econverso stare debet, que sibi collateralis esse refertur, ut patet hic: ♩♩♩♩♩ |♩♩♩♩♩♩ |♩♩♩♩♩|

P1 22va [47] In qua non nisi duo tempora conmorari tenentur ratione collateralis, que ab eadem sumitur a parte finis, unde versus:

[48] Ante vero longam tria tempora longa fatetur.

[49] Si brevis addatur, duo tempora longa meretur.

38–41 cf. Hugo de Sancto Victore, *Didascalicon de studio legendi*. III (Ch. H. Buttimer, 1939, p. 60, l. 6: 'opus Dei est, et quod creat potentia, et quod moderatur sapientia, et quod cooperatur gratia') ‖ **44** Anon. Emmeram. II (p. 196, l. 29–30) ‖ **48** Ioh. Garl. mens. 1, 29 ('Prima vero talis est: longa ante longam valet longam et brevem')

37 sonis] et sonis *Erf* | trina] trinam *P1* | tantum] tantummodo *Si* | existit] consistit *Hw* ‖ **38** consequntur] consequitur *Hw* ‖ **39** fuisse] finisse *Cs* ‖ **40** possit fieri] fieri possit *Si* prius sit factum *Hw* | nichil sapienter] vel sapienter *Hw* | et cum] etc. *Hw* | nullo] nullae *Hw* ‖ **41** manifestum] maximum *Hw* | et gratia] gratia *Erf* | essentia] ecclesia *Hw* ‖ **42** rerum] tunc *Hw* | sunt] tantum sunt *Hw* | principiorum principium] principium principiorum *ErfHw* | celestis] est celestis *Si* | spera] super *Hw* | motu] motus *ante corr. ? Si* | omnia] alia *(dub.)* omnia *Erf* | et agens particulare *om. Hw* | agens] agens ipsum *Erf* ‖ **43** breviter] brevius *Si* | ab ipsa figura *om. Erf* | eadem] eamdem *Erf* eandem *Si* | replicatur] resoluitur et replicatur *Erf* | ad eandem-retinendam] propter equipollenciam retinendam ad eandem *Erf* | recurrunt] recurritur *Si* recurrit *Hw* ‖ **44** eius autem] eiusdem *Erf* cuius *Hw* | longa *om. Hw* | longam] vel ante ligaturam sue perfectionis *add. Erf* | ut hic *om. Hw* | ex. *om. Erf* ‖ **45** sibi-efficitur] consimilis est sibi *Erf* | sibi *om. Si* | consimilis] ⁺ ... ⁺similis *Si* ‖ **46** brevem] unius temporis *add. Hw* | econverso] post *Hw* | ut patet hic] verbi gratia ut hic *Si* verbi gratia *Hw* ‖ **46–47** que sibi-unde versus] a qua et ipsa huius brevis est abstracta ut patet in presenti exemplo sic: *ex. om.* Unde in hac longa ubi duo ⁺que a⁺ (tempora ?) conmorantur, tercium autem tempus continetur in sua collaterali videlicet altera *(dub.)* brevi ab ea sumpta unde versus *Erf* ‖ **47** conmorari] communicari *Hw* | eadem] eodem *Hw* ‖ **48** ante-tempora] longa[m] precedens duo tempora *Erf* | tria-fatetur] minima longa faciunt *Hw* ‖ **49** Si-meretur] Si brevis accedens sic in uno dimietur *(dub.)* *Erf*

Lambertus, 'Ars musica' – 'Musica mensurabilis'

[37] Also in pitches, sounds, and all things, a threefold consonance is manifest, namely, the diatessaron, diapente, and diapason. [38] Therefore, all things formed by nature mirror this Trinity; [39] since it is right for the inexperienced to believe that, with respect to all things since creation, the Trinity has been naturally inherent in the highest and first artist [40] since nothing can be made except if it first exists within the power of the Creator making it, and since nothing can be done wisely without wisdom, since He desires nothing, so He makes nothing from it, except through grace. [41] Therefore, since they make all things from it, it is clear to wise people that these three things, namely, wisdom, power, and grace, are in the divine essence, because many things are not necessary for the highest and perfect good. [42] And the first of all things are the three principles: the immobile principle; God, the principle of principles; and the mobile principle – the heavenly sphere whose motion moves all things, and the particular agent.

[43] And so in brief let us say this: every measurable song arises from and is divided by this figure and is revealed in this same figure, and all figures subsequent [to it] return to this same figure according to the same equipollence retained. [44] But it has the following rule and nature: whenever a long is found before a long it is always held for three *tempora*, for example as here: ♩♩♩ |♩♩♩♩ |♩♩♩♩♩♩|

[45] Now follows its [the perfect long's] affinity, which is fashioned in a very similar form to it. Its rule and nature is as follows: [46] it ought to stand before a breve (and *vice versa*), which is brought back to be adjacent to it, as is shown here: ♩■■♩■ |♩■■♩■■♩ |♩■♩■♩|

[47] A delay of just two *tempora* is held in it, by reason of the adjacent [breve] that is removed from it (from its last part), whence the verse:

[48] Before a long, a long professes three *tempora*.

[49] If a breve is added, a long is worth two *tempora*.

Cs 271a [50] Unde notandum est quod quandocumque inter | duas longas sola brevis evenerit, semper ad imperfectam reducetur precedentem, et merito cum ab eadem procreatur. Consimili modo fit econverso. [51] Unde considerandum est quod imperfecta fieri nequit nisi mediante brevi sequente seu precedente, quoniam longa et brevis et econverso semper unam perfectionem faciunt.

P1 22vb [52] Unde si querat aliquis utrum posset fieri modus sive | cantus naturalis de omnibus imperfectis sicut fit de omnibus perfectis, responsio cum probatione quod non, cum puras imperfectas nemo pronunciare possit. [53] Verumtamen quidam in artibus suis referunt, perfectam figuram se habere per ultramensuram, [54] et quosdam etiam modos sicut primum et quartum esse per ultramensurabiles, id est non rectam mensuram habentes, quod falsum est, [55] quia si verum esset, tunc posset fieri cantus naturalis de omnibus imperfectis, quoniam imperfectam dicunt esse perfectam. [56] Sicut

▶ p. 119

▶ p. 119

Erf 89v enim res | quelibet naturalis ad similitudinem divine nature ex
P1 23ra tribus constare invenitur, et in vocibus et sonis trina tantum existat | consonantia, [57] sic omnis cantus mensurabilis ad similitudinem divine nature ex tribus constare invenitur. Cuius probatio patet in mensura ubi ternarius numerus reducitur ad perfectum.

▶ p. 120

[58] Et ne in ambiguum procedamus, sciendum est quod perfecta figura multiplici cognoscitur regula.

[59] Prima igitur sicut prefati canunt versiculi.

▶ p. 120

[60] Secunda: quandocumque inter duas longas due breves omni proprietate carentes evenerint, affinitatem in forma tenentes, verbi gratia ut hic:

O Maria beata genitrix

P1 23rb [61] prima profert unum | tempus, que recta brevis dicitur, secunda
Cs 271b duo, que altera brevis appella|tur, et sumitur a parte finis figure |
Si 26r   precedentis, unde versus:

▶ p. 120

---

52 Anon. Emmeram. I (p. 104 'Et hoc asserunt tali siquidem ratione: nullus cantus perfectus potest fieri de imperfectis figuris, et hoc est quia nemo puras imperfectas pronuntiare potest per se, quod concedimus, nam ex puris et veris imperfectis non posset cantus perfectus absque perfectarum consortio compilari') ‖ **53** Ioh. Garl. mens. 1, 7–9; cf. Anon. Emmeram. II, passim (p. 186, l. 39–40; 188, l. 43; 190, l. 7–9; p. 204, l. 15–20) ‖ **60** (O Maria...) RISM B IV/2 Ba 76, Da 9; and further on [166]

50 est *om. Erf* | quod imperfecta] quando perfecta *Hw* | fieri nequit] nequit fieri *Si* | seu] et *Erf* ‖ **52** posset] possit *ErfHw* | omnibus perfectis] perfectis omnibus *Si* | cum probatione] brevis *Erf* | nemo *om. Erf* ‖ **53** perfectam figuram] perfectas *Erf* ‖ **54** per ultramensurabiles] perultramensurales *Hw* | falsum] faciendum *Hw* ‖ **55** tunc] hoc tunc *Erf* | imperfectam ... perfectam] imperfectum ... perfectum *Hw* ‖ **56** quelibet *om. Si* | tantum] tantummodo *Si* | existat] existit *Erf* ‖ **57** perfectum] perfectam *Hw P1 (ante corr. ?)* ‖ **58** quod] quod quod *Si* ‖ **59** igitur] gratia *dub. Si om. ErfHw* | prefati canunt] predicti canuntur *Erf* ‖ **60** secunda] secunda est *Erf* | breves] breus *ante corr. P1* | evenerint] evenerunt *Hw* | tenentes] carentes *Hw* | verbi gratia *om. Si* | verbi-hic] ut hic patere possit *Erf* | ut hic *om. Hw* | *ex. om. Erf* ‖ **61** secunda] faciens *Hw* | appellatur] dicitur *ErfSi* | parte finis] fine *Erf* | unde versus *om. Hw*

Lambertus, 'Ars musica' – 'Musica mensurabilis'

⁵⁰ Now it should be noted that whenever a single breve should occur between two longs, it will always be led back to the preceding imperfect [long], and deservedly so, since it is begotten from the same. The converse shall be made in a very similar way. ⁵¹ Now it should be considered that the imperfect does not know how to be made except through the following or preceding breve in the middle, because the long and the breve [together] (and *vice versa*) always make one perfection.

⁵² Now if anyone asks whether a mode or a natural song can be made from all imperfect longs – just as it can be made from all perfect longs – the response (with a proof) is no, since no-one could utter pure imperfect longs. ⁵³ However, certain people in their *Artes* say that the perfect figure holds itself through 'ultra'-measure, ⁵⁴ and also that certain modes, such as the first and fourth, exist through 'ultra-measurables', that is, not having a 'proper' measure. This is false, ⁵⁵ because if it were true, then a natural song could be made from all imperfects, because they call the imperfect 'perfect'. ⁵⁶ For just as any natural thing is found to accord with the likeness of the divine nature in threes, and likewise in pitches and sounds there exists a threefold consonance, ⁵⁷ thus every measurable song is found to accord with the likeness of the divine nature in threes. The proof of this is shown in measure where the ternary number is rendered as perfect.

⁵⁸ And so that we should not proceed in ambiguity, it should be understood that a perfect figure is known by a rule of many parts.

⁵⁹ First, just as in the aforesaid little verse.

⁶⁰ Second, whenever two breves lacking all *proprietas* occur between two longs, and holding affinity in form, for example as here,

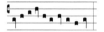

O Maria beata genitrix

⁶¹ the first produces one *tempus*, which is said to be a *recta* breve, the second, two, which is called an *altera* breve, and it is taken from the part of the figure last preceding [it], whence the verse:

The 'Ars musica' Attributed to Magister Lambertus/Aristoteles

⁶² Inter perfectas si bis brevis una locetur,
⁶³ Temporis unius fit prima, secunda dupletur.
⁶⁴ Et quoniam in tali binario tria tempora commorari reperiuntur, ideo longarum quevis predictarum adeo perfectionem retinere meretur, nisi tantummodo sola brevis primam precesserit longam, sicut per hanc patet clausulam:

Hw 422   Vilains leves sus

P1 23va
⁶⁵ <et> tunc duo tempora longa tenebit. Et sic perfectio ante perfectionem coniunctam | sive disiunctam nunquam diminui potest quoniam longa [perfecta] nequit habere perfectionem nisi aliqua mediante perfectione sequente.

⁶⁶ Tertia: si tres inter predictas quandoque reperiantur et in forma consimiles, ut patet hic:

Trop y use ma vie

Erf 90r
⁶⁷ quelibet unum tempus observat et tamen nichilominus nulla longarum virtutem | sive gratiam sue perfectionis amittet, nisi ut predictum est.

⁶⁸ Quarta: si IIII°ʳ inter predictas evenerint, omnes breves petantur et equales, sed ultima oriatur a subsequenti, ⁶⁹ et tunc
P1 23vb unum parvum | tractulum in forma et longitudine semisuspirii   ▶ *p. 120*
obtineat precedens longa iuxta latus suum a parte finis, ⁷⁰ qui divisionem modorum seu perfectionem semper et ubique significabit, ut hic:

Cs 272a   Deus ⁺ele ma to<r>menter ? tra ?⁺

62–63 Nɪᴄ. Wᴇʏᴛs p. 262b ‖ **64** (Vilains leves sus) cf. Vilain, lieve sus o RISM B IV/2 Mo 296 T ‖ **66** (Trop y...) RISM B IV/2 Mo 26 (Joliement en douce / Quant voi la florete... (56v ...trop use ma vie...) / Je suis loiete / Aptatur) ‖ **70** (Deus...) Not identified (cf. Ludwig, *Repertorium*, p. 293).- cf. Dex ele ma tolu? (Aɴᴏɴ. Emmeram, p. 352)

62–63 om. *Hw* ‖ **63** temporis] pars *Si* | dupletur] locetur *Si* ‖ **64** binario] binaris *Erf* | adeo] a Deo *Hw* | retinere meretur] retinet *Si* | precesserit] precessit *Si* | sicut-clausulam] sicut patet in clausula *Erf* | patet clausulam] clausulam patet *Hw* | Vilains leues sus *om. Hw* | Vilains leves sus *sine notis Erf* ‖ **65** tunc duo-sequente] tunc duo tempora illa brevis a<ltera> tenebit et sic ex illa et brevi ipsam precedente, que a principo eius sumpta est, perfectio fit, et sic perfectio ante perfectionem coniunctam sive disiunctam nunquam potest diminui *Erf* | perfectio] perfecto *Si* | perfectionem¹] profectionem *Hw* ‖ **66** et] etiam ? *P1* om. *Si* | patet *om. SiHw* | Trop y use ma vie] Trop use ma vie *Si* (*om. Hw*, *Erf sine notis*) ‖ **67** quelibet] et licet *Hw* | observat] conservat *SiHw* | tamen] tum *Hw* | nulla] nullam *Si* ‖ **68** quarta] regula talis est *add. Erf* | petantur] sunt *Erf* putantur *Hw* | subsequenti] longa *add. Erf* ‖ **69** tunc] etiam *Hw* | parvum] parvulum *Erf* | tractulum] tractum *Hw* | longitudine] longitudinem *P1* | semisuspirii] suspirii *Erf* | a parte] aperte *Hw* ‖ **70** divisionem] differentiam *Hw* | modorum] numerorum *Si* | perfectionem-hic] perfectionem precedentis figure signabit ut hic *Erf* perfectorum significat ut hic *Hw* perfectionum significat verbi gratia ut hic *Si* | Diex elema conc mon c'reb'l' *Erf sine notis* Diex elle ma tot mon cuor tubre (?) *Si* Deus ele ma tomteera ? *om. Hw* | tempora-duo] nisi duo tempora *Erf*

Lambertus, 'Ars musica' – 'Musica mensurabilis'

[62] If one breve should be found between two perfects, [63] The first would be of one *tempus*, the second would be doubled.

[64] And because three *tempora* are found to dwell in these two, so it deserves to retain the perfection of the aforesaid longs, except if a single breve should lead in such a way before the first long, as is evident in this *clausula*:

Vilains leves sus

[65] and then the long will hold two *tempora*. Thus a perfection before a perfection, conjunct or disjunct, can never be diminished, because a [perfect] long does not know how to retain perfection except through some mediating perfection that follows it.

[66] Third, whenever three [breves] are found between the aforesaid longs, and in a very similar form, as is shown here:

Trop y use ma vie

[67] any long will observe the one *tempus* but nevertheless, none of the longs will part with the virtue or grace of its perfection, except as was said before.

[68] Fourth, if four [breves] should occur between the aforesaid longs, all the breves will desire to be equal, but the last originates from the [long] following [it], [69] and then the first long acquires one short little stroke, in the form and length of the half-breath [rest], its side near to the part of the last [figure], [70] which will always and everywhere signify a division of the modes or a perfection, as here:

Deus elema tormenter ? tra- ?

[71] et tunc longa subsequens tempora nisi duo tenebit. Et hoc est secundum ordinem quarti et quinti modi imperfecti. [72] Nam si ▶ *p. 120* tractus ille deficeret, tunc prima brevium procederet a precedenti secundum ordinem secundi imperfecti, ut hic:

Mammelettes a si dur<ettes>

P1 24ra   [73] Quinta: vero si quinque in forma consimiles evenerint, tres prime dabunt unam perfectionem, et binarius subsequens non equalis unam, et quelibet longarum, prout superius dictum est, tenebit, verbi gratia:

Sen dirai chanconette

[74] Et si plures evenerint secundum imparem numerum, consimili modo fiat. Et sic de facili quisque scire poterit differentiam inter longam perfectam et imperfectam si bene consideratur.

P1 24rb   [75] Preterea notandum est quod perfecta figura in uno corpore quandoque duplicari vi|detur cuius latitudo transit longitudinem, ut hic:

---

72 (Mammelettes...) Extrait de 'Quant florist' (RISM B IV/2 Mo 3, 42) ‖ **73–74** Ioh. Garl. mens. 1, 30 ('Secunda vero talis est: si multitudo brevium fuerit in aliquo loco, semper debemus facere, quod aequipolleant longis') ‖ 73 (Sen dirai...) RISM B IV/2 Mo 26 (Joliement en douce / Quant voi la florete... (55v ... S'en dirai chançonete...) / Je suis loiete / Aptatur)

71 tenebit] tenebant *Hw* | hoc] hec *Si* | est secundum] etiam secundum *Hw* | quarti et quinti modi] quarti modi et quinti *Si* | modi *om. Erf* ‖ 72 ille *om. Si* | procederet] precederet *Si* | precedenti] longa *add. Erf* | secundum] per *Hw* | secundum-imperfecti] secundum secundi *Si* | secundi] modi *add. Erf* | ut hic] verbi gratia ut hic *Si* | verbi gratia *Hw* | Mammelettes a si dure *om. Hw* | *ex. om. Erf* ‖ 73 quinque] quando *Si* quandoque *Hw* | in forma] informatur *Si* | consimiles evenerint] consimilis evenerit *Hw* | unam[1]] una *Si* | perfectionem] perfectam *Hw* | superius-est] dictum est superius *Si* | Sendirai chanconette] Sen dirai canchounete *Si* (*om. Hw*) | *Erf:* Quinta regula talis est quod si quinque [quod si quinque] in forma consimiles evenerunt inter longas ut dictum est, prime tres dabunt unam perfectionem et alie due faciunt aliam. Nam prima recta brevis erit, sequens vero altera brevis, et quelibet longarum, sicut superius dictum est, se tenebit (*ex. om.*) ‖ 74 modo fiat] modo non fiat *Hw* | fiat] fiet *Erf* | quisque scire poterit] quis poterit habere *Hw* | scire poterit] poterit scire *ErfSi* | et imperfectam *om. Si* | consideratur] supradicta *add. Erf* ‖ 75 De duplatione perfecte figure *tit. P1* | preterea] propterea *Hw* | quandoque *om. Si* | duplicari] duplicare *Hw* | cuius latitudo] quae tunc latitudo eius *HwSi* cuius tunc latitudo *Erf* | transit] ex<c>edit *Erf* | ut hic] sic *ErfHwSi* | *ex. om. Si*

[71] and then the following long will hold but two *tempora*. And this is according to the *ordo* of the fourth and fifth imperfect mode. [72] For if that stroke were to be absent, then the first of the breves would proceed from the [long] preceding [it], according to the *ordo* of the second imperfect mode, as here:

Mammelettes a si durettes

[73] Fifth, if five [breves] very similar in form should occur, the first three will give one perfection, and the two subsequent unequal breves [will give] one [perfection], and each of the longs, just as was said above, will hold [its perfection], for example,

Sen dirai chanconette

[74] and if more of an unequal number should occur, let it be done in a very similar way. And thus, from this easy rule, anyone will be able to know the distinction between the perfect and imperfect long, if it is considered well.

[75] Beyond this it should be noted that whenever a perfect figure (within one body) seems to be doubled, with its width greater than its length, [it is] as here:

The 'Ars musica' Attributed to Magister Lambertus/Aristoteles

Erf 90v   [76] Que non ad aliarum figurarum spectat originem nisi ex | gratia,   ▶ *p. 120*
quoniam nunquam duplaretur [77] nisi ne in compositione sive
Cs 272b   ordinatione tenoris | plana musica frangatur, super quam omnes
Hw 423   motelli et omne organum | fundari tenentur.

[78] Recta brevis autem, que superius pluries cum pluribus
Si 26v   denominatur, adhuc in forma | propria describitur in hunc modum: ▪
continens igitur unum in se tempus – unde versus:

[79] Solo recta brevis moderatur tempore quevis –

Pl 24va   [80] seipsamque in duas diminuit partes non equales | vel in tres
tantummodo equales et indivisibiles. [81] Quarum prima pars duarum
semibrevis minor appellatur, secunda vero maior, et econverso.
[82] Tres autem semibreves minores equales et indivisibiles nuncupari
tenentur. [83] Unde notandum est quod nulla semibrevis sola reperitur,
quoniam per se sola significare nequit, sed bine et bine non equales,
ut patet hic: ◆◆ ◆◆ ◆◆

vel tres et tres equales inveniri debentur, ut hic: ◆◆◆ ◆◆◆ ◆◆◆ ◆◆◆

[84] Et sic binarius non equalis seu ternarius equalis semibrevium
figurarum semper ad rectam brevem equipollere debet, ⁺recta brevis   ▶ *p. 120*
Pl 24vb   ad imperfectam | ad alteram brevem, imperfecta cum brevi seu
brevis cum altera brevi ad perfectam⁺.

---

77 (ne in-frangatur) Iac. Leod. spec. 7, 21, 6 ('Haec figura vel notula non est de
essentia huius artis, etiam nec musicae planae, sed ex geometria propterea ab
auctoribus inter notulas recepta est, ut ait Aristoteles, ne in ordinatione tenoris
plana musica frangatur ut de notula una plani cantus duae fiant'.) ‖ **89** (plica-
diverso) Ioh. Garl. mens. 3, 9 ('quia plica nihil aliud est quam signum dividens
sonum in sono diverso'); Anon. Emmeram. I (p. 92, l. 2–3); Iac. Leod. spec. 7,
22, 2.- (videlicet-diapente) Anon. Emmeram. I (p. 96, l. 16–18 'et sic mobilis in
sonos varios subtiliter transmutata aut per tonum vel semitonum aut ditonum
vel semiditonum vel dyatessaron et si licuerit dyapente, scematorum plurium
quaerit amicabiliter armoniam'.)

76 que non] quod non *Pl* | ad-nisi] ad originem aliarum spectat figurarum
nisi *Erf* | spectat] spectatur *PlSi* | quoniam] quia *Erf* | nunquam duplaretur]
nunquam hec figura duplicatur *Erf* | duplaretur] duplicaretur *Hw* ‖ **77** nisi ne]
nisi quod ne *HwPlSi* | sive *om. Erf* | frangatur] non frangatur *Erf* |super] supra
Erf | tenentur] tenetur *Erf* ‖ **78** De recta brevi *tit. Pl* | autem] aut *Hw* | hunc] hinc
Si | igitur-tempus] in se unum tempus *Erf* in se igitur unum tempus *Si* | unde
versus *om. Hw* ‖ **79** *om. Hw* ‖ **80** seipsamque] seipsam *Hw* | duas] duos *Erf* |
diminuit] diminuens *Si* | vel-equales *om. Erf* ‖ **81** Quarum] Sciendum quod partes
sunt tres breves quarum *Erf* | pars *om. Erf* | semibrevis] semibreves *ante corr. Pl*
| appellatur] dicitur *Erf* | secunda] altera (?) *Erf* | et econverso] vel econverso *Erf*
‖ **82** indivisibiles-tenentur] ut dictum est nuncupantur *Erf* ‖ **83** est *om. Erf* | sola
significare nequit] nichil significat *Erf* | significare] si grate *Pl* | sed bine-(*fig.*)] sed
bine et (*fig.*) bine ut hic et iste sunt non equales *Erf* | **83** patet *om. HwSi* | inveniri-ut
hic *om. Erf* ‖ **84** sic] si *Si* | imperfectam] imperfectas *Si* | vel] et *Erf* | imperfecta]
imperfectam *ErfHw*

[76] this figure is not of the same order as the other figures, that is to say, it would never be doubled [77] except so that the plainchant is not broken up by the the arrangement or patterning of the tenor, on top of which we consider all motets and every *organum* to to be built.

[78] But a *recta* breve, mentioned above many times in many examples, is copied this way in its correct form: ∎

containing within itself one *tempus* – whence the verse:

[79] Any *recta* breve is governed by a single *tempus* as you wish –

[80] and divides itself into two unequal parts, or into just three, equal and indivisible. [81] The first of these two parts is called a minor semibreve, the second major, and *vice versa*. [82] But three equal and indivisible semibreves are considered to be called minor. [83] Now it should be noted that no semibreve is found alone, because no-one knows how to interpret it alone by itself, but as two and two unequal [semibreves], as shown here: ♦♦ ♦♦ ♦♦

or three and three equal [semibreves] ought to be found, as here: ♦♦♦ ♦♦♦ ♦♦♦ ♦♦♦

[84] And thus the two unequal or the three equal semibreve figures always ought to be equipollent [rest of passage corrupt].

The 'Ars musica' Attributed to Magister Lambertus/Aristoteles

[85] Cum dictum sit de simplicibus figuris, nunc autem dicendum est de simul ligatis seu coniunctis, qualiter inter se differunt, rursus incipiendo ab unitate, et sic distinguendo longitudinem et brevitatem secundum quod multiplicantur in numero. [86] Unde notandum est quod quedam sunt species quibus omnis cantus ▸ *p. 120* eufonie causa decoratur. [87] Que etiam in divisione quinque partium dividuntur, quarum quelibet divisio multas continet differentias et diversas.

Cs 273a/*P1* 25ra   [88] Prima [igitur] divisio. Prime partis est quedam figura, quam ▸ *p. 120* plicam communiter appellamus. [89] Unde notandum quod plica nichil

Erf 91r | aliud est quam signum dividens sonum in sono diverso per diversas vocum distantias, tam ascendendo quam descendendo, videlicet per semitonium et tonum, per semiditonum et ditonum, et per diatessaron et diapente. [90] Que plica 4 differentiis explicatur, nam quedam perfecta dicitur, quedam imperfecta, quedam recta brevis et quedam altera brevis.

[91] Prima differentia plice perfecte descendendo est quedam figura duos habens tractus, quorum ultimus longior est primo, sicut patet hic: ⌐

P1 25rb   ascendendo autem unum solum retinet ut ibi: ⌐

Hw 424   [92] Habet autem omnem potestatem, regulam et naturam quam habet perfecta longa, nisi quod in corpore duo tem|pora tenet et unum in ▸ *p. 120* membris. [93] Fit autem plica in voce per compositionem epygloti cum ▸ *p. 120* repercussione gutturis subtiliter inclusa.

[94] Secunda differentia est plica imperfecta in forma perfecte similis, sed regulam imperfecte tenet et naturam, et continet unum tempus in corpore et reliquum in membris: ⌐

[95] Tertia differentia descendendo est illa que duos habet tractus, quorum primus longior est ultimo sicut patet hic: ⌐

---

92 (in corpore-membris) Iac. Leod. spec. 7, 22, 6 ‖ 93 cf. Iac. Leod. spec. 7, 22, 2

85 Cum dictum sit] iam dictum est *Hw* | autem *om. Erf* | est] videtur *Hw* | seu] et *Erf* | inter se *om. Si* | differunt] differant *Hw* | sic *om. Si* | secundum quod multiplicantur] vel (*dub.*) quod multiplicatur *Erf* | in numero] in necessario *dub. P1* innuere *Hw* ‖ 86 quod *om. Si* | eufonie] euphonye *Erf* | decoratur] decantatur *Hw* ‖ 87 dividuntur] dividitur *Si* ‖ 88 De prima divisione *tit. P1* | divisio] differentia *Hw* | plicam communiter] communiter plicam *Erf* ‖ 89 notandum] est *add. Si* | 89 distantias *om. P1* | per semiditonum et ditonum *om. Si* | et per] per *Erf* ‖ 90 quedam²] et quedam *ErfHw* ‖ 91 duos *om. Hw* | longior] longatur *ante corr. Erf* | sicut] ut *Si* | sicut patet hic] ut hic *Erf* ut patet *Hw* | autem] vero *Hw* | retinet ut ibi] retinet tractum ut patet *Hw* | ibi] hic *ErfSi* ‖ 92 Habet-potestatem] omnem igitur habens potestatem *Hw* | quam] quasi *Hw* | perfecta-membris] perfectam figuram excepto quod si longam precesserit in corpore duo tempora tenebit reliquum autem in membris *Hw* | in membris] in plica *Erf* ‖ 93 compositionem] compositione *Si* | epiglotti *Hw* | epygloty *Si* | inclusa] inclusam *Hw* ‖ 94 in forma-similis] quae etiam cum praemissa proprietate consimilem retinet formam *Hw* | sed-tenet] sed imperfecte tenet regulam *Si* | imperfecte] imperfectae figurae *Hw* | et continet] nisi quod continet *Erf* | et continet-membris] scilicet in corpore unum tempus reliquum in membris ut patet descendendo (*fig.*) patet et ascendendo ut (*fig.*) *Hw* | et reliquum in membris] et alium in plica *Erf* ‖ 95 descendendo *om. HwSi* | que duos habet] habet duos *Erf* | est *om. Si* | ultimo-hic] ultimo descendendo sicuti patet *Hw* ultimo sic patet hic descendendo *Si*

Lambertus, 'Ars musica' – 'Musica mensurabilis'

[85] Since simple figures have been discussed, now figures bound or joined together must be discussed: how they differ from each other, beginning again from unity, and thus distinguishing their length and shortness according to how they are multiplied in number. [86] Whence it should be noted that there are particular types by which every song is decorated for the sake of euphony. [87] And these types are separated into a division of five parts, which each contain many diverse distinctions.

[88] The first division. Of the first part is a certain figure that we commonly call a plica. [89] Now, it should be noted that the plica is nothing other than a sign dividing a sound into a different sound through a different interval of pitches, either ascending or descending, namely: through a semitone and tone, through a semiditone and ditone, and through a diatessaron and diapente. [90] This plica is set forth in four distinctions: a certain one is said to be perfect, a certain one imperfect, a certain one a *recta* breve, and a certain one an *altera* breve.

[91] The first distinction of a perfect plica, descending, is a certain figure with two strokes, the last of which is longer than the first, just as is shown here: ⌐

Ascending, however, it retains a single stroke, as here: ⌐

[92] But it has all the power, rule, and nature that the perfect long has, except that it holds two *tempora* in its body and one in its limb. [93] A plica is made in the voice through the combination of the epiglottis along with a subtle vibration of the throat.

[94] The second distinction is an imperfect plica similar in form to the perfect, but it holds the rule and nature of the imperfect, and it contains one *tempus* in its body and the remainder in its limb. ⌐

[95] The third distinction, descending, is that which has two strokes, the first of which is longer than the last, just as is shown here: ⌐

The 'Ars musica' Attributed to Magister Lambertus/Aristoteles

P1 25va   [96] Ascendendo autem duos habet diversos: unum in | dextra parte ascendendo, significans plicam, alium in sinistra parte descendendo, significans brevitatem, ut hic: |

[97] Potestatem autem hec observat regulam et naturam recte brevis et illius que vocatur altera brevis.

Si 27r   [98] Secunda divisio. Partis secunde est quedam ligatura duarum
Cs 273b   figurarum, que binaria vo|catur, IIII[or] habens differentias, quarum quelibet dupliciter habet fieri ascendendo videlicet et descendendo. [99] Sed notandum est quod si aliqua istarum descendendo proprietatem habuerit, tunc ascendendo carebit, et econverso,
Erf 91v   semibrevibus | exceptis.

    [100] Notandum est quod ascensus duplex est similiter et descensus, | ▶ *p. 120–*
P1 25vb   nam quidam perfectus dicitur, et quidam imperfectus. [101] Perfectus *21* autem ascensus dicitur cum in ternaria ligatura secundus punctus altior est primo et tertius secundo. [102] Imperfectus est quando secundus punctus altior est primo, et tertius secundo inferior reciprocando vel equalis. [103] Perfectus autem descensus dicitur ▶ *p. 121* quando secundus punctus inferior est primo et tercius secundo, [104] imperfectus quando secundus punctus inferior est primo, tercius autem secundo superior reciprocando vel equalis. ▶ *p. 121*

    [105] Prima differentia huius divisionis talis est, quod quandocunque duo figure simul ligate descendendo cum proprietate, ascendendo sine reperiuntur, ut hic:

P1 26ra   [106] prima recta brevis est, secunda vero longa imperfecta, ut manifeste patet in IIII°, V° modo et VI°, tam supra litteram quam ▶ *p. 121* sine. [107] In secundo tamen modo, tertio et septimo, ambe pronuntiantur equales tantummodo supra litteram, nisi longa precedat.

---

96 Anon. Emmeram. I (p. 92, l. 23–26) ‖ **96** ascendendo autem] ascendendo *Si* sed ascendendo *Hw* | diversos] divisos *P1* | in dextra parte] a parte dextra *Si* | significans] signantem *ErfSi* | plicam *om. Erf* | alium] alterum *Si* aliam *Hw* | significans] signantem *Erf* signans *Si* ‖ **97** Potestatem-observat] observantes igitur potestatem *Hw* | hec-naturam] regulam et naturam observat *Erf* | illius] ipsius *Hw* | altera brevis] altera ⁺ ... ⁺ ut dictum est *Erf* ‖ **98** De secunda divisione *tit. P1* | partis *om. Si* | partis secunde *om. Erf* | que] quae etiam *Hw* | differentias habens *Si* | dupliciter habet fieri] duplicem habet figuram *Hw* habet dupliciter fieri *Si* ‖ **99** sed] unde *Hw* | est *om. Si* | descendendo] in descendendo *Hw* | tunc ascendendo] in ascendendo vero *Hw* | ascendendo] in ascendendo *Erf* | semibrevibus exceptis] exceptae tantummodo semibreves *Hw* ‖ **100–104** Ascensus autem intelligitur quando secunda figura alicuius ligature fuerit altior prima. Descensus autem econverso. *Hw* ‖ **100** est¹] etiam *ErfSi* | quidam-dicitur] quidam est perfectus *Erf* ‖ **101** cum] ut *Erf* | est¹] *om. P1* | secundus punctus] secundus *Erf* punctus secundus *Si* | et tertius] tercius *Erf* ‖ **102** reciprocando vel] reciprocandum et *Erf* ‖ **103** dicitur *om. ErfP1* | secundus punctus] punctus secundus *Si* | et tercius] tercius autem *Si* | imperfectus] imperfectus est *Si* ‖ **104** punctus *om. Erf* | reciprocando *om. Erf* ‖ **105** prima] prima igitur *Hw* | huius divisionis *om. Hw* | duo] duae *Hw* | cum] est *Si* | ascendendo sine] ascendendo vero sine proprietate *Erf* vel cum proprietate ascendendo *Hw* | ex. *om. Erf* ‖ **106** brevis-imperfecta] brevis fit longa imperfecta *Hw* | est *om. Hw* | ut] tamen ut *Si* | IIII°-VI°] quarto quinto et sexto modo *ErfHw* |V°] vero *P1* V *Si* | sine] sine littera *Hw* ‖ **107** tamen *om. Hw* | septimo] vi° *Si* | ambe-precedat] tales omnes fiunt equales tantummodo supra literam secundum usum *Hw* | nisi longa precedat *om. ErfSi*

80

Lambertus, 'Ars musica' – 'Musica mensurabilis'

[96] Ascending, however, it has two varieties: one, ascending, in the right part, signifying a plica; another, descending, in the left part, signifying brevity, as here: ⌐

[97] This figure, however, observes the power, rule, and nature of a *recta* breve, and of the one called an *altera* breve.

[98] The second division. Of the second part is a certain ligature of two figures, which is called a binary ligature, having four distinctions, of which each is made in a twofold manner, namely ascending or descending. [99] But it should be noted that if any descending ligature has *proprietas*, then the ascending one will lack *proprietas*, and *vice versa*, with the exception of semibreves.

[100] It should be noted that an ascent and similarly a descent is twofold, for one is called perfect, and one imperfect. [101] The ascent, moreover, is called perfect when the second notehead in a ternary ligature is higher than the first and the third higher than the second. [102] An ascent is imperfect when the second notehead is higher than the first, and the third is lower than the second, or equal by returning [to the first]. [103] But the descent is said to be perfect when the second notehead is lower than the first and the third [is lower than] the second; [104] it is imperfect when the second notehead is lower than the first, but the third is higher than the second, or equal by returning [to the first].

[105] The first distinction of this division is as follows: that whenever two figures are found joined together, descending with *proprietas*, ascending without, as here:

[106] the first is a *recta* breve, but the second an imperfect long, as is clearly shown in the fourth and fifth mode and the sixth, both with text and without. [107] But in the second mode, and the third and seventh, both are uttered equally above the text, except if a long precedes.

The 'Ars musica' Attributed to Magister Lambertus/Aristoteles

Cs 274a

[108] Secunda differentia tam ascendens quam descendens per contrarium prime differentie constat tam in proportione quam in proprietate. [109] <Descendendo prima figura caret proprietate> secunda autem figura ascendens prime non directe supraponitur, sed quasi averso capite ab ea declinat, ut patet hic:

Prima longa est imperfecta, secunda recta brevis.

P1 26rb

[110] Tertia differentia descendendo est ligatura duarum figurarum | quarum secunda non directe subponitur prime, sed est a prima continue protracta in obliquum. Tenet autem prima proprietatem in fronte. [111] Ascendendo vero secunda non directe supraponitur prime, sed aversum ab eadem declinat, omni proprietate carens, ut patet hic:

Erf 92r

[112] Harum autem potestas et natura equalitas | appellatur quoniam utraque recta brevis dicitur et equali tempore mensuratur.

[113] Quarta differentia est ligatura duarum figurarum tam ascendendo quam descendendo proprietatem tenens non propriam, ▶ p. 121 ut hic:

P1 26va

[114] Prima autem minor | semibrevis dicitur, secunda vero maior vel econverso, ita quod ambe nisi <uno> tempore mensurantur, nisi ▶ p. 121 quod aliquando pro altera brevi ponantur, tunc enim duo tempora compleantur.

Si 27v

[115] Tertia divisio. Tertie partis est quedam ligatura seu coniunctura trium figurarum novem habens differentias, quarum quelibet fit dupliciter, ascendendo videlicet et descendendo, ut patebit.

108–109 Secunda differentia tam ascendens quam descendens per contrarium primae differentiae constat ut hic: (ex.) tam in proportione quam in proprietate. *Hw* ‖ **108** ascendens quam descendens] ascendendo quam descendendo *Si* | differentie constat] constat differentie *Si* | in² *om. P1* ‖ **109** secunda-supraponitur] secunde autem figure ascendendo non directe prime supraponitur *Erf* | ascendens] ascendendo *Si* | quasi averso] quod adverso *Si* | ea] eadem *Erf* | patet *om. Si* | ex. *om. Erf* ‖ **110–112** Tertia differentia tam ascendens quam descendens sub tali forma sequitur quod secun<425>dum aequalitatem proferuntur (ex.) Et notandum est quod talis ligatura vocatur equalitas, quoniam reddit aequalitatem: omnes aliae, quarum prima fuerit longior seu brevior, sunt non aequales. *Hw* ‖ **110** descendendo (*ErfSi*)] desc' *P1* | non] vero *Erf* | subponitur] supponitur *Erf* supraponitur *P1Si* | protracta-obliquum] in obliquum protacta *Erf* ‖ **111** vero secunda] autem *Erf* autem secunda *Si* | supraponitur] supponitur *Si* aversum] adversum *Si* | omni-hic] omni carens proprietate ut hic *Erf* | ex. *om. Erf* ‖ **112** recta] tota *Si* ‖ **113–114** Quarta differentia tam ascendens quam descendens retinet proportionem non propriam, sub tali forma (ex.) Quae semibreves appellantur, non aequales etiam proferuntur, ut predictum est, quod duae semibreves, quarum prima minor est et econverso constituunt unam brevem et quandoque pro altera brevi ponuntur. *Hw* ‖ **113** proprietatem] proprietate *Si* | tenens] habens *Erf* | non propriam *om. P1* ‖ **114** vel econverso] et econverso *Erf* | ita quod] nisi quod *P1* | uno] solo Σ | nisi quod] nisi *Erf* quod si *P1* | ponantur] ponatur *Si* | tunccompleantur] tunc enim sunt duorum temporum sicut et ipsa videlicet altera brevis duo tempora in se continet *Erf* | enim] ut *post corr. marg. Si* ‖ **115** tertie partis *om. Erf* | novem] 14 (4 ?) *ante corr. Si* | seu] cui *Hw* | ascendendo] ascendens *Hw* | videlicet] scilicet *Erf* | descendendo] descendens *Hw* | ut patebit *om. Hw*

[108] The second distinction, both ascending and descending, contrary to the first distinction, accords both in proportion and in *proprietas*. [109] Descending, the first figure lacks *proprietas* but the second figure, ascending, is placed not directly above the first, but it turns away, as if its head is reversed to it, as is shown here:

The first long is imperfect, the second a *recta* breve.

[110] The third distinction, descending, is a ligature of two figures of which the second is placed not directly under the first, but is continuously stretched out from the first into an oblique [notehead]. The first, however, holds the *proprietas* in its front. [111] The second, ascending, is not directly placed above the first, but reversed, it turns away from it, lacking all *proprietas*, as is shown here:

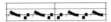

[112] The power and nature of these is called 'equality' because each is said to be a *recta* breve and measured by an equal *tempus*.

[113] The fourth distinction is a ligature of two figures, both ascending and descending, and with a *proprietas* that is not proper, as here:

[114] Now the first is called a minor semibreve, but the second major (or *vice versa*), so that both are only measured by one *tempus*, except when they are in the place of an *altera* breve, since then two *tempora* will be filled.

[115] The third division. Of the third part, there is a certain ligature or *coniunctura* of three figures having nine distinctions, of which each can be made in a twofold manner, namely, ascending and descending, as will be shown.

Cs 274b

[116] Prima autem differentia huius divisionis tam supra litteram quam sine talis est, quod quandocumque ternaria ligatura tam descendendo cum proprietate quam ascendendo sine proprietate reperta fuerit, binaria ligatura sequente, ut hic:

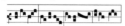

Pl 26vb

[117] prima longa est imperfecta, secunda recta brevis, tertia prime similis si brevis eam sequatur, si autem longa tunc tertia trium temporum iudicatur.

[118] Secunda differentia tam in proportione quam in proprietate omnino per oppositum prime differentie, tam supra litteram quam sine, iudicatur, ut hic:

[119] Tertia differentia tam supra litteram quam sine talis est quod quandocunque ternarie ligature continuantur, longa per se posita precederet, ut hic:

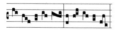

Pl 27ra

[120] prima profert unum | tempus, secunda duo, tertia tria, et hoc secundum ordinem quarti modi dum tamen in primo gradu longa ponatur.

Erf 92v

[121] Quarta differentia descendendo cum proprietate, ascendendo sine, tam supra litteram quam sine, talis est quod quandocumque binaria ligatura precedit ternariam, ut hic:

Hw 426

[122] prima binarie profert unum tempus, secunda duo et prima ternarie profert unum tempus, secunda duo, tertia tria secundum ordinem quinti modi.

116 autem *om. Si* | huius divisionis *om. Hw* | tam¹-talis est] talis est tam supra literam quam sine *Si* | tam¹-sine] tam sine litera quam cum litera *Hw* | ternaria] trinaria *Hw* | quam ascendendo sine proprietate] ascendendo vero sine *Erf* | sine proprietate reperta] sine reperta *Si* | binaria ligatura] ligatura binaria *Si* | binaria-hic] in primo gradu de bina ligatura sequente *Hw* | *ex. om. Erf* ‖ 117 prima longa est-iudicatur ut hic] prima fiet longa imperfecta, secunda recta brevis, tertia sicut prima si ante <brevis, sed longa perfecta si> longa sequatur. Tunc tria tempora tertia donat *Hw* | iudicatur] iudicabitur *Si* ‖ 118 sine] sine litera *Hw* | iudicatur] regnat *Hw* | ut hic] velud hic patet *Erf* | *ex. om. Erf* ‖ 119 ternarie] trinariae *Hw* | continuantur] adinvicem contineantur *Hw* | longa-ut hic] quamvis longa praecedat seu sequatur sicut hic tam ascendendo quam descendendo *Hw* | precederet] precedente *Erf om. Si* | ut hic] sic *Erf* | *ex. om. Erf* ‖ 120 tertia] tertia vero *Erf* | hoc] hic (*dub.*) *Erf* | hoc est *Hw* | ordinem-modi] quarti modi ordinem *Si* | modi *om. Hw* | in primo-ponatur] longa in primo gradu consistat *Hw* | longa ponatur] ponitur longa sic *Erf* ‖ 121 Quarta differentia est quod quandocunque binaria ligatura praecedit ternariam, prima binarie profert unum tempus, secunda duo, ternaria ut supra continetur in proxima. Verbi gratia: (ex.) Et hoc secundum ordinem quinti modi. *Hw* | sine¹] vero sine *Erf* | *ex. om. Erf* ‖ 122 binarie] binaria *ErfHw* binare *Pl* | et prima-secunda duo *om Erf* | secundum] ⁺ … ⁺ *Erf*

[116] But the first distinction of this division, both with text and without, is as follows whenever a ternary ligature, both descending with *proprietas* and ascending without *proprietas*, should be found with a binary ligature following, as here:

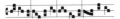

[117] the first long is imperfect, the second [figure] is a *recta* breve, the third is similar to the first if a breve follows it, but if a long [follows it], then the third [figure] should be judged to be of three *tempora*.

[118] The second distinction, both in proportion and *proprietas*, is judged to be in complete opposition to the first distinction, both with text and without, as here:

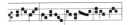

[119] The third distinction, both with text and without, is as follows whenever ternary ligatures are joined, a long, placed by itself, would precede [them], as here:

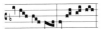

[120] the first [figure of the ternary ligature] produces one *tempus*, the second two, the third three, and this is according to the *ordo* of the fourth mode (while nevertheless the long is placed in the first degree).

[121] The fourth distinction, descending with *proprietas*, ascending without, both with text and without, is as follows whenever a binary ligature precedes a ternary as here:

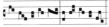

[122] the first [figure] of the binary [ligature] produces one *tempus*, the second two, and the first [figure] of the ternary produces one *tempus*, the second two, the third [figure] three [*tempora*] according to the *ordo* of the fifth mode.

Cs 275a
P1 27rb

¹²³ Quinta differentia tam ascendendo quam descendendo, tam etiam supra litteram quam sine, | talis est, quod quandocunque ternaria ligatura | reperta fuerit ut hic:

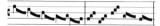

omnes equales secundum ordinem septimi proferuntur.

¹²⁴ Sexta differentia tam supra litteram quam sine, talis est, quod quandocumque ternarie ligature tam ascendendo quam descendendo cum proprietate non propria reperiuntur, ut hic:

¹²⁵ due prime semibreviantur, ultima duo tempora donat si brevis sequatur, si autem longa tunc trino tempore mensuratur.

P1 27va

¹²⁶ Septima differentia tam ascendendo quam descendendo, tam etiam supra litteram quam sine, talis | est quod quandocumque ternarie ligature seu coniuncture reperiuntur ut patet hic:

Si 28r

¹²⁷ due prime semibreviantur, ultima profert unum | tempus si brevis sequatur, si autem longa tunc bino tempore modulatur.

¹²⁸ Octava differentia tam ascendendo quam descendendo omnino per oppositum precedenti contrariatur:

Cs 275b

¹²⁹ Nona differentia tam ascendendo quam des|cendendo talis est quod quandocumque ternarie ligature seu coniuncture reperiuntur ut hic:

123 tam ascendendo-sine] ascendit et descendit tam supra literam quam sine litera *Hw* | ligatura] ligatura confecta *Hw* | reperta-ut hic] invenitur sic *Erf* | fuerit] est *Si* | ex. om *Erf* | omnes-proferuntur] omnes proferuntur equales secundum ordinationem septimi *Hw* | proferuntur *om. Si* ‖ 124 ternarie ligature] ligature ternarie *Erf* | ligature-reperiuntur] ligature contineantur proprietates non proprias habentes tam ascensum quam descensum *Hw* | reperiuntur] reperiantur *Si* | ex. om. *Erf* ‖ 125 due prime] prime due *Erf* | ultima-donat] ultima longa duorum temporum profertur *Hw* | si-mensuratur] si ante longam tria tempora donat *Hw* | duo tempora donat] continente (*dub.*) duorum temporum *Erf* | si] sin *Erf* | tunc-mensuratur] trium temporum iudicatur *Si* | mensuratur] mensurantur *P1* ‖ 126 tam-descendendo] ascendens et descendens *Hw* | tam etiam *om. Erf* | etiam *om. Hw* | est *om. Erf* | ternarie-coniuncture] ternaria tam coniuncte quam ligate *Hw* | patet *om. SiHw* | ut patet hic] sicut hic *Erf* | ex. om. *Erf* ‖ 127 si brevis-longa *om. Erf* | longa] sequatur *add. Si* | bino-modulatur] duo tempora donat *Hw* | modulatur] mensuratur *Erf* ‖ 128 tam-descendendo] tam ascendens quam descendens *Hw* | descendendo] descendendo talis est quod *add. Si* | per oppositum-contrariatur] oppositionem (*dub.*) precendi sunt *Erf* | precedenti contrariatur] praecedentia tam scriptura quam proprietate *Hw* | ex. om. *Erf* ‖ 129 tam-descendendo} tam ascendens quam descendens *Hw* | seu] vel *Si* | seu coniuncture] tam coniunctae quam compositae *Hw* | ut] sicut *Erf* | ut hic *om. Hw* | ex. om. *Erf*

[123] The fifth distinction, both ascending and descending, and both with and without text, is as follows whenever a ternary ligature is found, as here:

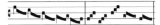

all are produced as equals, according to the *ordo* of the seventh [mode].

[124] The sixth distinction, both with and without text, is as follows whenever ternary ligatures (both ascending and descending) are found with a *proprietas* that is not proper, as here:

[125] the two first are made into semibreves, the last gives two *tempora* if a breve follows, but if a long follows, then it is measured by a threefold *tempus*.

[126] The seventh distinction, both ascending and descending, also both with text and without, is as follows whenever ternary ligatures or *coniuncturae* are found, as is shown here:

[127] the two first are made into semibreves, the last produces one *tempus* if a breve follows, but if a long [follows], then it is measured by a twofold *tempus*.

[128] The eighth distinction, both ascending and descending, is in every way contrasted through its opposition to the previous distinction:

[129] The ninth distinction, both ascending and descending, is as follows whenever ternary ligatures or *coniuncturae* are found, as here:

The 'Ars musica' Attributed to Magister Lambertus/Aristoteles

P1 27vb/*Erf* 93r   [130] omnes semibreves equales et indivisibiles proferuntur, nisi in tertio loco quarti modi pro altera brevi reperiantur. [131] Nam sicut altera brevis tenet affinitatem recte brevis, sic etiam tales affinitatem inter se tam in forma quam in proprietate tenebunt.

   [132] Quarta divisio. Quarte partis est quedam ligatura seu coniunctura IIII^{or} figurarum, IX habens differentias, quarum quelibet

Hw 427 | dupliciter habet fieri, ascendendo videlicet et descendendo. [133] Sed notandum quod plures fiunt <potius> descendendo quam ascendendo propter difficultatem ascensus, nam facilius est descendere quam ascendere.

P1 28ra   [134] Prima igitur eius differentia talis est, quod quandocumque | aliqua coniunctura descendendo seu ligatura ascendendo inventa fuerit quatuor figurarum – descendendo dico, cum prime figure proprietas tantum descendat quantum ultima figura coniuncture – ut hic:

prima erit longa perfecta, subsequentium due prime semibreves, ultima vero duo tempora possidebit.

   [135] Secunda differentia de talibus talis est quod si predicta proprietas brevietur ad distantiam secunde figure descendendo, asc<endendo> vero talis scribatur ligatura, ut hic:

Cs 276a

P1 28rb   [136] prima duo tempora dabit, relique autem tres semibreves erunt indivisibiles et equales.

130 equales et indivisibiles] et indivisibiles et equales *Si* | proferuntur] proferunt *Erf* | nisi *om. Hw* | pro] quod *Hw* ‖ 131 tales] talis *Erf* | tenebunt] tenent *Hw* ‖ 132 quarte partis *om. Erf* | differentias] differentia *Erf* | fieri-descendendo] figuram descendentem videlicet et ascendentem *Hw* | videlicet] scilicet *Erf* ‖ 133 fiunt] sunt *Erf* | fiunt descendendo] descendendo inveniuntur *Hw* | difficultatem-est] gravem ascensum quoniam levius est *Hw* ‖ 134–136 Prima differentia talis est quod quandoque aliqua iunctura descendit, seu ligatura ascendit, quatuor figurarum alicubi reperiuntur quarum proprietates primae figurae tangit longitudinem trium sequentium figurarum, verbi gratia: (ex.) prima erit longa perfecta, subsequentium duae primae semibreves, et ultima duo tempora debet. *Hw* ‖ 134 prima] primo *Erf* | eius *om. Si* | coniunctura] iunctura *Si* | seu] et *Erf* | cum] quadra *dub. Erf* | prime-descendat] proprietas prime figure tantum descendit *Erf* | ultima-ut hic] figura ultima alius ligature ut patet hic *Erf* | coniuncture] subiunctur *dub. Si* | *ex. om. Erf* | subsequentium] et subsequentium *Erf* ‖ 135–136 Secunda differentia ex talibus talis est, quod si praedicta longitudine dictae proprietatis abbreviatur ad distantiam secundae figurae illorum quatuor subsequentium, verbi gratia: (ex.) prima duo tempora dabit, reliquae semibreves erunt indivisibiles et aequales *Hw* ‖ 135 predicta] precedens (predens *ante corr.*) *Si* | proprietas brevietur] brevietur proprietas *Erf* | distantiam] instantiam *Si* | vero *om. Erf* | ut hic *om. Erf* | *ex. om. Erf* ‖ 136 prima] primo *Erf* | erunt] eruat *dub. Si* | indivisibiles] indivisibilis *Erf*

[130] all semibreves are produced as equals and indivisible, except in the third position of the fourth mode [when] they are found in place of an *altera* breve. [131] For just as the *altera* breve holds an affinity with the *recta* breve, so too such [figures] will hold an affinity among themselves, both in form and *proprietas*.

[132] Fourth division. Of the fourth part is a certain ligature or *coniunctura* of four figures, having nine distinctions, of which each can be made in a twofold manner, namely, ascending and descending. [133] But it should be noted that many make them descending rather than ascending on account of the difficulty of the ascent, for it is easier to descend than to ascend.

[134] So, the first of its distinctions is as follows whenever any descending *coniunctura* or ascending ligature of four figures is found – by descending I mean when the *proprietas* of the first figure descends as far as the last figure of the *coniunctura* – as here:

the first [figure] will be a perfect long, and the first two of the following [figures] will be semibreves and the last will occupy two *tempora*.

[135] The second distinction of this sort is as follows: if descending, the aforesaid *proprietas* should be shortened to the distance of the second figure; but ascending, the ligature would be written as follows, as here:

[136] the first will give two *tempora*, but the remaining three semibreves will be indivisible and equal.

The 'Ars musica' Attributed to Magister Lambertus/Aristoteles

[137] Tertia differentia talis est, quod si tales evenerint, quarum prima cum proprietate per se, et alia tres cum proprietate non propria colligate consequantur ut patet hic:

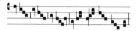

Erf 93v

[138] prima longa imperfecta erit, et due prime subsequentes semibreves, ultima duo tempora | dabit si brevis sequatur, si autem longa tunc tempori trino pollebit.

Si 28v
P1 28va

[139] Quarta differentia talis est quod si in fronte prime IIII[or] figurarum coniunctarum descendentium | cum proprietate propria, simul in fronte secunde ascendentium non propria proprietas ascribatur ut patet hic:

[140] prima dabit unum tempus, due medie semibreviabuntur, et ultima tantum temporis est unius.

[141] Quinta differentia talis est, quod si proprietas in fronte prime figure IIII[or] coniunctarum reperiatur, ut hic:

[142] tres prime semibreves sunt equales, ultima brevis si brevis sequatur, si autem longa tunc duplici tempore mensuratur.

Cs 276b/P1
28vb

[143] Sexta differentia talis est quod | si in coniunctura IIII[or] figurarum prima formam recte brevis habeat, relique autem tres formas semibrevium et hoc dico descendendo, [144] ascendendo autem ▶ *p. 121* copula trium cum plica ad ultimam figuram ascendente, proprietatem non propriam retinens ad secundam, ut hic:

Hw 428

[145] prima recta brevis, alie autem semibreves equales et indivisibiles proferuntur.

---

137 evenerint] creverint *Hw* | alia] alie *Si* | non propria-hic] simul compositae fuerint *Hw* | colligate consequantur] sequantur *Erf* | conligantur *Si* | patet om. *ErfSi* | ex. om. *Erf* ‖ 138 ultima] ultima vero *Si* | autem om. *Hw* | tempori trino pollebit] trine tempore mensurabitur *Erf* tria tempora donat verbi gratia (ex.) *Hw* ‖ 139 coniunctarum om. *Hw* | descendentium-propria] cum proprietate propria descendunt *Erf* | cum proprietate propria simul om. *Hw* | non propria proprietas ascribatur om. *Hw* | proprietas ascribatur] ascrtibatur proprietas *Erf* | ut patet hic] verbi gratia *Hw* | patet om. *ErfSi* | ex. om. *Erf* ‖ 140 et ultima-unius] et ultima dabit unum tempus *Hw* ‖ 141 *ex. om. Erf* ‖ 142 semibreves sunt] semibreviabuntur *Hw* | equales] et equales *Si* | ultima] vero add. *Si* | duplici] bino *Erf* | duplici tempore mensuratur] duo tempora donat *Hw* ‖ 143 Sexta differentia talis est quod si prima quadrangulatur et aliae syncopantur, verbi gratia: (ex.) prima recta brevis, reliquae semibreves efficiuntur ‖ 144 ascendendo] et ascendendo *Si* | copula] co⁺ ... ⁺a *Erf* | ascendente] ascendendo *ErfSi* | ex. om. *Erf* ‖ 145 alie autem] alie *Si*

[137] The third distinction is as follows: if the following figures should occur, where the first has *proprietas* through itself, the other three, with a *proprietas* that is not proper, would follow joined together, as shown here:

[138] the first long will be imperfect, and the first two following [will be] semibreves, the last [figure] will give two *tempora* if a breve follows, but if a long [follows] then it will flourish as a threefold *tempus*.

[139] The fourth distinction is as follows: if the front of the first figure of a four-note descending *coniuncturae* is with proper *proprietas*, or in front of the second [figure] of the ascending figures a *proprietas* that is not proper is added, as shown here:

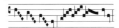

[140] the first figure will give one *tempus*, the two middle ones will be made into semibreves, and as such the last is of one *tempus*.

[141] The fifth distinction is as follows: if *proprietas* is found in front of a figure of four *coniuncturae*, as here:

[142] the three first semibreves are equal, the last is a breve if a breve follows, but if a long, then it is measured by a twofold *tempus*.

[143] The sixth distinction is as follows: if the first [figure] in a *coniunctura* of four figures has the form of a *recta* breve, but the remaining three [have] the forms of semibreves (and here I am speaking of descending), [144] but ascending, a threefold *copula* with a *plica* ascending from the last figure, retaining a *proprietas* that is not proper from the second [figure], as here:

[145] the first [will be] a *recta* breve, but the other semibreves are uttered as equal and indivisible.

P1 29ra

[146] Septima differentia est, quod si quaternaria ligatura ▶ *p. 121* descendendo cum proprietate, ascendendo sine reperiatur, ut hic:

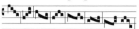

[147] tres prime breves erunt equales, quarta longa imperfecta si brevis sequatur, si autem longa, tunc perfecta longa iudicatur.

Erf 94r

[148] Octava differentia de eisdem talis est, quod si omnes equales esse debeant, et quelibet recta brevis, tunc ultima trahatur oblique a penultima descendendo, ascendendo autem ultima non directe superponatur | penultime sed ab eadem quasi averso capite declinando, ut hic:

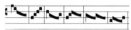

P1 29rb

[149] Nona differentia talis est quod | si in fronte precedentis ligature proprietas addatur non propria, ut hic:

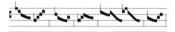

Cs 277b

[150] prime due semibreves erunt, alie vero due recte breves et equales, nisi quod si ultima longa fuerit, tunc penultima duo tempora possidebit, ut hic:

Si 29r

P1 29va

[151] Quinta divisio. Quinte partis est quedam ligatura quinque figurarum, duas habens differentias, que dupliciter habent fieri, ascendendo videlicet et descendendo, [152] quarum prima differentia tam ascendendo quam econverso talis est, quod si | in fronte prime figure quinarie ligature proprietas extiterit <non propria>, ut hic:

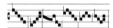

[153] due prime semibreves sunt inequales, due autem sequentes breves sunt et equales, ultima longa imperfecta si brevis sequatur, si autem longa tunc trium temporum teneatur.

146 est quod-reperiatur] quaternae ligaturae tam descendentis causa et proprietate quam ascendentis scientiae *Hw* | *ex. om. Erf* ‖ **147** erunt] et *Hw* | tunc-iudicatur] tunc et tercia iudicatur (*dub.*) perfecta longa *Erf* tunc erit perfecta *Hw* tunc tercia perfecta longa iudicatur *P1* tunc tercia longa perfecta iudicatur *Si* ‖ **148** de eisdem talis] taliter *Erf* | quod si-ut hic] quod si ultima vult breviari varietur hoc modo *Hw* | oblique] obliqua *P1* | superponatur] supponatur *Si* | penultime] ultime *P1Si* | sed-ut hic] sed quasi averso capite ab ea declinet sic (*ex. om.*) Omnes breves sunt et equales *Erf* | quasi] quod *Si* ‖ **149–150** Nona differentia talis est quod si duae primae volunt semibreviari, habeant proprietam semibrevitatis: (ex.) et si ultima longa fuerit tunc penultima duo tempora tenebit, verbi gratia: (ex.) *Hw* ‖ **149** addatur] ponatur *Erf* | *ex. om. Erf* ‖ **150** erunt] sunt (et equales *add. ante corr.*) *Erf* | vero *om. Erf* | breves] sunt *add. Erf* | longa fuerit] fuerit longa *Si* | possidebit-hic] habuerit sic *Erf* ‖ **151** quinte partis *om. Erf* | duas-descendendo] duas habens figuras ascendentes videlicet et descendentes *Hw* | videlicet] scilicet *Erf* ‖ **152** quarum-quod] quarum prima talis est differentia tam ascendendo quam descendendo *Si* | tam ascendendo-ut hic] tam ascendit quam descendit, talis est, quasi proprietas in fronte primae quinariae ligaturae extiterit, verbi gratia *Hw* | extiterit ut hic] extiterit quedam sicut hic (*ex. om.*) *Erf* ‖ **153** prime-teneatur] primae non aequales semibreviabuntur, et duae sequentes breves aequales, ultima longa si imperfecta fuerit sequatur, si autem longa tunc erit perfecta *Hw* | tunc] tunc illa quinta *Erf*

92

[146] The seventh distinction is that if a quaternary ligature should be found, descending with *proprietas*, ascending without, as here:

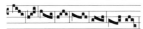

[147] the first three breves will be equal, the fourth an imperfect long if a breve follows it, but if a long, then it is judged to be a perfect long.

[148] The eighth distinction of these is as follows: if they all ought to be equal, and each a *recta* breve, then the last should be dragged out obliquely descending from the penultimate; but ascending, the last figure should not be placed directly above the penultimate but away from the same, as if turning away from the back of its head, as is shown here:

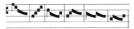

[149] The ninth distinction is as follows: if a *proprietas* that is not proper is added at the front of the preceding ligature, as here:

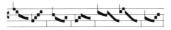

[150] the first two will be semibreves, and the other two *recta* breves and equal, except if the last [figure] were a long, then the penultimate will occupy two *tempora*, as here:

[151] Fifth division. Of the fifth part is a certain ligature of five figures, having two distinctions, which have to be made in a twofold manner, that is, ascending and descending, [152] of which the first distinction, both ascending and *vice versa* [i·e·, descending] is as follows: if at the front of the first figure of a five-figure ligature the non-proper *proprietas* turns up from it, as here:

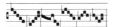

[153] then the two first semibreves are unequal, but the two following are breves and equal, [and] the last [is] an imperfect long if a breve should follow, but if a long [should follow], then it would be held for three *tempora*.

[154] Secunda differentia talis est, quod si predictis ligaturis sexta apponatur figura et similem habeant proprietatem <non propriam> sicut prius, ut hic:

[155] tres prime semibreves sunt et equales, due vero sequentes breves equales, | ultima longa imperfecta si brevis sequatur, si autem longa tunc trium temporum iudicatur.

[156] Cum dictum sit de figuris simul ligatis et coniunctis | qualiter inter se differunt, nunc autem dicendum est de plicis in eisdem existentibus figuris. [157] Quoniam sicut in qualibet scientia speculativa sunt quedam que debent supponi, ita in hac | scientia necessarium est [158] quod diversa tempora per diversas figurationes de|signentur, et quod plice explicentur et varientur secundum variationem temporis et mensure.

[159] Cum igitur primo sit declaratum de singulis plicis in prima divisione nullatenus | propter hoc omittemus, quin adhuc manifestius se presentant, ut hic:

[160] Nota quod si a parte finis ligature duarum vel plurium figurarum ultima breviatur et tractus in fine tam ascendendo quam descendendo extiterit, erit plica brevis, sicut patet hic:

154 predictis ligaturis *om. Hw* | et] etiam *Hw* | sicut prius *om. Hw* | sicut-hic] ut prius hic (*ex. om.*) *Erf* ‖ **155** tres *om. Erf* | tres prime-iudicatur] tres primae aequaliter semibreviabuntur et duae sequentes breves aequales ultima vero longa ut declaratum est *Hw* | semibreves sunt] sunt semibreves *Si* | vero] autem *Erf* | breves equales] breves sunt et equales *Erf* | tunc trium] tunc illa sexta trium *Erf* ‖ **156** simul ligatis] vel ligaturis *Hw* | inter se differunt] differunt inter se *Si* | differunt] differant *Hw* | autem *om. Erf* | existentibus figuris] figuris existentibus *Hw* ‖ **157** ita in hac] ita quod in hac *Erf* ‖ **158** tempora *ill. Erf* | quod plice] cum plice *Si* | explicentur et *om. Hw* ‖ **159** cum] quum *Hw* | sit declaratum] declaratum sit *Hw* | divisione] prime partis *add. HwP1Si* | nullatenus-omittemus *om. Hw* | propter hoc *om. Erf* | omittemus] omittettentes *P1* obmittentes *Si* | quin-se] quae adhuc manifeste se *Hw* | se presentant] require (*exp.*) representant *Erf* | se presentat *P1* (*Cs*) se representent *Si* se repraesentat *Hw* | ut hic *om. Erf* | ex. om. ErfHw ‖ **160** *om. Hw* | si *om. Erf* | ultima breviatur-patet hic *om. Erf* (4 *lineae vacuae*) | ex. om. *Erf* | ultima breviatur] ultima si breviantur *P1* | hic *om. Si* | ex. om. *Si*

[154] The second distinction is as follows: if a sixth figure should be added to the aforesaid ligatures and they would have a similar *proprietas* that is not proper just as before, as here:

[155] then the three first semibreves are equal, and the two following are equal breves, the last an imperfect long if a breve should follow, but if [it is] a long then it is judged to be of three *tempora*.

[156] Since we have discussed the figures, as well as the ligated and conjoined [figures], and how they differ among themselves, now, however, we must discuss the plicas in these very same figures. [157] Since, just as in any speculative science, there are certain things that ought to be understood, so in this science it is necessary [158] that diverse *tempora* should be designated through diverse figurations, and that plicas should be set forth and varied according to the variation of *tempus* and measure.

[159] So, although single plicas in the first division have been demonstrated so that we will omit nothing whatsoever, why not let them present themselves more clearly, as here:

[160] Note that if, from the end part of a ligature of two or more figures, the last figure is shortened and the stroke at the end turns up from it, ascending and descending, it will be a plicated breve, just as shown here:

P1 30va   [161] Quoniam fieri posset | questio quid sit tempus, ad quod respondendum est quod tempus, ut hic sumitur, est quedam proportio iusta in qua recta brevis habet fieri, [162] in tali videlicet proportione, quod possit dividi in duas partes non equales, vel in tres tantummodo equales et indivisibiles, ita quod vox non ulterius in tempore | discretionem habere possit.

[163] Unde sciendum est quod tempus habet fieri tripliciter: aliquando enim voce recta, aliquando cassa, aliquando omissa.

P1 30vb   [164] Voce enim recta, ut vox humana procedens a pulmone. [165] Cassa vero est sonus, non vox, id est vox artificialis que fit secundum aliquod instrumentum, et ideo dicitur 'cassa' quoniam non vera sed ficta dicitur | esse. [166] Etiam et vox pueri non mutata dicitur esse cassa, quia cum recta voce rectam non potest dare concordantiam.

[167] Omissa autem vox est illa proportio sive mora, in qua quelibet figura superius prenominata secundum magis et minus proportionaliter habet fieri, et hoc tacite rectam mensuram excogitando secundum quod quelibet figura pro sua parte continet in se.

161–162 Ioh. Garl. mens. 1, 21–22; Iac. Leod. spec. 7, 11, 5 ‖ **163** Ioh. Garl. mens. 1, 23 ('Sed huiusmodi tempus habet fieri tripliciter: aliquando enim per rectam vocem, aliquando per vocem cassam, aliquando per vocem amissam'.) ‖ **163–165** cf. Anon. Emmeram. I (p. 102 'Et nota quod tempus potest tripliciter considerari et hoc proportionaliter, quoniam aut per vocem rectam aut cassam aut omissam. Vox recta est vox instrumentis naturalibus procreata. Vox cassa idem est quod sonus, non vox, aritificialiter procreatus, sicut patet in musicis instrumentis, in quibus sonus nunc proportionaliter accipitur et habetur; vel vox quassa a *quassa* dicta est idem quod vox imperfecta aut etiam semiplena per sonos varios diminuta. Vox omissa fit per recreationem spirituum et per pausationem aliquam praedictae voci aequipollentem'.)

161 quoniam] b⁺ (*marg. ab alia manu*) Quoniam *P1* | ad quod *om. Si* | respondendum est] respondendum *Hw* | fieri] figuram *Hw* ‖ **162** videlicet *om. Si* | vel in tres tantummodo equales *om. Si* | ita quod-possit] ita quod vox ulterius non possit habere discretionem in tempore *Erf* | ita quod] itaque *Si* | ulterius] alterius *Hw* | discretionem] discretionum *Hw* ‖ **163** unde] etiam *Hw* | fieri tripliciter] figuram triplam *Hw* | voce recta] recta voce *Si* | recta aliquando cassa] recta aliquando recta aliquando cassa *Si* | omissa] demissa *Hw* ‖ **164** enim] *om. Erf* vero *Hw* | vox] vere *Erf* ‖ **165** artificialis] non articulata *Hw* | secundum] per *ErfSi* | et ideo] ideo *Erf* | non vere-esse] natura non hic dicitur ficta esse *Hw* | non vera-esse] non est vera sed ficta *Si* ‖ **166** etiam-esse *om. Erf* | etiam-mutata *om. Si* | et vox pueri] vox parva *Hw* | esse] etiam *Hw* | cassa] vox cassa *Erf* | rectam *om. Si* | concordantiam] rectam concordiam *Erf* ‖ **167** omissa autem] demissa vero *Hw* | vox *om. ErfSi* | in qua] qua *Hw* | prenominata] nominata *Erf* denominata *Si* | proportionaliter] proportionabiliter *Erf* | habet fieri] habet figuram *Hw* | et hoc] hic *Hw* | mensuram excogitando] excogitando mensuram *Erf*

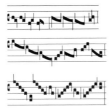

[161] Because one could pose the question of what *tempus* is, to which one must answer that a *tempus*, as it is understood here, is a certain proper proportion in which a *recta* breve has to be made, [162] that is, in such a proportion that is divisible into two unequal parts, or into three, always equal and indivisible, because in a *tempus* there can be no separation of pitch beyond this.

[163] Whence it should be understood that a *tempus* can be made in a threefold manner: now with a proper voice, now with an empty voice, now with an omitted voice. [164] A voice is proper when it is a human voice proceeding from the lungs. [165] But an empty voice is a sound, not a voice, that is an artificial voice, which is made by some instrument, and thus it is said to be 'empty' because it is said to be not true, but false. [166] And also the unchanged voice of a boy is said to be empty, because he is not able to produce a proper concord with a proper voice.

[167] An omitted voice is that proportion or delay, in which any figures named above can be made proportionally according to more and less, and by this silent thinking-out of the proper measure that any figure for its part contains within itself.

P1 31ra

Cs 278b

^{168} Unde notandum est quod huiuscemodi tacita mensura discernenda est per V^e virgulas graciles longas et breves de quibus patent quinque differentie, ^{169} quarum prima perfecta pausa vocatur continens in longitudinem V lineas a summo usque deorsum, habens omnem potestatem, | regulam et naturam, quam habet perfecta figura. ^{170} Secunda vero pausula imperfecta nominatur, que summitatem continet IIII^{or} linearum habens potestatem imperfecte figure et illius que vocatur altera brevis. ^{171} Tertia vero suspirium breve nuncupatur continens summitatem trium linearum et ponitur pro recta brevi. | ^{172} Quarta est semisuspirium maius continens summitatem duarum et ponitur pro semibrevi maiore. ^{173} Quinta est semisuspirium minus quod inter duas lineas medium tenet, et ponitur pro semibrevi minore, quod est indivisibile. ^{174} De quibus manifeste formule patent:

P1 31rb

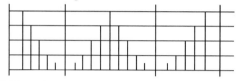

Erf 95v

^{175} Notandum autem quod perfecta | pausa nunquam ponitur nisi in ⁺pari⁺ loco post ⁺imparem⁺ figuram et perfectam, dum tamen naturalis extiterit cantus. ▶ p. 121

^{176} Pausula vero inter duas breves ponitur.

^{177} Suspirium ponitur ubique. Cuius probatio patet in *O quam* ▶ p. 121
sancta et in ceteris omnibus naturaliter compositis. ^{178} Et sic tempus in tempore semper equipollentiam donat, quoniam nichil potest proferri quin possit omitti. ^{179} Nam | licet vox omitti|tur, tempus vero non, unde versus:

Si 30r – Hw 430

^{180} Tempora pretereunt more fluentis aque.

P1 31va

^{181} Sequitur de mensura, | que per totam musicam locum optinet necessarium, que etiam non solum in musica, sed et in omnibus perutilis invenitur, unde versus:

^{182} Sicut in omne quod est, mensuram ponere prodest,

^{183} Sic sine mensura deperit omne quod est.

177 (O quam sancta <quam benigna fulget mater salvatoris …>) cf. RISM B IV/2 *ArsB* 8, *Ba* 74, *Châlons* 5, *Cl* 28, *Hu* 72, *LoC* 7, *Ma* 86, *Mo* 28. ‖ 180 Hans Walther, *Proverbia sententiaeque latinitatis medii aevi* (Göttingen, 1963), n° 31213 ‖ 182–183 cf. S. Singer, *Thesaurus proverbiorum*, p. 129

168 huiuscemodi] hiis *P1* huius *ErfSi* | discernenda *om. Hw* | per *om. Erf* | graciles *om. Hw* ‖ 169 deorsum] ad deorsum *Si* | omnem *om. Si* | naturam] mensuram *Hw* | perfecta figura] longa perfecta *Hw* ‖ 170 pausula] pausa *Hw* | continet *om. Erf* | illius] aliud *Erf* | altera] alia *Si* | brevis] basis *Hw* ‖ 171 vero suspirium] suspirium vero *Erf* | nuncupatur breve *Si* | recta brevi] brevi recta *Hw* ‖ 173 inter *om. Erf* ‖ 174 fomule] forme *Si* | patent] inferius *add Erf* | *fig. om. Erf* ‖ 175 notandum] est *add. Si* | autem] etiam *Hw* | in loco pari *Si* | dum] cum *Hw* | cantus] et ponitur per eadem *add. Hw* ‖ 176–179 Pausula vero in loco ponitur perfectae figurae, suspirium in loco brevi<s>. Cuius probatio est in *O quam sancta* et in caeteris hymnis aut aliter compositis. Et sit tempus in tempore propter aequipollentiam donatam, quoniam nec post propriam quantitatem possit obtinere, nam licet vox obmutatur, tempus tamen non, unde versus *Hw* ‖ 177 suspirium] autem *add. Si* | cuius-omnibus] ut patet in omnibus motellis (motalis ? *cod.*) *Erf* ‖ 178 nichil *om. Si* ‖ 179 nam-versus] licet <vox> omittatur tempus tamen omitti (*dub.*) non (vero *cod.*) *Erf* ‖ 180 *om. Erf* ‖ 181 sed et] sed etiam *Erf* | perutilis] particulis *Si* ‖ 182 est mensuram *om. Erf* | mensuram] musicam *Hw*

Lambertus, 'Ars musica' – 'Musica mensurabilis'

[168] Whence it should be noted that a silent measure of this sort is discerned from five thin *virgulas*: five distinctions of which show the longs and breves. [169] The first of which is called a perfect rest, containing in its length the five lines from the top to the bottom, having all the power, rule, and nature that a perfect figure has. [170] But the second little rest is called imperfect, which contains in sum four lines, having the power of an imperfect figure and of that called an *altera* breve. [171] The third is called a short 'breath' (*suspirium*), containing in sum three lines, and is placed for a *recta* breve. [172] The fourth is a major 'half-breath' (*semisuspirium*), containing in sum two lines, and is placed for a major semibreve. [173] The fifth is a lesser 'half-breath' that holds the middle space between two lines, and it is placed for a minor semibreve, which is indivisible. [174] These rules show these [rests] clearly:

[175] But it should be noted that the perfect rest is only ever placed in a [corrupt] position after a [corrupt] perfect figure, provided that the song observes a perfect measure, however.

[176] A *pausula*, however, is placed between two breves.

[177] A *suspirium* is placed wherever. An example of it is shown in *O quam sancta* and in all the others composed naturally. [178] And so a *tempus* always gives equipollence in time, because nothing can be uttered that someone could not omit. [179] For a pitch can be omitted, but not the *tempus*, whence the verse:

[180] Time flows beyond, in the manner of flowing water.

[181] Measure follows, which occupies a crucial place in all music, and which is found in all useful things, not only in music, whence the verse:

[182] Just as it is good to consider measure in everything that is,

[183] So without measure, everything that is perishes.

The 'Ars musica' Attributed to Magister Lambertus/Aristoteles

[184] Unde videndum est quod mensura duplex in hac arte continetur, scilicet localis et temporalis, [185] et videndum est quod ars ista mensurabilis musica nuncupatur ad differentiam plane musice, [186] quia cum ipsa plana musica locali mensura, que est ad distantiam vocum mensurandam, solummodo mensuratur, [187] isti non solum localis sufficit, sed requirit etiam et temporalem. [188] Temporalis |

P1 31vb – Cs   autem, ut hic sumitur, est duarum, trium vel plurium | figurarum
279a   secundum quod sunt in numero, ad aliquam perfectionem relata equalitas. [189] Nam ut si quis aliquam proportionem iustam seu consonantiam duorum cantuum sive trium diversorum generum ▸ *p. 121-* alicuius loci determinati scire desiderat, [190] ab aliquo sibi noto *2* principio ad locum usque deputatum per tria tempora vel per equipollentiam semper ad perfectionem figuram diligenter studeat computando referre.

[191] Cum superius declaratum sit de omni genere figurarum et de
Erf 96r   temporibus et de mensura, ac etiam | de plicis, et in huiusmodi
P1 32ra   <discantu> | consistit modus seu maneries, et modus consistat in ▸ *p. 122* sonorum modulatione et vocum discretione, [192] nunc autem videndum est quid sit modus et quot sint, et qualiter a principali ▸ *p. 122* figura omnes modi constare videntur.

[193] Modus autem seu maneries, ut hic sumitur, est quidquid per debitam mensuram temporalem longarum breviumque figurarum et
P1 32rb   semibrevium transcurrit. [194] Unde notandum, quod ad similitudinem novem naturalium instrumentorum, novem modos esse dicimus ▸ *p. 122*

184+186 (localis mensura) cf. *supra* mp 25 ‖ **191** (et in huiusmodi …) Ioh. Garl. mens. 1, 5 ('Sed quia in huiusmodi discantu consistit maneries sive modus, in primis videndum est quid sit modus sive maneries …'); (modus-discretione) Iac. Leod. spec. 7, 18, 2 ('ideo vult Aristoteles quod modus consistit in modulatione et dispositione vocum') ‖ **193** Ioh. Garl. mens. 1, 6 ('Maneries eius appellatur, quidquid mensuratione temporis, videlicet per longas vel per breves, concurrit'); Anon. Couss. VII 1, 2 ('modus est quicquid currit per debitam mensuram longarum notarum et brevium'); Anon. Emmeram. II (p. 184, l. 26–27 'quo modus sive species es quicquid currit per debitam mensuram longarum vel brevium notularum …'); Iac. Leod. spec. 7, 18, p. 39 ('Ideo vult Aristoteles [sc. Lambertus] … est enim, ut ait, modus seu maneries, ut hic sumitur, quicquid per debitam mensuram temporalem longarum breviumque figurarum ac semibrevium decantatur') ‖ **194–195** Anon. Emmeram. II (p. 212, l. 28–30 'Dicebant et enim in suo modorum capitulo novem esse modos sive spieces huius artis … ad quorum modum … primus quartus et septimus')

184 videndum] sciendum *Erf* | est *om. Si* | mensura duplex] duplex mensura *Si* | duplex] dupliciter *Hw* | in hac arte] in arte ista *Erf* ‖ **185** et videndum est] et inde est *dub. Si* et idem est *Hw* | plane] plenae *Hw* ‖ **186** plana] plena *Hw* | mensura] musica *ante corr. P1* | distantiam vocum] vocum distantiam *Erf* | mensurandam] mensurandarum *Hw* | mensuratur] mensuretur *ErfHw* ‖ **187** sed-etiam et] sed et requirit *Erf* | requirit etiam] etiam requirit eam *Hw* | temporalem] temporalis *Erf* ‖ **188** temporalis-sumitur] temporalis ut hic vel mutatio *Hw* | autem *om. Erf* ‖ **189** nam *om. Hw* | consonantiam] consonantem *Cs* | cantuum (*Cs*)] cantus *ErfP1Si* cantantium *Hw* | generum] vocum *Hw* | determinati] destinati *Hw* ‖ **190** principio] principaliter *Hw* | semper] aut semper *Hw* | perfectionem] perfectiorem *post corr. Si* perfectam *ErfHw* ‖ **191** temporibus] temporebus *ante corr. P1* | de mensura] mensura *Si* | ac] et *ErfHw* | et in] in *Erf* | in huiusmodi] nihilominus *Hw* | huiusmodi] huius *P1 ante corr. Si* | consistit] autem consistit *Erf* | consistit-consistat] consistit maneries sive modus qui eciam consistit *Erf* ‖ **192** autem *om. Erf* | quot sint et *om. Erf* | modi] numeri *Hw* ‖ **193** autem-maneries] vero maneriesve *Hw* | seu-sumitur] ut hic sumitur seu maneries *Erf* | seu maneries *om. Si* | temporalem] temporaliter *Hw* | transcurrit] transcurrent *Hw* ‖ **194** notandum] notandum est *Si* | ad similitudinem novem] ad constitutionem *Hw* | esse dicimus adinventos] damus *Hw*

Lambertus, 'Ars musica' – 'Musica mensurabilis'

[184] Now it must be seen that measure is contained in this art in a twofold manner, namely, locally and temporally, [185] and it must be seen that this art is named 'measurable music' to distinguish it from *musica plana*, [186] because although *musica plana* itself is measured only by a local measure, that is, by the measuring of the distance between pitches, [187] for that other [type of music] local [measure] does not suffice, but it also requires temporal measure. [188] But temporal [measure], as it is understood here, is of two, three, or more figures, or whatever number they are, equality related to some perfection. [189] For if anyone wishes to know some correct proportion or consonance of some determined position between two vocal parts, or between three different voice ranges, [190] let them study diligently how to return from some beginning note to it, by computation through three *tempora* or through its equipollent figure always through a perfection, all the way back to the estimated position.

[191] Since we have discussed above every class of figure and *tempora* and measure, and also plicas, and mode or rhythmic schemes (*maneries*) set forth in discant of this sort, and mode set forth in the modulation of sound and the separation of pitches, [192] now it must be seen what a mode might be, and how many there might be, and how all modes seem to be established from the first figure.

[193] But a mode or rhythmic scheme, as it is understood here, is anything which traverses through an appropriate temporal measure of long and breve and semibreve figures. [194] Whence it should be noted that we say the nine modes were found as a mirror of the nine natural instruments.

adinventos. [195] Ad quorum cognitionem discernendum et multorum etiam errorem | destruendum, tres liberaliores excipiuntur, scilicet primus, quartus et VII^{us}, [196] a quibus alii sex, quasi clientes, bini et bini a quolibet exoriuntur, quorum etiam quilibet perfectus dicitur aut imperfectus. [197] Perfectus vero est ille qui habet fieri et finire recto moderamine per talem quantitatem, numerum et maneriem sicut per qualem incipit. [198] Imperfectus vero est ille qui in diversis locis variatur, prout in sequentibus patebit.

[199] Primus modus dicitur
qui tantum componitur
perfectis figuris,
[200] ut monstrat qui sequitur
cantus, qui colligitur
ex perfectis puris:

P1 32va

Sancti spiritus

Cs 279b   [201] Ex hoc patet igitur
quod nunquam comprimitur

Si 30v   hic in ligaturis,

Hw 431*   [202] sed liber excipitur
et solus non patitur
unquam a pressuris,
[203] regit et non regitur.
Imperans non utitur
aliorum curis.

<Alma redemptoris mater>

197 Ioh. Garl. mens. 1, 32 ('Modus perfectus dicitur esse, quandocumque ita est, quod aliquis modus desinit per talem quantitatem vel per talem modum sicut per illam, qua incipit'); Anon. Emmeram. II (p. 194, l. 40–42) ‖ **198** Ioh. Garl. mens. 1, 34 ('Omnis modus dicitur imperfectus quandocumque ita est, quod aliquis modus desinit per aliam quantitatem quam per illam, qua incipit ... ') ‖ **199–252** Ed. *Anderson, Lambertus*, p. 60–63 ‖ **199** Anon. Emmeram. II (p. 212, l. 32–33) ‖ **199–203** Iac. Leod. spec. 7, 19, 10–11: 'Hoc approbans Aristoteles dicit sic: Primus modus dicitur qui tantum componitur perfectis figuris, ut monstrat qui sequitur cantus qui colligitur ex perfectis puris, ut hic: *Sancti Spiritus. Adsit.* Ex hoc patet igitur quod nunquam comprimitur hic in ligaturis sed liber excipitur et solus non patitur unquam a pressuris. Regit et non regitur; imperans non utitur aliorum curis. Ex hoc patet doctorem hunc negare longam perfectam esse ligabilem nec per se quaelibet debet poni. Quodsi simplex longa omni cum alia consimili immediate non est ligabilis, multo minus longa duplex vel triplex, perfecta vel imperfecta sic est ligabilis'.

195 discernendum] descernendum *Erf* discernendam *Hw* | multorum] maiorum *Erf* | liberaliores] principaliores *Erf* ‖ **196** quasi clientes] quod dividentes *Si* | quolibet] qualibet *Erf* | aut] vel *Si* ‖ **197** fieri et finire] figuram *Hw* | moderamine per talem] moderamine finitam et per talem *Hw* | maneriem] mensuram *Hw* | qualem] qualitatem *Hw* ‖ **198** prout-patebit *om. Hw* ‖ **200** ut monstrat-puris *om. Hw* | *ex. om. Erf* ‖ **201** quod-ligaturis] quod hoc nunquam componitur in ligaturis *Hw* ‖ **202** excipitur] exipitur *P1* | unquam] nunquam *Si* ‖ **203** aliorum] aliarum *Hw* | *ex. om. Erf*

Lambertus, 'Ars musica' – 'Musica mensurabilis'

[195] So that the knowledge of these modes can be discerned, and the error of many destroyed, three freer modes are laid out first, namely the first, fourth, and seventh, [196] from which the other six, as if vassals, arise from the first, two and two, which are also said to be perfect or imperfect. [197] Perfect is that mode which must be made and finished with proper control, through a similar quantity, number, and manner with which it begins. [198] Imperfect is that mode which changes when in various positions, just as will be shown in the following.

[199] First mode is the name of
the one that is composed
of only perfect figures,
[200] as shown in the composition
that follows, which is assembled
from perfects without admixture:

Sancti spiritus

[201] From this therefore is it obvious
that it is never compressed
in ligatures,
[202] but it is received in a free state:
and alone it never suffers
from harassments,
[203] it rules and is not ruled.
It controls, and does not experience
the concerns of others.

Alma redemptoris mater

Erf 96v

P1 32vb

[204] Iste primus dicitur
et iuste preponitur
aliis venturis.
[205] Nam ad hunc reducitur
et in hunc resolvitur
quivis ex futuris.
[206] In hoc si pausabitur,
longe pause dabitur
par locus in | figuris.
[207] Aliter errabitur,
nec non sincopabitur
multum sui iuris.
[208] Secundus tunc sequitur
in quo primo ponitur
longa imperfecta
[209] cui mox subiungitur
ab ea que sumitur
quedam brevis recta:

Veni sancte spiritus
[210] Iste si ligabitur
ei prius dabitur
trinitas collecta
[211] quam concomitabitur,
si continuabitur,
dualitas adiecta:

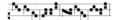

[212] Citius perficitur
levius addiscitur

P1 33ra

eius | imperfecta
[213] Hic post primum igitur
esse ex hoc arguitur
secundus in secta.
[214] Tercius contrariatur
ipsi precedenti.
[215] Ex hoc tercius dicatur.
Ex causa decenti

205 futuris] figuris *Hw* ‖ **206** par locus] per locos *Hw* ‖ **207** nec non] necessarium *Hw* ‖ **208** secundus] modus *add. Hw* | ponitur] inter *dub.* (*sc.* <po>nitur ?) *Erf* ‖ **209** mox] vox *Erf* | quedam] wedam *Erf* | *ex. om. Erf* ‖ **210** iste] ista *Hw* | prius] primo *HwSi* | trinitas collecta] trinae adiecta Veni sancte sancte spiritus etc. collecta *Hw* ‖ **211** quam-adiecta] quam comitabitur dualitas *Hw* | quam concomitabitur *om. Si* | adiecta] adisca *dub. P1* | *ex. om. Erf* ‖ **212** citius perficitur] tertius modus perficietur *Hw* | citius] circulus *Si* | imperfecta (*Hw*)] vi perlecta *ErfP1* vi perfecta *Hw* ‖ **213** in secta] insecta *P1* ‖ **214** ipsi precedenti] ipsa praecedentia *Hw* ‖ **215** ex hoc] contra *add. Si* | decenti] dicente *Hw*

[204] That is the one called first
and justly it is placed before
others to come.
[205] For to the first is reduced
and into the first is resolved
any of those to be.
[206] If there is to be a rest in it,
an equal position in figures
will be given to the long rest.
[207] Otherwise errors will be made
and there will be much syncopation
subject to no control.
[208] The second then follows,
in which there is first placed
an imperfect long
[209] to which is soon subjoined,
taken from the aforesaid,
a certain *recta* breve:

Veni sancte spiritus
[210] If the mode is ligated
to it will first be given
the assembled threesome,
[211] with which will be associated,
if it is prolonged,
the adjacent duality.

[212] More quickly is it perfected,
more easily learnt
is its imperfect.
[213] Here after the first, therefore,
from this is proved to be
the second in sequence.
[214] The third is contrasted
to this preceding one.
[215] From this let it be called 'third'
from a suitable cause.

The 'Ars musica' Attributed to Magister Lambertus/Aristoteles

[216] huic primo brevis datur,
longa subsequenti
[217] atque brevis comitatur
hanc incontinenti:

Marie preconio

Cs 280a [218] Iste modus colligatur
bina precedenti
[219] ligatura, consummatur
trina finienti:

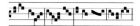

[220] Quartus quaternarium
P1 33rb   tenet figu l rarum,
[221] et ob hoc post tercium
collocatur parum.
[222] Finis et principium
perfecte sunt harum.
[223] Medie sunt brevium
non adequatarum.

O Maria beata genitrix
[224] Quedam per se stantium
atque perfectarum
[225] semper sit initium
hic ligaturarum.
[226] Postea ternarium
sumet ligatarum
Erf 97r   [227] unum et l post alium
totum erit clarum.

Si 31r

Hw 432* [228] Quintus modus nuncupatur
qui ex quinque congregatur
P1 33va   et completur l vocibus,
[229] cuius prima breviatur

---

217 hanc] hunc *Hw* | *ex. om. Erf* | Marie preconio] Mariae praeconio devotio etc. *Hw* ‖ **218** *om. Erf* | consummatur] consociatur *Hw* | trina] a tritina *P1* ‖ **220** quaternarium] quat<er>narum (quatuarum *cod.*) *Erf* | figurarum] figuratum *Si* | et ob] ab *Erf* ‖ **223** medie-brevium] mediae sunt finitimi *Hw* | *ex. om. Erf* ‖ **225** sit *om. Erf* | ligaturarum] ligaturum *Erf* ‖ **226** postea ternarium *om. Hw* | *ex. om. Erf* ‖ **228** qui ex-congregatur *om. Erf* | secunda] figura *Hw*

[216] To this first a breve is given,
the long to the following,
[217] and the breve is associated
with this immediately.

Marie preconio
[218] This mode is bound together
with binary ligatures,
[219] with the preceding it is completed
in the final ternary [ligature].

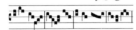

[220] The fourth holds
a foursome of figures,
[221] and for this reason,
it is placed just after [the third mode].
[222] The last and the first
are the perfect figures amongst these;
[223] the middle figures
are of unequal breves.

O Maria beata genetrix
[224] Let one of the standing and
perfect figures
[225] always be the beginning
here of the ligatures.
[226] Afterwards of the ligated figures
it will take a ternary;
[227] choose one [threesome] after another.
All will be clear.

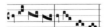

[228] The name 'fifth mode'
goes to the one that is gathered
and completed from 'five' pitches
[229] of which the first is shortened

The 'Ars musica' Attributed to Magister Lambertus/Aristoteles

    et secunda prolongatur
    ex binis temporibus,
[230] tercia corripiatur,
    quarta brevis appellatur
    non de rectis brevibus,
[231] quinte trinum tempus datur,
    ergo longa teneatur
    illa modis omnibus:

    Demenant grant ioie
[232] Iste modus cum ligatur,
    tunc ex binis preponatur
    ligatura vocibus
[233] et ternaria subdatur,
    quam bis bina consequatur
    necnon trina postponatur
    istis precedentibus:

Cs 280b

P1 33vb   [234] Sextus modus figu | rarum
    non caret senario,
[235] sed perfecte sunt earum
    due sine dubio,
[236] necnon quatuor illarum
    ponuntur in medio.
[237] Duas quoque primas harum
    semibreves facio,
[238] sed quamcumque sequendarum
    rectam brevem nuntio:

    O virgo virginum celi domina.   ▶ *p. 122*
[239] Huiusmodi ligaturarum
    pones in principio
[240] illam per se perfectarum
    que est de consortio.
[241] Quatuorque ligatarum
    sequantur confinio

---

231 (Demenant …) *P1* f. 38r.
230 tertia corripiatur] propterea corripiat *Hw* | corripiatur] corripitur *Si* | rectis] recte *P1* certis *Hw* ‖ **231** trinum tempus] trium temporum *Hw* | *ex. om. Erf* ‖ **232** cum ligatur] colligatur *HwSi* | preponatur] proponatur *Hw* ‖ **233** subdatur] subditur *Si* | trina] tertia *P1* | postponatur] preponatur *Si* | *ex. om. Erf* ‖ **234** figurarum] figuratum *Si* | sed] si *Erf* ‖ **238** quamcumque] quarumcunque *Hw* quandocumque *Si* | O virgo virginum celi] Suaut voile dont tans vnd, etc. (*cum not. Hw* | *ex. om. Erf* ‖ **239** huiusmodi] huiusque *Erf* huius quoque *P1* huiusmodi *Hw* huius *Si* | que] quem *P1*

and the second prolonged
[consisting] of two *tempora*.
[230] Let the third be shortened,
and the fourth is called a breve,
not [one] of the *recta* breves.
[231] The fifth is given a threefold *tempus*,
therefore let it be held for a long
in all modes;

Demenant grant ioie
[232] When this mode is ligated,
then let a two-note
ligature be placed before it
[233] and a *ternaria* set down after it,
[after] which let twice two follow,
and likewise let a threesome be placed after
those preceding ones:

[234] The sixth mode of figures
is not devoid of the number six,
[235] but two of these figures are
perfect without a doubt,
[236] and four of these figures
are placed in the middle.
[237] Also, the first two of these [four] figures
I make into semibreves,
[238] but any one of those following
I declare a *recta* breve:

O virgo virginum celi domina
[239] Of such ligatures
you shall place at the start
[240] that one of the figures perfect in themselves:
that is of the group,
[241] and let four of those ligated figures
follow it close by,

109

[242] sicut est in subscriptarum
notatum collegio:

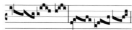

P1 34ra
[243] Septimus ex vocibus
septem componetur
[244] necnon rectis brevibus
hic ergo locetur:

O Maria virgo davitica
[245] Sese colligantibus
quatuor ligetur
[246] binis concurrentibus
iste finietur
[247] ast earum finibus
semper plica detur:

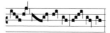

Erf 97v
[248] et sic iste septimus
merito dicetur.
[249] Octavus imparibus
binis semibrevibus
semper potietur:

Cs 281a
Si 31v
A ma dame que iavoe
[250] Binis coeuntibus
cum proprietatibus
ipse copuletur:

Hw 433/ P1
34rb

[251] Nonus semibrevibus
tribus et equalibus
sic perficietur:

244 (O Maria ...) Gennrich, *Bibliographie*, n° 448–450 [11 sources]; Anderson, *Lambertus*, p. 67 et n. 42. ‖ **251** (Domine ...) same example in ANON. Emmeram., I (p. 182, l. 8). Not identified (cf. *Ludwig, Repertorium*, p. 293; ANON. Emmeram, p. 352).

242 sicut-collegio] sicut etiam in collegio scripturarum notatum *Hw* | subscriptarum] subscripturarum *P1* | notatum] notarum *Cs no (cum abr.) Si* | ex. om. *Erf* ‖ 243 septimus] modus *add. Hw* | septimus modus *ante corr. Si* | componetur] componitur *Si* ‖ 244 *ex. om. Erf* ‖ 246 iste] est *Erf* ‖ 247 ast] est *Hw* | ex. om. *Erf* ‖ 248 dicetur] dicitur quod in triplis optimis sic usus facetur *Erf* ‖ 249 imparibus] inequalibus *ErfHwP1Si* | binis] bis *Si* | potietur] patietur *Hw* ponetur *P1* | A ma dame que iavoe] O ma dame que i'auoye *Hw* | ex. om. *Erf* ‖ 250 (binis coeuntibus ...)–267 *om. Erf* ‖ 251 nonus] modus *add. Hw* nonus modus *ante corr. Si* | perficietur] proficietur *P1*

²⁴² just as it is noted in the collection
[of ligatures] written below:

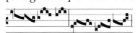

²⁴³ The seventh will be composed
from seven pitches
²⁴⁴ and also of *recta* breves.
Let it therefore be placed here:

O Maria virgo davitica
²⁴⁵ When the figures join themselves together
let a quartet be bound.
²⁴⁶ With two running together
it will be ended,
²⁴⁷ but to their ends
always let a plica be given:

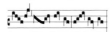

²⁴⁸ and thus will that one
deservedly be called 'seventh'.
²⁴⁹ The eighth will always
possess pairs of
unequal semibreves:

A ma dame que iavoe
²⁵⁰ let this one be coupled together
with pairs coming together
with *proprietas*:

²⁵¹ The ninth by semibreves
three and equal
thus will be perfected:

The 'Ars musica' Attributed to Magister Lambertus/Aristoteles

Hw 434

Domine domine domine rex glorie
[252] quibus tribus omnibus
unum de temporibus
equale dicetur.

[253] Notandum autem quod nullus aut raro cantus aliquis perfectus sive motellus ex istis duobus ultimis invenitur propter difficultatem semibrevitatis.

P1 34va

[254] Cum dictum sit superius de diversitate multiplicium figurarum et de modis et multis aliis | precedentibus, nunc autem dicendum est de quadam armonia resecata, que quantum ad nos 'hokettus' vulgariter appellatur. [255] Circa quam considerandum est quod unam et eandem retinet mensuram sicut in predictis modis continetur, sed in opere sonoque diversificatur.

[256] Unde notandum est quod resecata musica, id est ipsa hoccitatio, est illa que fit secundum rectam vocem et omissam, videlicet quando ab aliqua perfectione tempus sit resecatum. [257] Et hoc dico dupliciter: nam aliquando a parte principii fit resecatio, aliquando a parte finis, prout in scriptura plane sub breviloquio per tractus et figuras declaratur. [258] Verbi gratia | quandocumque inter duas longas figuras suspirium non in medio sed iuxta latus alicuius figure positum invenitur, illa figura cuius tractus propinquior erit, suspirium obtinet: [259] utpote si tractus propinquior figure precedentis extiterit, a parte finis eiusdem sumetur, si autem propinquior figure subsequentis extiterit, tunc a parte principii sumetur eiusdem ut hic:

P1 34vb

Si 32r
P1 35ra

[260] Et per hoc intelligendum est quod nullus tractus inter duas figuras medium tenere debet, sed iuxta | illam a qua sumitur stare tenetur, ut patet in *In seculum* | et in eiusdem tertia conversione secundi modi, [261] quoniam si medium teneret, tunc fieri posset ambiguitas utrum tempus sumeretur a precedenti figura vel a subsequenti. [262] Unde si querat aliquis cuius <modi> sit talis armonia, ad quod respondendum est, quod in genere cuiuslibet modi referre tenetur equipollentialiter, et illius esse modi possit, in quo mensurari videtur.

258–261 ANON. Emmeram. III (p. 252, l. 29–37 'Quidam tamen in suis artibus contrarium asserere sunt reperti sic dicentes "quandocumque ..."')

252 quibus] ex quibus *Hw* | dicetur] dicitur *P1* ducetur *Hw* ‖ **253–267** *om. Hw* ‖ **253** Notandum est autem *Si* | sive] sine *Si* ‖ **254** Cum] Quoniam *Si* | hokettus] hokectus *P1* hoccettus *Si* ‖ **255** quam] quem *Si* ‖ **256** ipsa] in ipsa *Si* | hoccitatio] hoccettatio *Si* | rectam] totam *ante corr. Si* | omissam] obmissam *Si* | sit] fit *Si* ‖ **257** principii] percipii *P1* | resecatio] rescecatio *P1* ‖ **258** quandocumque] quandoque *Si* | obtinet] obtinebit *Si* ‖ **260** in in seculum] in seculum *Si* ‖ **261** teneret] tenerent *Si* | a subsequenti] subsequenti *Si* ‖ **262** mensurari] mensurare *Si*

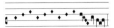

Domine domine domine rex glorie
[252] all of which three
to one *tempus*
will be called equal.

[253] But it should be noted that there is no song or only a rare perfect song or motet found in these last two modes, on account of the difficulty of its short notes (*semibrevitas*).

[254] Since we have discussed above the variety of multiple figures and modes and many other things, now, however, we must discuss a particular 'cut-up' harmony (*armonia resecata*), inasmuch as we commonly it call *hokettus*. [255] On this, it should be considered that it retains one and the same measure as is contained in the aforesaid modes, but is varied in the [written] composition and sound.

[256] Whence it should be noted that 'cut-up' music, that is, this *hoccitatio*, is made according to a proper voice and an omitted voice, that is, whenever there is a *tempus* cut back from some perfection. [257] And I say this in two ways: for sometimes the cutting-up is made from a beginning part, and sometimes from an ending part, just as it is declared clearly in writing with abbreviations through strokes and figures. [258] For example, whenever a *suspirium* [rest] is found between two long figures, it is not placed [exactly] in between them, but next to the side of one of these figures; this figure whose stroke will be closer gets the *suspirium*: [259] since if the stroke is closer to the preceding figure, existing through the preceding figure, it will be taken from its last part, but if the stroke is closer to the following figure, then it will be taken from its initial part, as here:

[260] And from this, it should be understood that no stroke ought to occupy the midpoint between two figures, but it is understood to stand next to that figure from which it is taken, as is shown in *In seculum* and in the third alteration of it in the second mode, [261] because if it were to occupy the midpoint, then there could be an ambiguity about whether the *tempus* should be taken from the preceding figure or from the subsequent. [262] Whence if someone were to ask what mode such a harmony is in, it must be answered that it is held to return within a class of some mode in an equipollent manner, and to the mode in which it seems to be measured.

P1 35rb
²⁶³ Deinde querendum est qualiter se habet in opere sive in cantu. ²⁶⁴ Responsio: quod a duobus cantatur vel saltim a tribus propter consonantiam perficiendam. ²⁶⁵ Sed a duobus tantummodo fit truncatio alternando unusquisque vocem suam tam rectam quam omissam, ita quod | inter eos pausula vel aliquod suspirium maius et minus non remaneat vacuum, sicut in sequentibus patebit exemplis:

²⁶⁶ Exemplum secundum ordinem et mensuram primi modi.

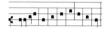

²⁶⁷ Patet altrinsecatio contra eundem.

---

265 truncatio] cantantio *Si* | *ex. om. Si*‖ **266–267** <In seculum> cf. RISM B IV/2 *Mo* 3; ANON. Emmeram, p. 353

[263] Then it must be asked how it is contained in a work or in a song. [264] The answer: that it may be sung from twos or sometimes from threes according to a perfecting consonance. [265] But let a truncation from twos only be made by alternating one of its pitches between a proper voice and an omitted voice, so that between these a *pausula* rest or any major or minor *suspirium* or a *minus* rest does not leave a vacuum, just as will be shown in the following examples:

[266] An example according to the *ordo* and measure of the first mode.

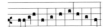

[267] An alternate 'cutting-up' against this one.

Translated by Karen Desmond

Critical and Explanatory Notes

Christian Meyer

Musica Plana

4 consistentiam] conscientiam in other recensions of this text (cf. Compil. Ticin. A1).

54 In the text of Gundissalinus (ed. Baur, p. 100), the theoretical definition of *instrumentum* (means, activity) is lost. Lambertus's prologue allows this lacuna to be filled: the text, in this case, is concerned with the discovery and demonstration of the proportions of instrumental and vocal sounds.

55 'Omnis enim sermo his novem rebus formatur: primo appulsu quattuor dentium, repercussione duorum labrorum, plectro linguae, cavo gutturis, adiutorio pulmonum' (Gloss. Mart. Cap. 27/12, 20). Cf. Berno prol. 2, 1; Iac. Leod. spec. 6, 34, 2; etc.- (epyglotus) for more, see below, [mm93] and Haines, Epyglotus.

112 'illo' (and not 'uno') since it indeed concerns the eighth upper or lower position, at the octave, using the same letter as the first.

114 (secunda … tenent) These two rules, which the table of solmisation just clarified, have just been stated: 'unde sequitur per numerum naturalem (1) quod si …. (2) Ergo si primum sit …'.

131 (non duplicantur per …) This formulation is found again in all sources of the text and in the treatises that set forth this doctrine (see the apparatuses here). One must understand that two syllables authorise two mutations, three authorise six: *sc.* 'et hac ratione due voces vero duplicantur in quatuor, sicut tres in sex'.

135 This table presents a series of twenty medallions disposed in five horizontal rows. Each medallion contains the name of a scale degree (consisting of a letter and of one or more solmisation syllables) and all of the possible hexachordal mutations between these syllables (from four to six depending on the number of syllables). This table thus contains the same information as that of the scalar type of solmisation table. The disposition of the medallions highlights a series of five tetrachords: Γ-C, D-G, a-d, e-a', b flat'-e'. This disposition in medallions is nevertheless atypical and seems to have been cultivated in a French tradition of which the *Musica plana* of Lambertus is the first known witness. It is reproduced in Iac. Leod. spec., VI (ed., vol. 6, p. 184), and one finds it

The 'Ars musica' Attributed to Magister Lambertus/Aristoteles

again in a treatise originating in the German-speaking region around the end of the fourteenth century. On this treatise, see Christian Meyer, 'Une "dissertation" sur la musique autour de 1400 "*Circa musicam est notandum* ..."' (München, BSB, Clm 18800, f. 134r–138r)' [http://hal.archives-ouvertes.fr/hal-00876117] and on this type of figure, Stefano Mengozzi, *The Renaissance Reform of Medieval Music Theory* (Cambridge, 2010), pp. 76–79.

165 (non est de origine ...) The expression remains obscure, but the meaning is quite clear: it seems to want to indicate that the B flat is not a note, but of another order. All of the sources here and all of the treatises that bring up this point (cf. this apparatus) agree in this formulation, however. Perhaps it should be read as: 'non est de ordine'? as comparable to the explanation 'non ad aliarum figurarum spectatur originem' concerning the *duplex longa* ([mm58b]).

190 (aliquis numerus ... ad IV) This relationship is that of the double-octave and not that of the octave.

194 (cum probatione) This expression is abundantly used in the teaching tradition of Johannes de Garlandia and refers to verification by practice.

200 The verb of the principle proposition is not expressed.

202 (quia ... meliores) This remark can be compared to the idea of the distance of consonances from the unity, such as it appears, for example, in the diagrams of harmonic numbers (cf. *Meyer, Mathématique; Meyer, Diagramme; Meyer/Wicker, Leo Hebraeus*). In this Platonic Pythagorean perspective, which asserts that the relationships the closest to the unity are the best, one must therefore understand: 'quia quanto propinquiores inveniuntur eo tanto meliores, et quanto remotiores tanto peiores'.

202–203 Thirds are generally qualified as imperfect consonances, sixths as dissonances (cf. *Sachs, Elementarlehre*, p. 140). This classification is, in addition, in disagreement with what is stated further on **[197–198]**.

205 (genera generalissima) With Johannes de Garlandia, the 'most general genres' of all the concords are the unison, octave, fifth, fourth, major third, and minor third (IOH. GARL. mens. 9,13).

206–207 Classification of consonances:

Imperfect consonances: fourth, fourth redoubled at the octave

Medium consonances: fifth, fifth redoubled at the octave

Perfect consonances: octave, double-octave

208 On this point, see BOETH. mus. V, c. 7.

Critical and Explanatory Notes

<De modis>

218 (secunde speciei) The tone belongs in the second position, after the unison, in the classification of intervals.

303 The six psalm terminations are not in the order adopted in what follows.

317 The psalm termination is incorrect in the two manuscripts. For the antiphons beginning with the formula G ac, Jacobus (Iac. Leod. spec. VI, xcl, p. 263) gives the following psalm termination:

318 The two manuscripts agree in giving this psalm termination, which seems incorrect. It should probably be corrected as follows:

Musica mensurabilis

6 (Discantus, hokettus et organum). Hocket is examined later on [**254–267**]. The treatise tells readers nothing about organum.

13 (neumatibus conductorum) This concerns ornamental sections of melismatic character – still called *caudae* – that are interpolated into polyphonic conductus. See, for example, Andreas Traub, 'Conductus', in: *Die Musik in Geschichte und Gegenwart*, ed. Ludwig Finscher, *Sachteil*, vol. 2 (1995), cols 987–91.

16 (etiam in forma et quantitate consimiles) The idea of quantity is not understood well, because quantity (duration) is precisely the distinctive element on the level of the signification of the figure. The Anonymous of St Emmeram evades this idea of quantity: 'quamvis sub bina significatione forma et eiusdem representatio sit consimilis et eadem' (Anon. Emmeram, p. 98, l. 38–39).

19 (in IX partes ...) cf. below [**199–253**].

20 (comam) coma -ae. In the meaning of stem. Still attested in Anon. Emmeram (cf. LmL I, col. 559).

52 (cantus naturalis) The expression is proper to Lambertus and designates singing in perfect measure (cf. 'cantus naturalis. 2' in LmL, vol. 1, col. 408).

53 (quidam in artibus suis) refers to the principles of notation illustrated by Johannes de Garlandia, who distinguishes the correct measure (*recta mensura*) from the excessive measure (*ultra mensura*), which each proceed from the breve (the unity of the *tempus*) and the long (two *tempora*). The first is that of the first mode (L B L, etc.), the second (B L B, etc.), and the sixth of Johannes de Garlandia (B B B B etc.). The second is

The 'Ars musica' Attributed to Magister Lambertus/Aristoteles

proper to the third mode (L B B L, etc.), the fourth (B B L B B, etc.), and the fifth mode (L L L L, etc.).

56 (trina ... consonantia) the fourth, the fifth, and the octave.

59 (prefati versiculi) here above **[48–49]**.

61 (a parte finis) that is, to the right of the figure in question.

69 (semisuspirii) see here below **[173–174]**.

71–72 (secundum ordinem quarti et quinti modi imperfecti ... secundi imperfecti) the distinction of the modes in perfections and imperfections is borrowed from Johannes de Garlandia; see the introduction to this edition and still further on **[196–198]**.

76 (ad aliarum figurarum spectatur originem) to be understood as 'ordinem'? See above, *Musica plana* **[165]**.

84 (recta brevis ... ad perfectam) Perhaps the author intends here to specify, in conclusion, that the *brevis recta* and the *brevis altera* observe, in the heart of a perfection, the same relationship as the *semibrevis minor* and the *semibrevis maior*. One should note, in fact, that the concept of the imperfect breve ('ad imperfectam vel ad alteram brevem') is foreign to the author's vocabulary: imperfection is reserved for the long (*longa imperfecta*); at question elsewhere are only the *brevis recta* and *brevis altera*. One must thus perhaps understand this as follows:

recta brevis <cum recta brevi> ad imperfectam <longam seu> ad alteram brevem, [imperfecta] <altera brevis> cum brevi seu brevis cum altera brevi ad perfectam <longam>.

86 (quedam sunt species): an allusion to the theory of the five consonances (fourth, fifth, octave, twelfth, and double octave) formulated, for example, in the *Alia musica* or in the *De harmonica institutione* of Regino (cf. *Sachs, Elementarlehre*, p. 130).

88–97 The textual tradition of this section derives from a corrupt archetype: the author announces four psalm terminations, but the fourth (*altera brevis*) is not stated as such. In addition, the physiological explanation of the realisation of the plica **[93]** seems not to be in the right place.

92 'corpus' designates the principal sound and 'in membris' the passing note.

93 On these physiological considerations, see Haines, Epyglotus.

100–103 [100] It should be noted that an ascent, and similarly the descent, is twofold, for one is called perfect, and one imperfect. [101] The ascent, moreover, is called perfect when the second notehead in a ternary ligature is higher than the first and the third higher than the second [*scandicus*]. [102] An ascent is imperfect when the second notehead is

120

Critical and Explanatory Notes

higher than the first, and the third is lower than the second, or equal by returning [to the first] [*torculus*]. [103] But the descent is called perfect when the second notehead is lower than the first and the third [is lower than] the second [*climacus*]; [104] it is imperfect when the second notehead is lower than the first, but the third is higher than the second, or equal by returning [to the first] [*porrectus*]'.

These remarks, which concern the classification of ternary ligatures (*ternaria*), seem out of place in this second division of the text, which only treats binary ligatures (*binaria*). One should note, in addition, that the term *punctus* used here several times is otherwise unknown in this exposition on measured music. The whole passage is perhaps an interpolation proper to the antigraph from which the tradition common to *P1* and *Si* derives.

102, 104 (reciprocando vel equalis) is a corrupt text: it means that the third note of a ligature of ascending and then descending movement, or the opposite (*torculus* ou *porrectus*), approaches the former or is found at the same height as that one.

106 (et VI°) The sixth mode (in Lambertus's typology) only consists of semibreves and breves.

113 (proprietatem … non propriam) in Lambertus, this expression designates 'opposite propriety'.

114 (nisi quod aliquando …) explains that this form of binary ligature can equally represent two breves that are equivalent to a *brevis altera*. This point was discussed by ANON. Emmeram. I (p. 144, l. 12–15: sicut quidam in suis artibus asserere non formidant, dicentes de ea 'prima autem …'; and p. 148, l. 4–5: unde magister Lambertus de tali figura dicit 'prima autem …'). Also see further on **[104–105]**.

144 In the case of ascending formulas, the last two notes are written in the form of a plica. There are thus certainly three and not two notes (the first *cum opposita proprietate*).

146 The second example is notated *cum opposita proprietate* in error.

175 As a general rule, the rest corresponding to the duration of a perfect long is not notated. The author nevertheless signals an exception ('nisi …') whose meaning remains obscure: the pause should be notated 'in an "even" position (*par*) after an "odd" perfect figure (*impar*)', provided that the song observes a perfect measure, however ('naturalis … cantus', cf. LML, vol. 1, col. 408).

177 (O quam sancta) Cf. Rebecca A. Baltzer, 'The Polyphonic Progeny of an *Et gaudebit*. Assessing Family Relations in the Thirteenth-Century Motet', in *Hearing the Motet. Essays on the Motet of the Middle Ages and Renaissance*, ed. Dolores Pesce (Oxford, 1997), pp. 17–27.- Text: AH 42,

The 'Ars musica' Attributed to Magister Lambertus/Aristoteles

n° 60; Susan Stakel and Joel C. Relihan, *The Montpellier Codex*, Part IV: *Texts and Translations* (Madison, 1985), p. 13.

189 ('duorum cantuum sive trium diversorum generum'). I adopt Coussemaker's conjecture (cantuum, i. *cantus* having the meaning of a vocal part). By 'genres' one should no doubt understand the different types of vocal parts constituting discant: the liturgical tenor, the *motetus* (in Latin or in the vernacular), *triplum*, etc.- 'Ad locum usque deputatum' i. 'adusque locum deputatum'.

191 ('discantu') conjecture, following IOH. GARL. mens. 1, 6: 'Sed quia in huiusmodi discantu consistit maneries sive modus, in primis videndum est, quid sit modus sive maneries ...'.

192 ('principali figura') a mental image, archetype. Cf., for example, 'Domus ad extra a domo que in mente figuratur, et vocatur alio nomine "architipos" ab *archos* quod est princeps et *tipus*: figura, quasi principalis figura, quia est figura principalis', Heymericus de Campo (1395–1460), Commentary of *De anima*, in: Maarten J.F.M. Hoenen, ed., *Speculum philosophiae medii aevi. Die Handschriftensammlung des Dominikaners Georg Schwartz (+ nach 1484)* (Amsterdam, 1994; *Bochumer Studien zur Philosophie*, 22), p. 94.

194 (novem naturalium instrumentum), cf. above, *De musica plana* **[55]**

238 (O virgo ...) unknown elsewhere; cf. *Ludwig, Quellen*, p. 293 and *Anderson, Lambertus*, pp. 67–8 et n. 43.

Translated by Barbara Haggh-Huglo

Indexes

LITURGICAL CHANTS AND POLYPHONIC COMPOSITIONS

MUSICA PLANA

Alma redemptoris mater mp**328**
Amavit mp**304**
Angeli archangeli mp**336**
Argentum mp**336**
Auro virginum mp**321**
Ave Maria mp**307**
Baptista mp**335**
Benedicta tu mp**324**
Benedictus mp**312**
Bethleem mp**322**
Christi virgo mp**307**
Cognoverunt omnes mp**306**
Crucem tuam mp**323**
Deo nostro mp**341**
Descendi in ortum mp**334**
Domine mi rex mp**316**
Dominus mp**308**
Dominus ab utero mp**339**
Dominus dixit mp**342**
Ecce nomen domini mp**305**
Ecce veniet mp**304**
Ego plantavi mp**339**
Estote mp**308**
Euge mp**306**
Felix namque mp**318**
Fidelia mp**323**
Hodie mp**340**
Hodierna mp**322**
In mandatis mp**323**
Lentis quidem mp**318**
Magnificat mp**312**
Nature mp**321**
O beata mp**304**
O pastor mp**305**

O vera mp**321**
Octo sunt beatitudines mp**337**
Pater mp**307**
Pontifices mp**334**
Primum querite regnum dei
     mp**301**
Quando natus es mp**315**
Quarta vigilia venit ad eos mp**319**
Querite dominum mp**325**
Qui sequitur me mp**317**
Quinque prudentes intraverunt
     ad nuptias mp**326**
Redemptionem mp**336**
Rubum quem viderat mp**321**
Sapientia mp**334**
Scio cui credidi mp**309**
Sede a dextris meis mp**305**
Septem sunt spiritus ante tronum
     dei mp**332**
Sexta hora sedit super puteum
     mp**329**
Surge mp**317**
Tertia dies est quod facta sunt
     mp**313**
Triduanum mp**321**
Unum opus feci mp**316**
Ut non delinquam mp**309**
Vidi dominum mp**309**
Vigilate mp**321**
Vivo ego mp**317**
Volo pater mp**308**

The 'Ars musica' Attributed to Magister Lambertus/Aristoteles

MUSICA MENSURABILIS

A ma dame que iavoe mm**249**
Alma redemptoris mater mm**203**
Demenant grant ioie mm**231**
Deus ele ma to<r>menter? tra?
   mm**70**
Domine domine domine rex
   glorie mm**251**
Mammelettes a si dur<ettes>
   mm**72**
Maria virgo davitica mm**244**
Marie preconio mm**217**

O Maria beata genitrix mm**223**
O Maria beata genitrix mm**60**
O virgo virginum celi domina
   mm**238**
Sancti spiritus mm**200**
Sen dirai chanconette mm**73**
Trop y use ma vie mm**66**
Veni sancte spiritus mm**209**
Vilains leves sus mm**64**

SOURCES AND PARALLEL READINGS

ANON. Carthus.
   pr. 5 mp**17**

ANON. Claudifor.
   3, 2, 6 mp**195**

ANON. Couss. VII
   1, 2 mm**193**

ANON. Emmeram.
   I, p. 102, l. 46 + p. 104, l. 1–5
      mm**18–19**
   I, p. 86, l. 11–16 mm**10–11**
   I, p. 86, l. 5–7 mm**8**
   I, p. 88, l. 1–9 mm**13–15**
   I, p. 92, l. 2–3 mm**89**
   I, p. 92, l. 23–26 mm**96**
   I, p. 96, l. 16–18 mm**89**
   I, p. 98, l. 38–42 mm**16**
   I, p. 102 mm**163–165**
   I, p. 104 mm**52**
   I, p. 182, l. 8 mm**251**
   II, p. 184, l. 26–27 mm**193**
   II, p. 194, l. 40–42 mm**197**
   II, p. 196, l. 29–30 mm**44**
   II, p. 212, l. 28–30 mm**194–195**
   II, p. 212, l. 32–33 mm**199**
   III, p. 252, l. 29–37 mm**258–261**
   IV, p. 258, l. 15–20 mp**196–198**

   IV, p. 268, l. 1–3 mp**200**
   VI, p. 282, l. 36 mp**41**

ARISTOTELES, Metaphysica
(Iacobus Veneticus transl.)
   I, 1 (Bekker 980a) mp**2**

AUGUST. MIN.
   BV 13, C 13, D 13 mp**23**
   BV 8 mp**25**

BOETH. arithm.
   I, 2 (p. 12, l. 14–17) mm**30–31**

BOETH. Cons.
   lib. 4, prosa 2, l. 96 mm**1**

BOETH. mus.
   I, 3 (p. 189, l. 22–23) mp**139**
   I, 34 (p. 223, l. 28–224, l. 18)
      mp**8–16**
   I, 34 (p. 224, l. 18–20) mp**31**
   I, 34 (p. 224, l. 20–25) mp**32–33**

COMM. Boeth. II
   p. 112, 18 mp**25**
   p. 134, 26 mp**25**

Compil. Ticin.
A 1 mp2–4
A 2 mp1
A 15 mp21
A 16 mp41
A 44 mp133
A 50–53 mp140–142
A 54 mp153
A 55 mp154
A 56 mp155
A 60–68, mp159–167
A 69–70 mp144–146
A 71 mp170
A 72 mp168–169
A 74–78 mp172–175
A 80–83 mp177–180

Guido micr.
20, 2 mp81
20, 2–3 mp82
20, 4–8 mp76–79
20, 19 mp83
20, 22 mp84

Guido prol.
6 mp6
14 mp19
34 mp5

Guido reg.
1–3 mp35–37

Gundissalinus, De divisione
philosophiae
p. 100 mp85
p. 100 mp86–90
p. 102 mp70–73
p. 95 mm32 + 33 + 34
p. 96 mp44
p. 96 mp45–46
p. 98 mp48
p. 99 mp27–30
p. 99 mp51–52
p. 99–100 mp53–56

Hugo de Sancto Victore,
Didascalicon de studio legendi III
p. 60, l. 6 mm38–41

Hugo Spechtsh.
comm. p. 19 mp21

Iac. Leod. spec.
1, 5, 10 mp57–58
1, 5, 13 mp63–64
2, 3, 4 mp6
6, 62, 12–13 mp101–106
6, 64, 18 mp118
6, 94, 8–11 mp321–325
7, 5, 8 mm7
7, 11, 5 mm161–162
7, 19, 10–11 mm199–203
7, 22, 2 mm89, 93
7, 22, 6 mm92
7, 18, 2 mm191, 193
7, 20, 5 mm12
7, 21, 6 mm77

Ioh. Garl. mens.
1, 4 mm12
1, 5 mm191
1, 6 mm193
1, 21–22 mm161–162
1, 23 mm163
1, 29 mm48
1, 30 mm73–74
1, 32 mm197
1, 34 mm198
2, 1 mm10–11
2, 2–6 mm12–15
3, 9 mm89
9, 13 mp205
9, 26 mp201

Ioh. Mur. comp.
6, 4 mp24, 25

Iohannes Scottus Eriugena, De
divisione naturae
III, p. 104 mm34–35

Isid. etym.
3, 16, 1 mp**74, 75**
3, 16, 2 mp**80**
3, 17, 1 mp**61–62**
3, 17, 1–2 mp**65–67**
3, 17, 3 mp**72–73**

Lad. Zalk.
A 14 mp**68–69**

Nic. Weyts
p. 262b mm**62–63**

Nicol. Cap.
p. 309 mp**2–4**

P. Vergilius Maro, Eclogae sive Bucolica
8, v. 73 mm**33**

Petr. Palm.
p. 518 mp**199**

Ps.-Boethius, Geometria
p. 397 l. 19–398 l. 1 mm**17**

Ps.-Phil. lib. mus.
p. **36**a mp**97**

Ps.-Thomas aqu. I
43 mp**39–40**
53 mp**62**

Quat. princ.
1, 1 mp**1, 2–4**
1, 2 mp**7**
1, 3 mp**17**
1, 4 mp**18**
1, 5 mp**21, 24**
1, 6 mp**25, 27–30**
1, 9 mp**39–40**
1, 11 mp**59–60**
1, 12 mp**44, 45**
1, 13 mp**47–50**
1, 14 mp**51–52**
1, 15 mp**53–56**
1, 16 mp**85**

1, 17 mp**86–90**
1, 18 mp**57–58**
1, 19 mp**61, 65–73**
3, 1 mp**92–95, 96**
3, 2 mp**98, 99, 100**
3, 7 mp**109–113**
3, 17 mp**187**
3, 8 mp**118, 120, 121–122**
3, 9 mp**123–129, 132, 134–135**
3, 13 mp**152**
3, 14 mp**139, 143, 145, 146–147**
3, 16 mp**185–186**
3, 18 mp**188–189**

Raimundus Lullus, Liber de venatione substantiae, accidentis et compositi
dist. 7, pars 4, l. 227 mp**213**

Sapientia
11, 20 mm**29–30**

Trad. Garl. plan. I
134 mp**119**
136 mp**135**
145–148 mp**109–113**
148 mp**114**
151 mp**123**
152 mp**124**
153–154 mp**125**
154 mp**126**
155 mp**127**
156–157 mp**128–129**
158 mp**130, 131**
159–160 mp**132**
161–162 mp**133**

Trad. Garl. plan. III
129–132 mp**109–113**
132 mp**114**
134 mp**116**
135 mp**117**
136 mp**118**
138 mp**120**
142 mp**98, 99, 100**
148 mp**127**
151 mp**131**

Trad. Garl. plan. IV
57 mp**119**
61–65 mp**109–113**
65 mp**114**
67–68 mp**116**
69 mp**117**
70 mp**118**
71 mp**120**
72 mp**121–122**
98 mp**142**
111–117 mp**159–167**

Trad. Holl. V
pr. 71–72 mp**64–65**
pr. 73 mp**66**
pr. 77 mp**68–69**
pr. 79 mp**72–73**

Trad. Holl. VI
1, 5–7 mp**2–4**
17, p. 46 mp**196–214**

Trad. Lamb.
1, 1 mp**61**, **63**, **64–65**
1, 1, 1 mp**21**

1, 2 mp**39–40**
1, 3 mp**41**, **96**
2, 2a mp**92–95**, **98**, **99**, **100**,
136–138
2, 2a, 8 mp**98**, **100**
2, 2b mp**108–114**
2, 2b, 2 mp**109–113**
2, 3 mp**115–119**, **120**, **121–122**,
165
2, 3, 3 mp**118**
2, 3, 5 mp**120**
2, 4 mp**123**, **124**, **125**, **128–129**,
131, **132**, **133–134**
3, 1 mp**139**, **193–194**
3, 10 mp**184**
3, 11 mp**187**
3, 14 mp**188–189**, **190**
3, 2 mp**140**
3, 3 mp**145**
3, 4a mp**154**
3, 4b mp**159–164**, **166–167**
3, 5 mp**160**
3, 8 mp**166–167**, **171–172**
3, 9 mp**177–180**

ROYAL MUSICAL ASSOCIATION MONOGRAPHS

General Editor: Simon P. Keefe

No. 1: *Playing on Words: A Guide to Luciano Berio's* Sinfonia (1985)
David Osmond-Smith

No. 2: *The Oratorio in Venice* (1986)
Denis and Elsie Arnold

No. 3: *Music for Treviso Cathedral in the Late Sixteenth Century: A Reconstruction of the Lost Manuscripts 29 and 30* (1987)
Bonnie J. Blackburn

No. 4: *The Breath of the Symphonist: Shostakovitch's Tenth* (1988)
David Fanning

No. 5: *The Song of the Soul: Understanding* Poppea (1991)
Iain Fenlon and Peter Miller

No. 6: *The Impresario's Ten Commandments: Continental Recruitment for Italian Opera in London 1763–64* (1992)
Curtis Price, Judith Milhous and Robert D. Hume

No. 7: *Institutional Patronage in Post-Tridentine Rome: Music at Santissima Trinità dei Pellegrini 1550–1650* (1995)
Noel O'Regan

No. 8: *Latin Poetry and Conductus in Medieval France* (1997)
Christopher Page

No. 9: *Orientalism, Masquerade and Mozart's Turkish Music* (2000)
Matthew Head

No. 10: *'Composing with Tones': A Musical Analysis of Schoenberg's Op. 23 Pieces for Piano* (2001)
Kathryn Bailey

No. 11: *Szymanowski, Eroticism and the Voices of Mythology* (2003)
Stephen Downes

No. 12: *Salomon and the Burneys: Private Patronage and a Public Career* (2003)
Ian Woodfield

No. 13: *Repetition in Music: Theoretical and Metatheoretical Perspectives* (2004)
Adam Ockelford

No. 14: *'To fill, forbear, or adorne': The Organ Accompaniment of Restoration Sacred Music* (2006)
Rebecca Herissone

No. 15: *MS Florence, Biblioteca Nazionale Centrale, Magl. XIX, 164–167* (2006)
Anthony M. Cummings

No. 16: *Bartók and the Grotesque: Studies in Modernity, the Body and Contradiction in Music* (2007)
Julie Brown

No. 17: *Sacred Repertories in Paris under Louis XIII: Paris, Bibliothèque Nationale de France, Vma ms rés. 571* (2009)
Peter Bennett

No. 18: *Rosa Newmarch and Russian Music in Late Nineteenth and Early Twentieth-Century England* (2009)
Philip Ross Bullock

No. 19: *Skryabin, Philosophy and the Music of Desire* (2012)
Kenneth M. Smith

No. 20: *The Politics of Plainchant in* fin-de-siècle *France* (2013)
Katharine Ellis

No. 21: *Brahms Beyond Mastery: His Sarabande and Gavotte, and its Recompositions* (2013)
Robert Pascall

No. 22: *Regina Mingotti: Diva and Impresario at the King's Theatre, London* (2013)
Michael Burden

No. 23: *Heinrich Schenker and Beethoven's 'Hammerklavier' Sonata* (2013)
Nicholas Marston

No. 24: *The Politics of Verdi's* Cantica (2014)
Roberta Montemorra Marvin

No. 25: *Johann Mattheson's* Pièces de clavecin *and* Das neu-eröffnete Orchestre (2014)
Margaret Seares

No. 26: *Singing Dante: The Literary Origins of Cinquecento Monody* (2014)
Elena Abramov-van Rijk